AMP

6

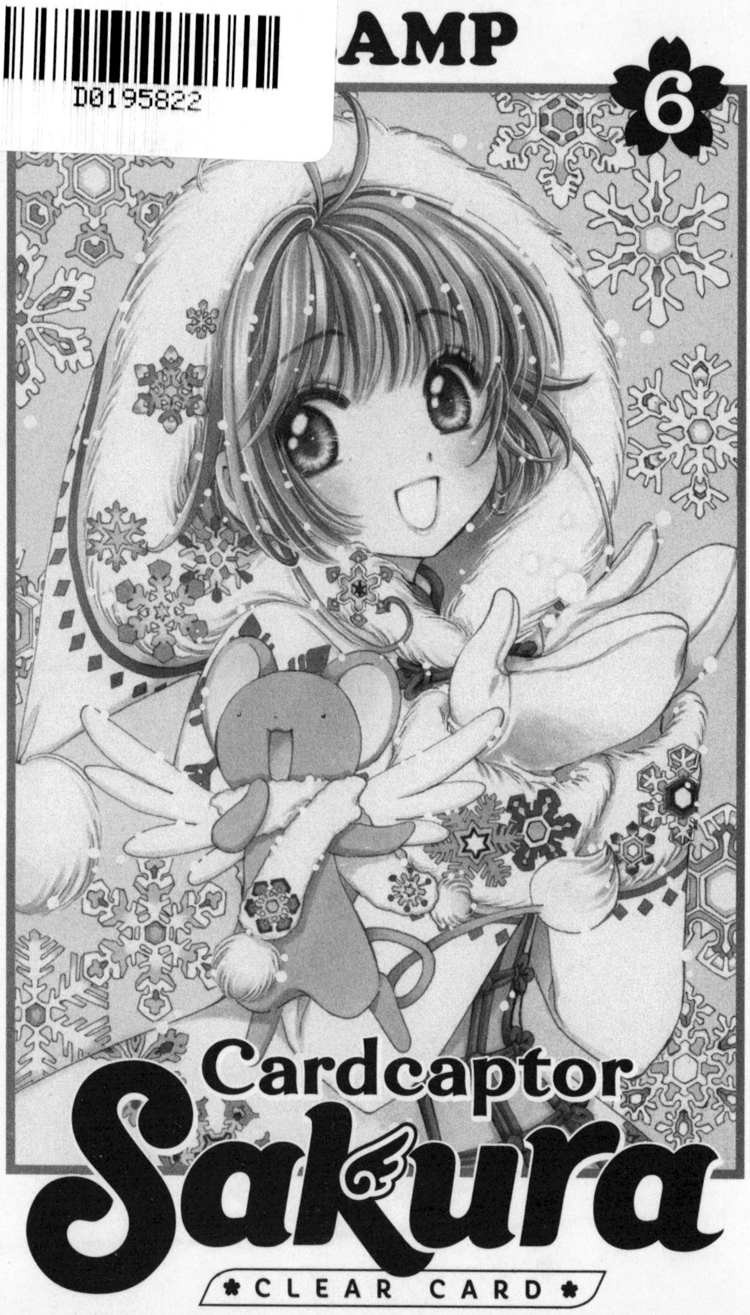

Cardcaptor Sakura

CLEAR CARD

Cardcaptor Sakura

CLEAR CARD

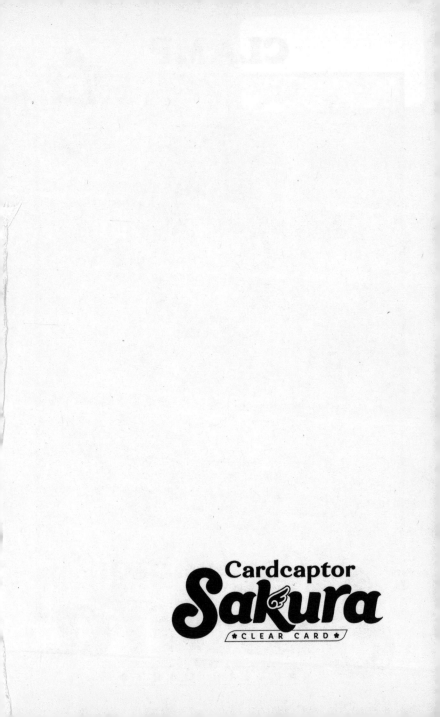

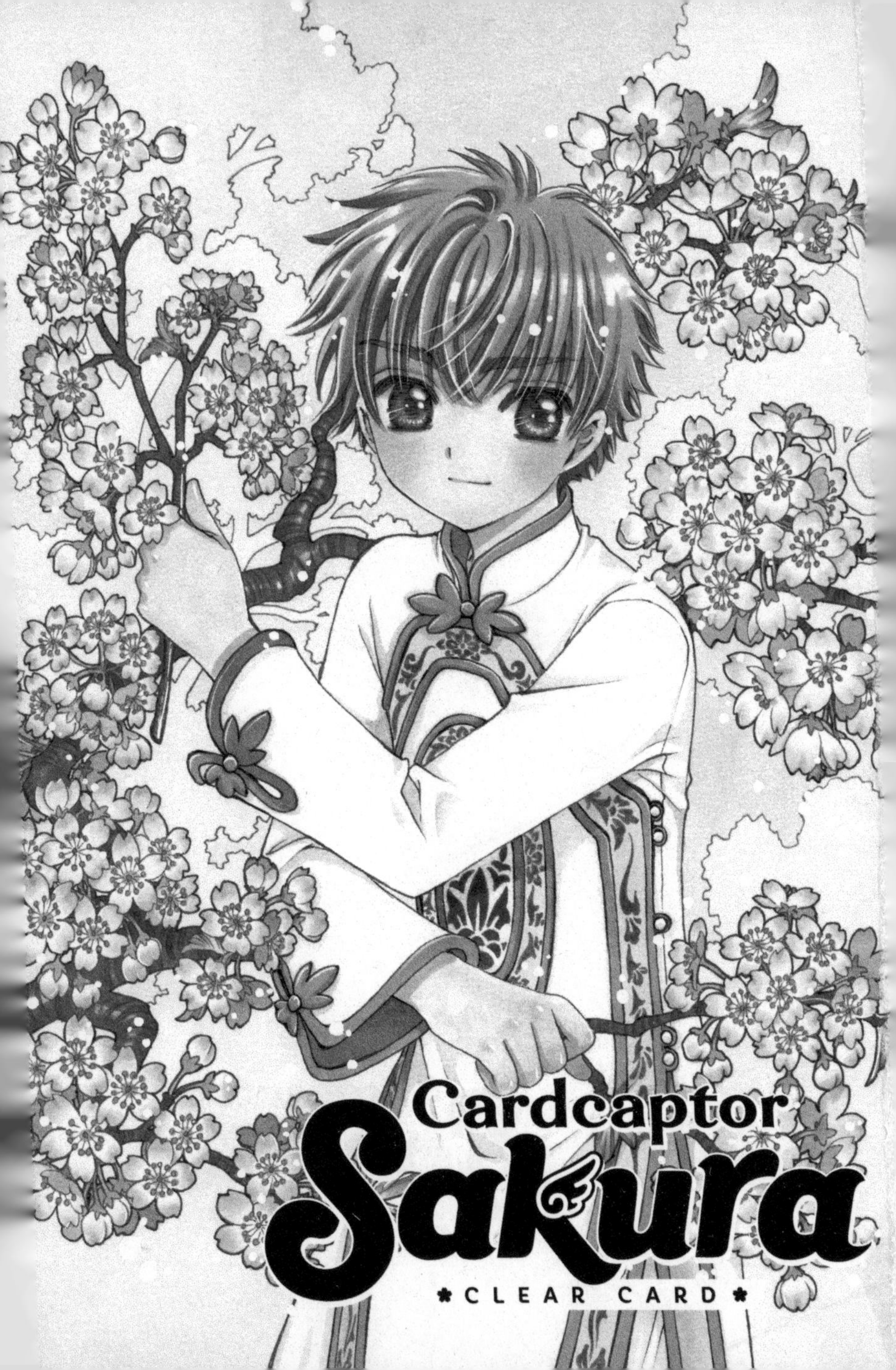
Cardcaptor
Sakura
CLEAR CARD

Cardcaptor
Sakura
CLEAR CARD

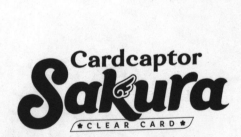

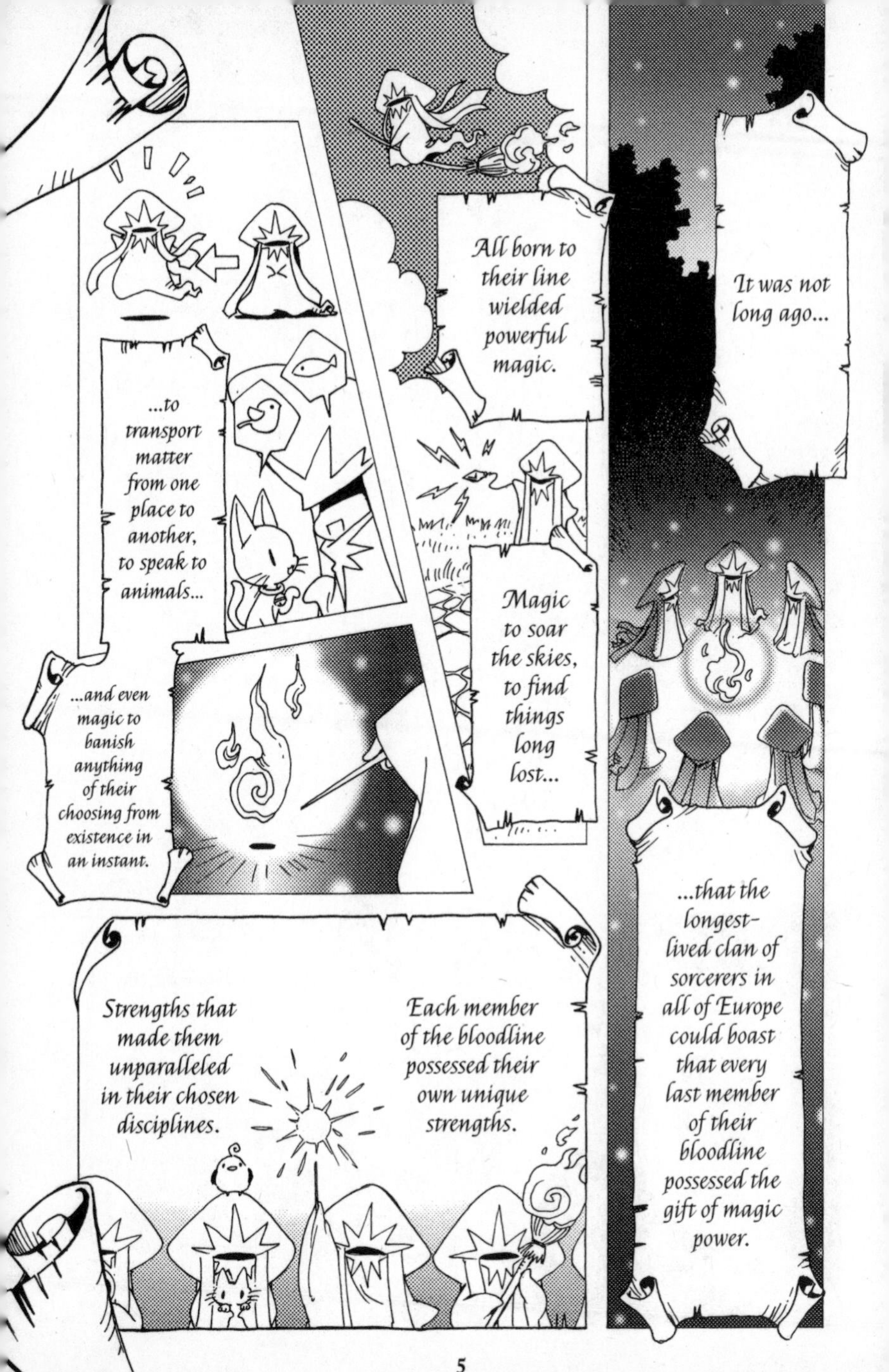
It was not long ago...
...that the longest-lived clan of sorcerers in all of Europe could boast that every last member of their bloodline possessed the gift of magic power.
All born to their line wielded powerful magic.
Magic to soar the skies, to find things long lost...
...to transport matter from one place to another, to speak to animals...
...and even magic to banish anything of their choosing from existence in an instant.
Each member of the bloodline possessed their own unique strengths.
Strengths that made them unparalleled in their chosen disciplines.

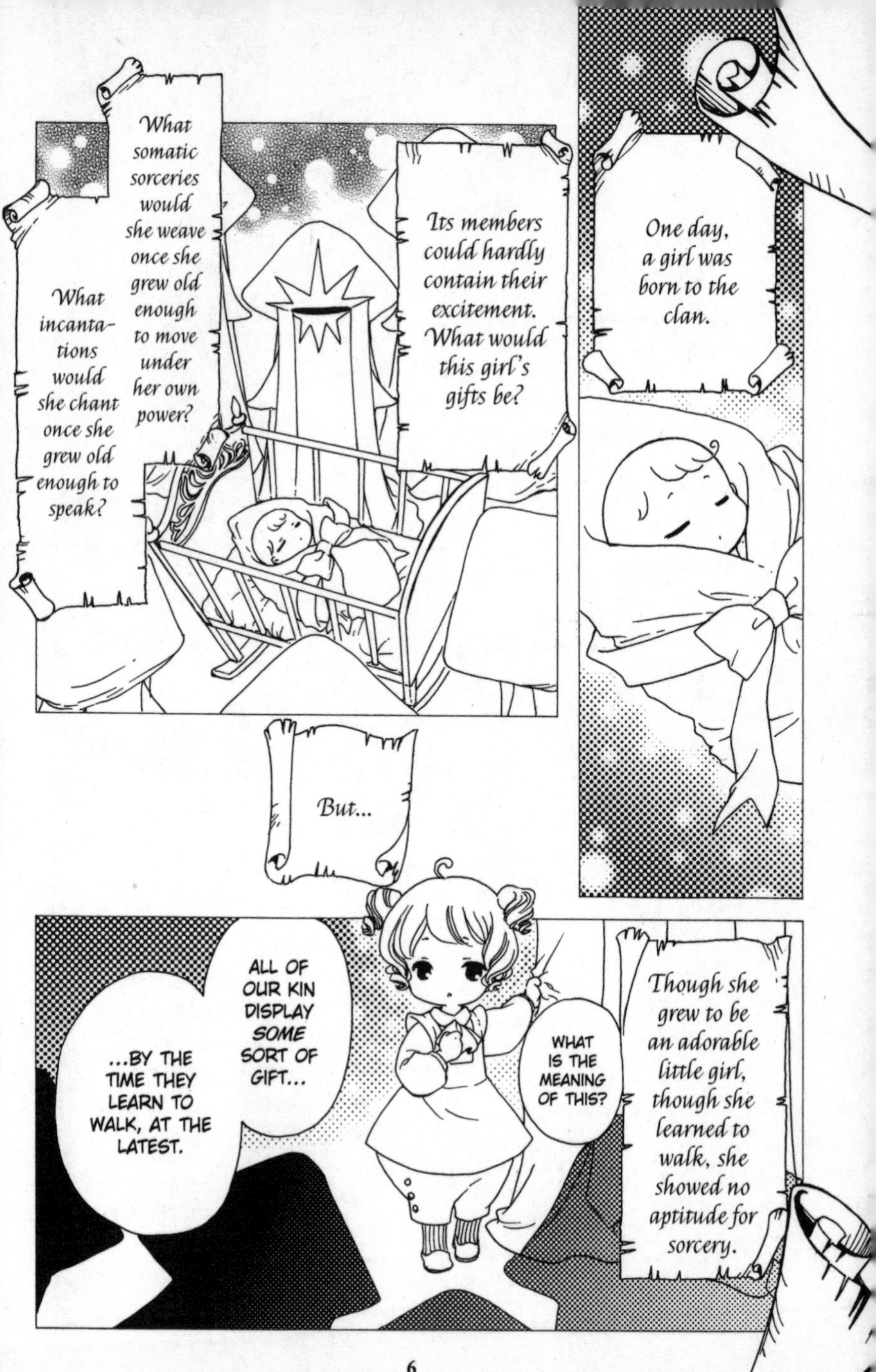
One day, a girl was born to the clan.
Its members could hardly contain their excitement. What would this girl's gifts be?
What somatic sorceries would she weave once she grew old enough to move under her own power?
What incantations would she chant once she grew old enough to speak?
But...
Though she grew to be an adorable little girl, though she learned to walk, she showed no aptitude for sorcery.
WHAT IS THE MEANING OF THIS?
ALL OF OUR KIN DISPLAY *SOME* SORT OF GIFT...
...BY THE TIME THEY LEARN TO WALK, AT THE LATEST.

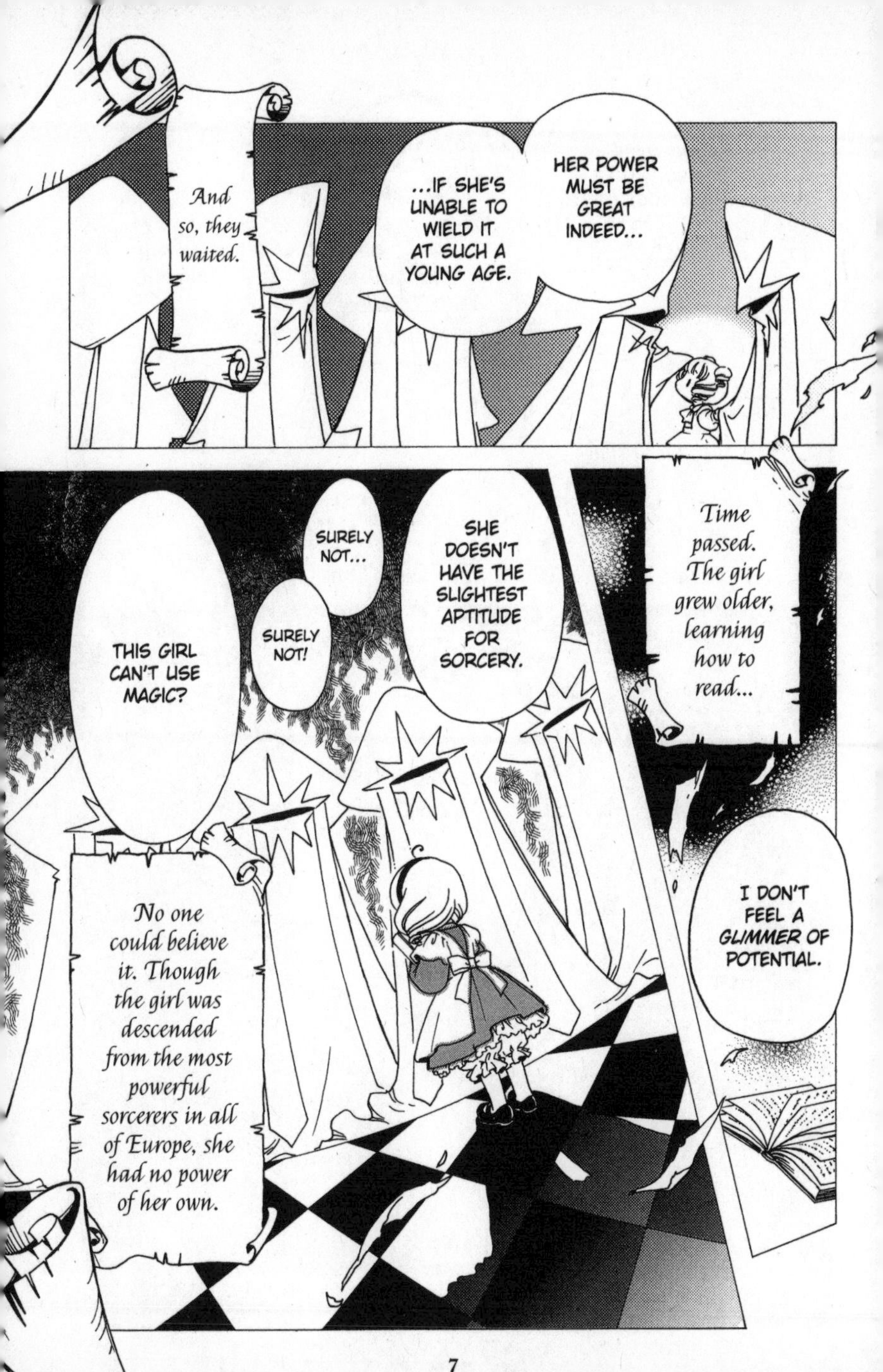
HER POWER MUST BE GREAT INDEED...
...IF SHE'S UNABLE TO WIELD IT AT SUCH A YOUNG AGE.
And so, they waited.
SHE DOESN'T HAVE THE SLIGHTEST APTITUDE FOR SORCERY.
SURELY NOT...
SURELY NOT!
THIS GIRL CAN'T USE MAGIC?
I DON'T FEEL A GLIMMER OF POTENTIAL.
No one could believe it. Though the girl was descended from the most powerful sorcerers in all of Europe, she had no power of her own.
Time passed. The girl grew older, learning how to read...

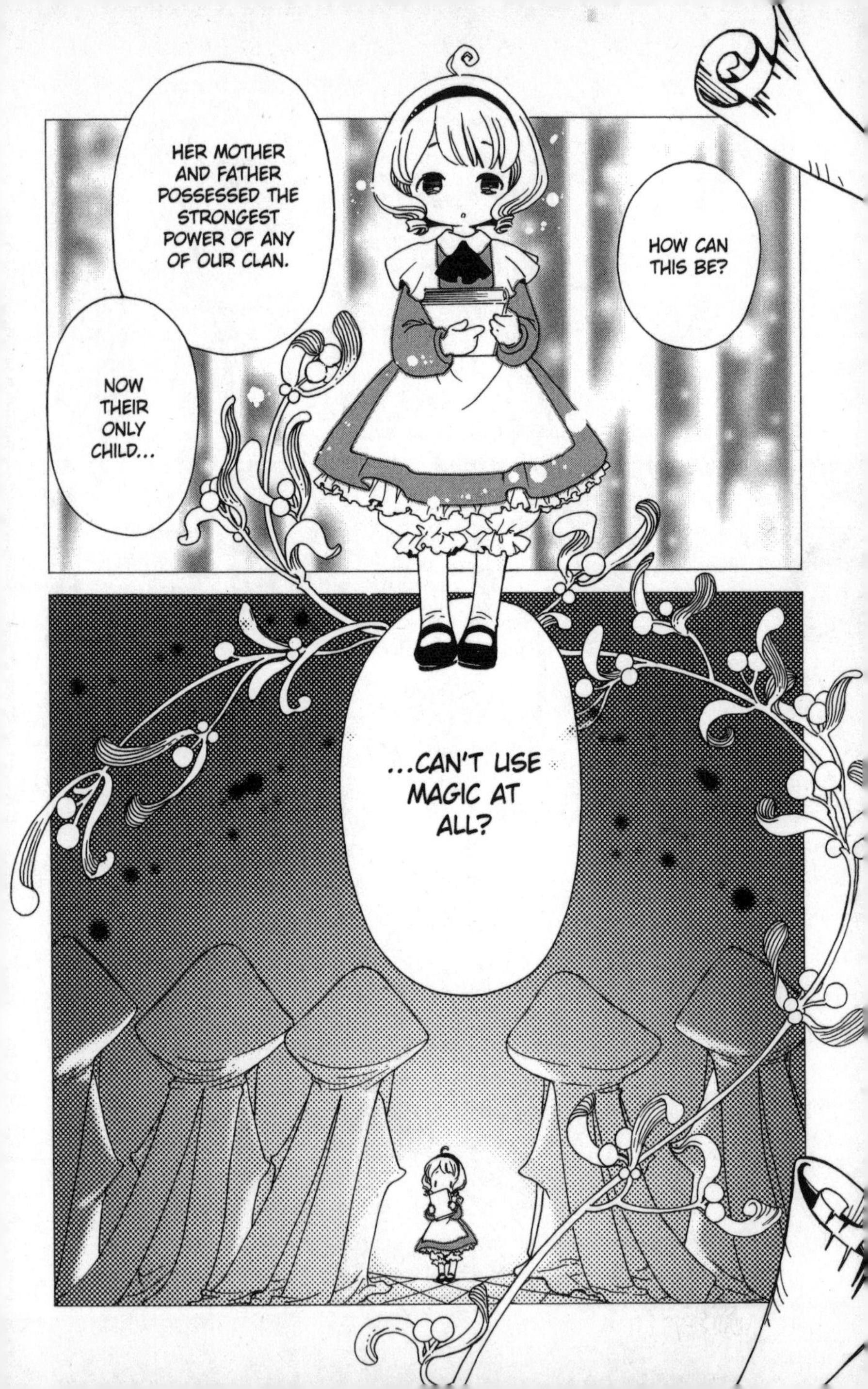
HOW CAN THIS BE?
HER MOTHER AND FATHER POSSESSED THE STRONGEST POWER OF ANY OF OUR CLAN.
NOW THEIR ONLY CHILD...
...CAN'T USE MAGIC AT ALL?

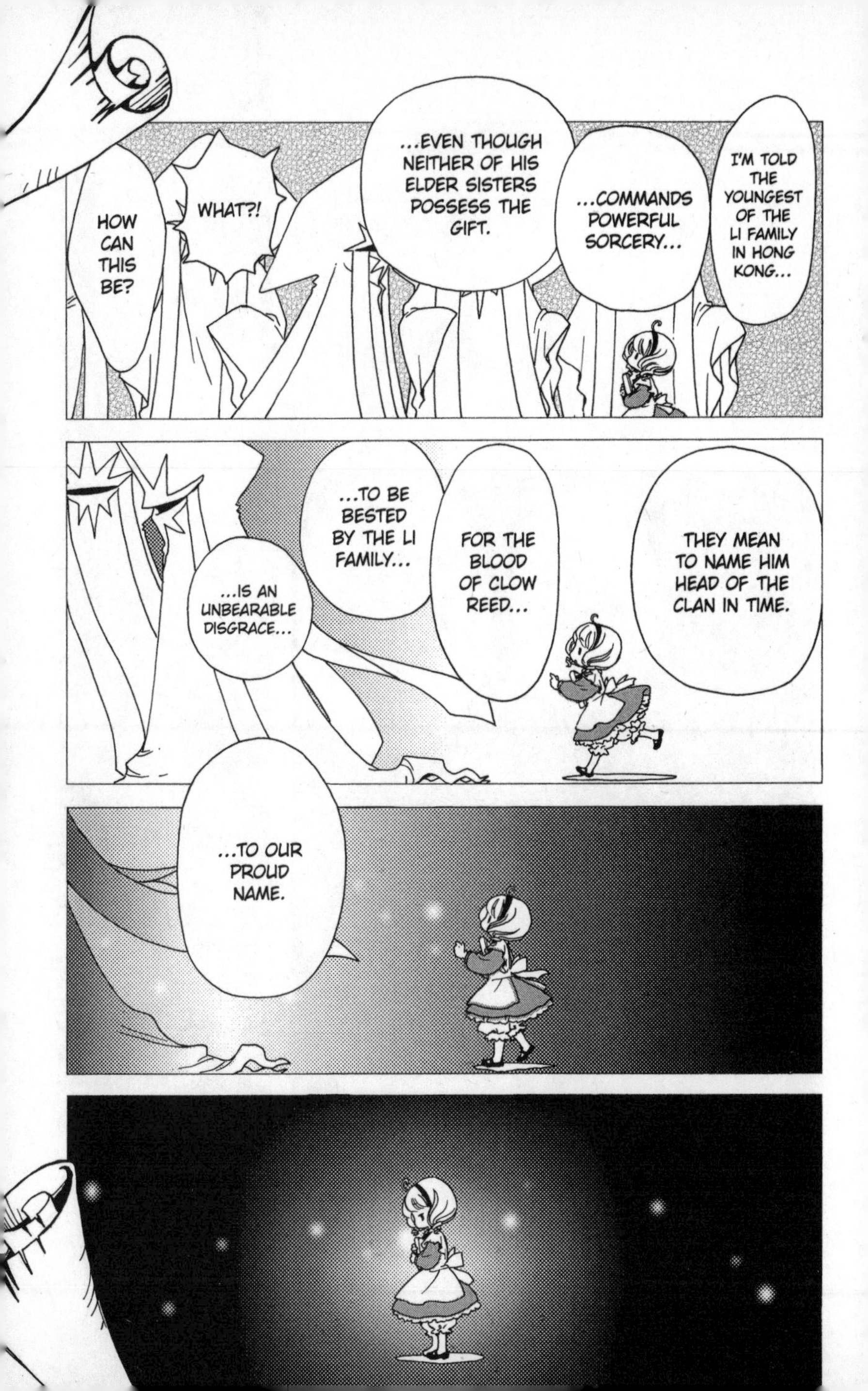
I'M TOLD THE YOUNGEST OF THE LI FAMILY IN HONG KONG...
...COMMANDS POWERFUL SORCERY...
...EVEN THOUGH NEITHER OF HIS ELDER SISTERS POSSESS THE GIFT.
WHAT?!
HOW CAN THIS BE?
THEY MEAN TO NAME HIM HEAD OF THE CLAN IN TIME.
FOR THE BLOOD OF CLOW REED...
...TO BE BESTED BY THE LI FAMILY...
...IS AN UNBEARABLE DISGRACE...
...TO OUR PROUD NAME.

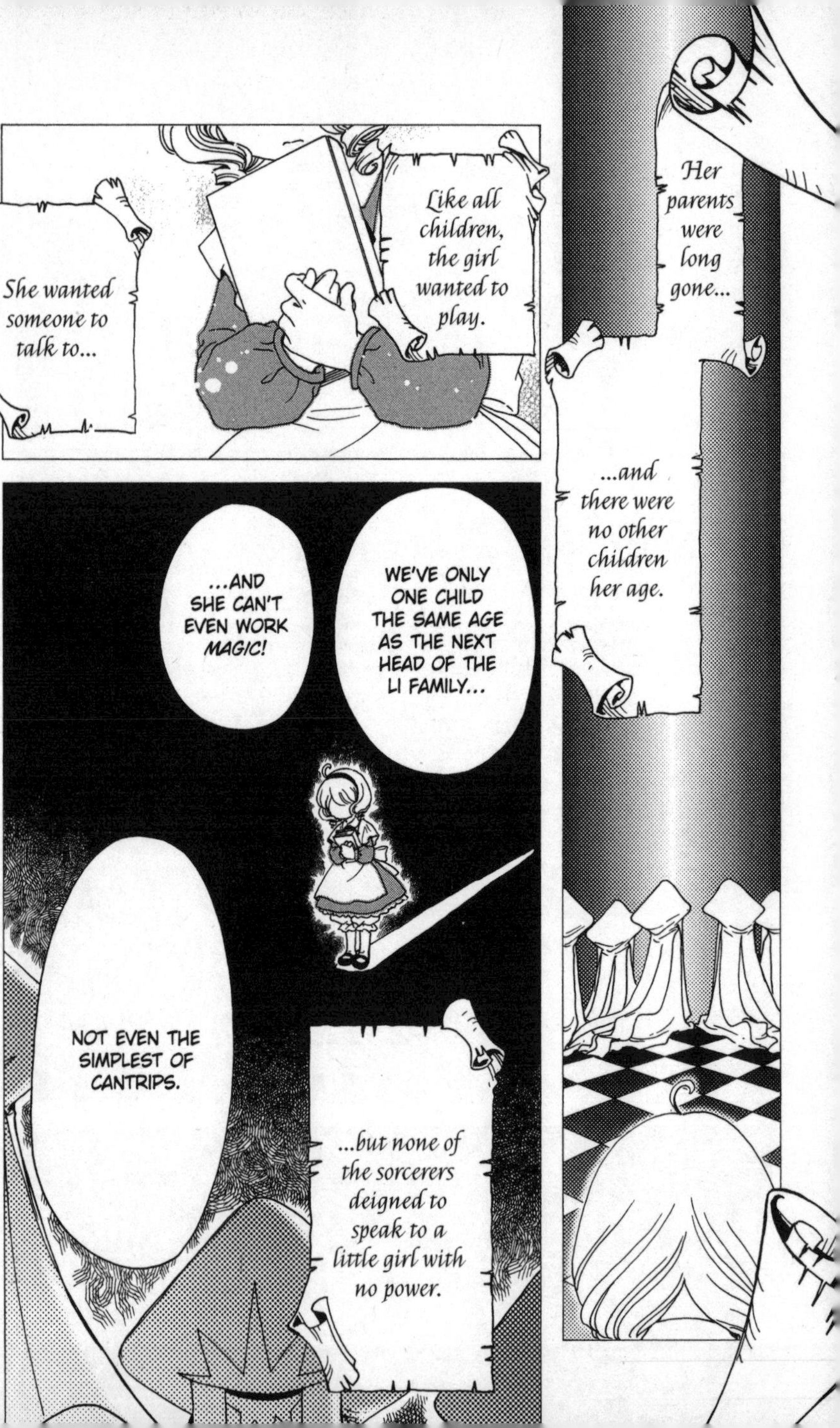
Her parents were long gone...
...and there were no other children her age.
Like all children, the girl wanted to play.
She wanted someone to talk to...
WE'VE ONLY ONE CHILD THE SAME AGE AS THE NEXT HEAD OF THE LI FAMILY...
...AND SHE CAN'T EVEN WORK MAGIC!
NOT EVEN THE SIMPLEST OF CANTRIPS.
...but none of the sorcerers deigned to speak to a little girl with no power.

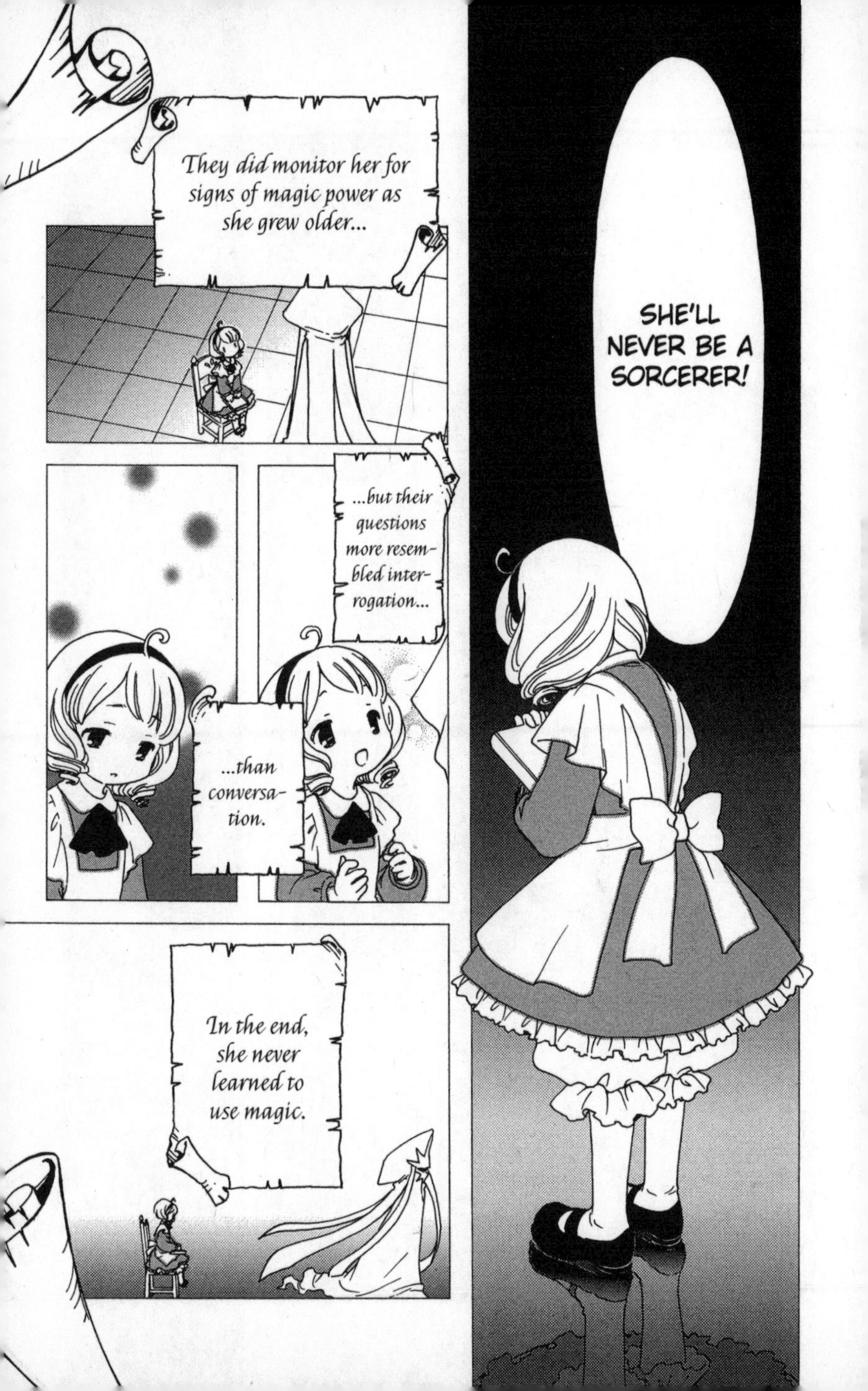
SHE'LL NEVER BE A SORCERER!
They did monitor her for signs of magic power as she grew older...
...but their questions more resembled interrogation...
...than conversation.
In the end, she never learned to use magic.

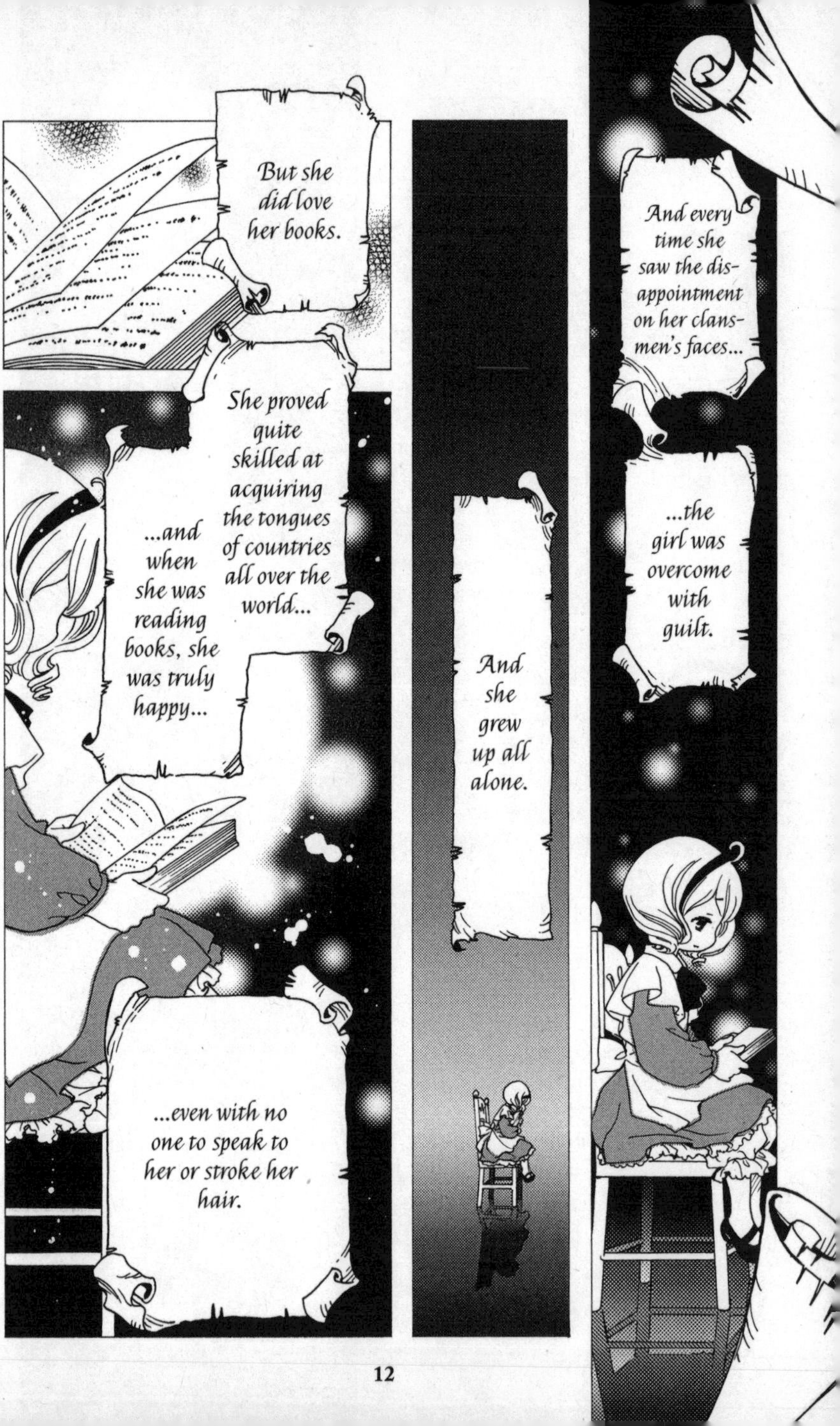
And every time she saw the dis-appointment on her clans-men's faces...
...the girl was overcome with guilt.
And she grew up all alone.
But she did love her books.
She proved quite skilled at acquiring the tongues of countries all over the world...
...and when she was reading books, she was truly happy...
...even with no one to speak to her or stroke her hair.

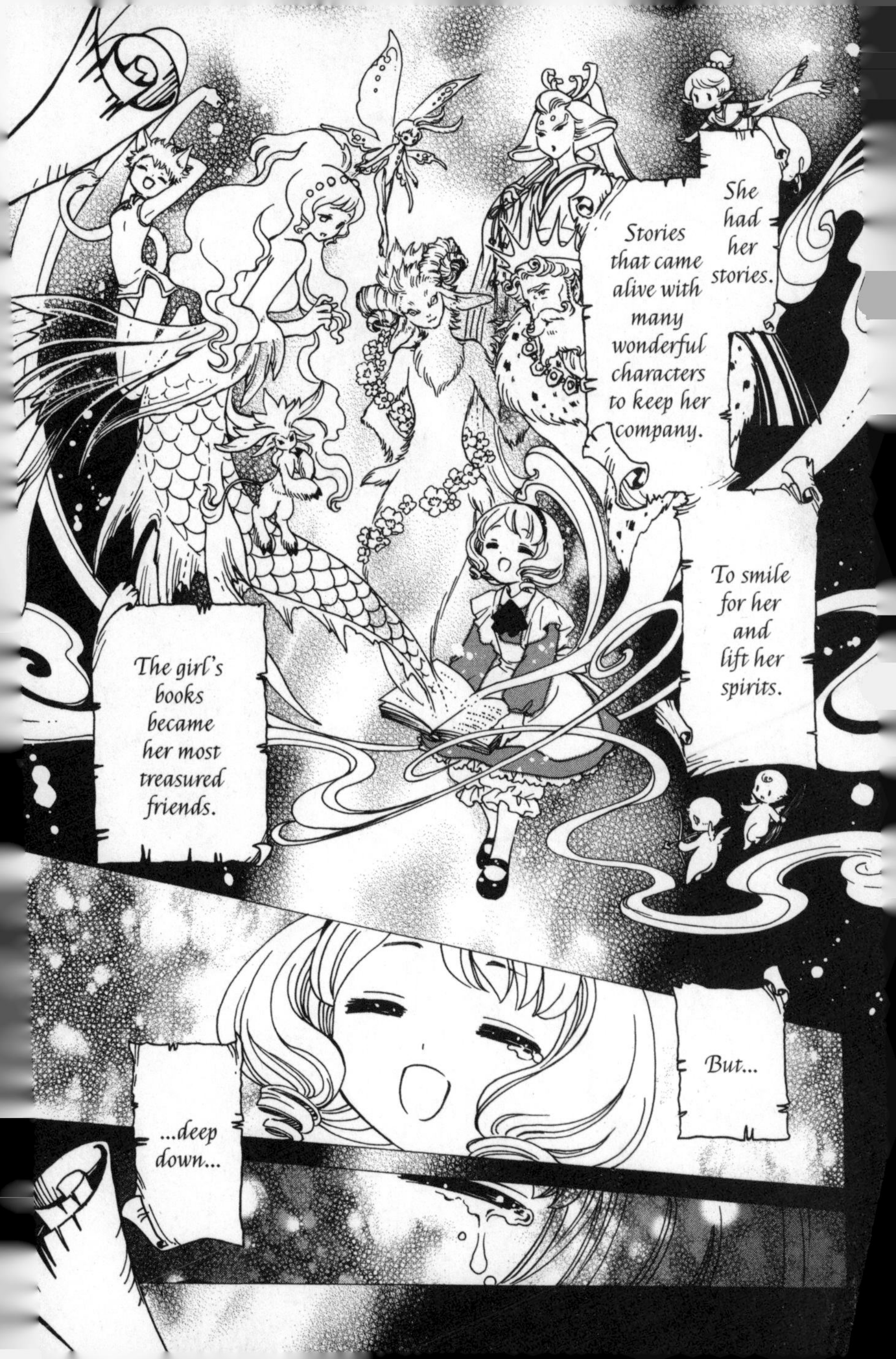
She had her stories.
Stories that came alive with many wonderful characters to keep her company.
To smile for her and lift her spirits.
The girl's books became her most treasured friends.
But...
...deep down...

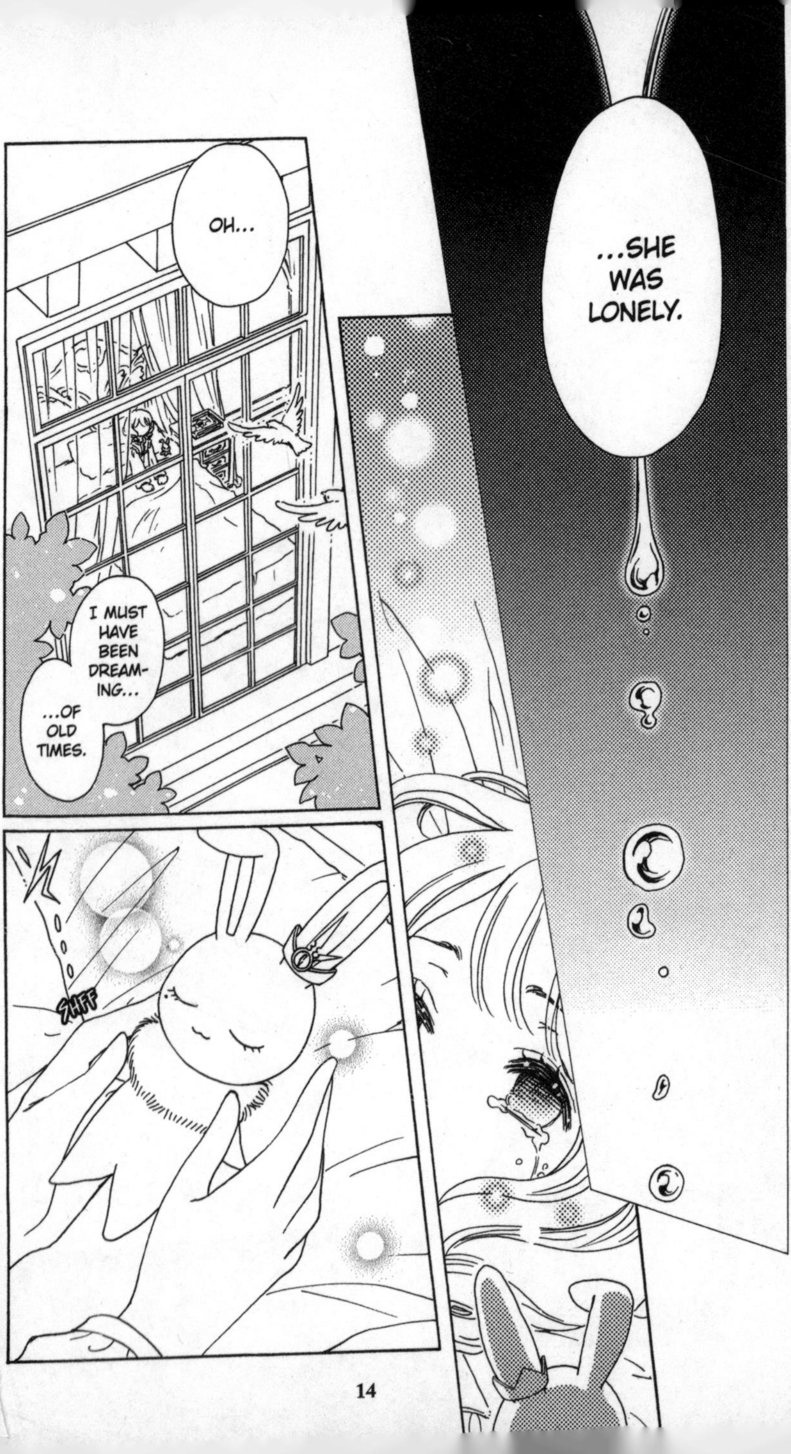
...SHE WAS LONELY.
OH...
I MUST HAVE BEEN DREAMING...
...OF OLD TIMES.
SHFF

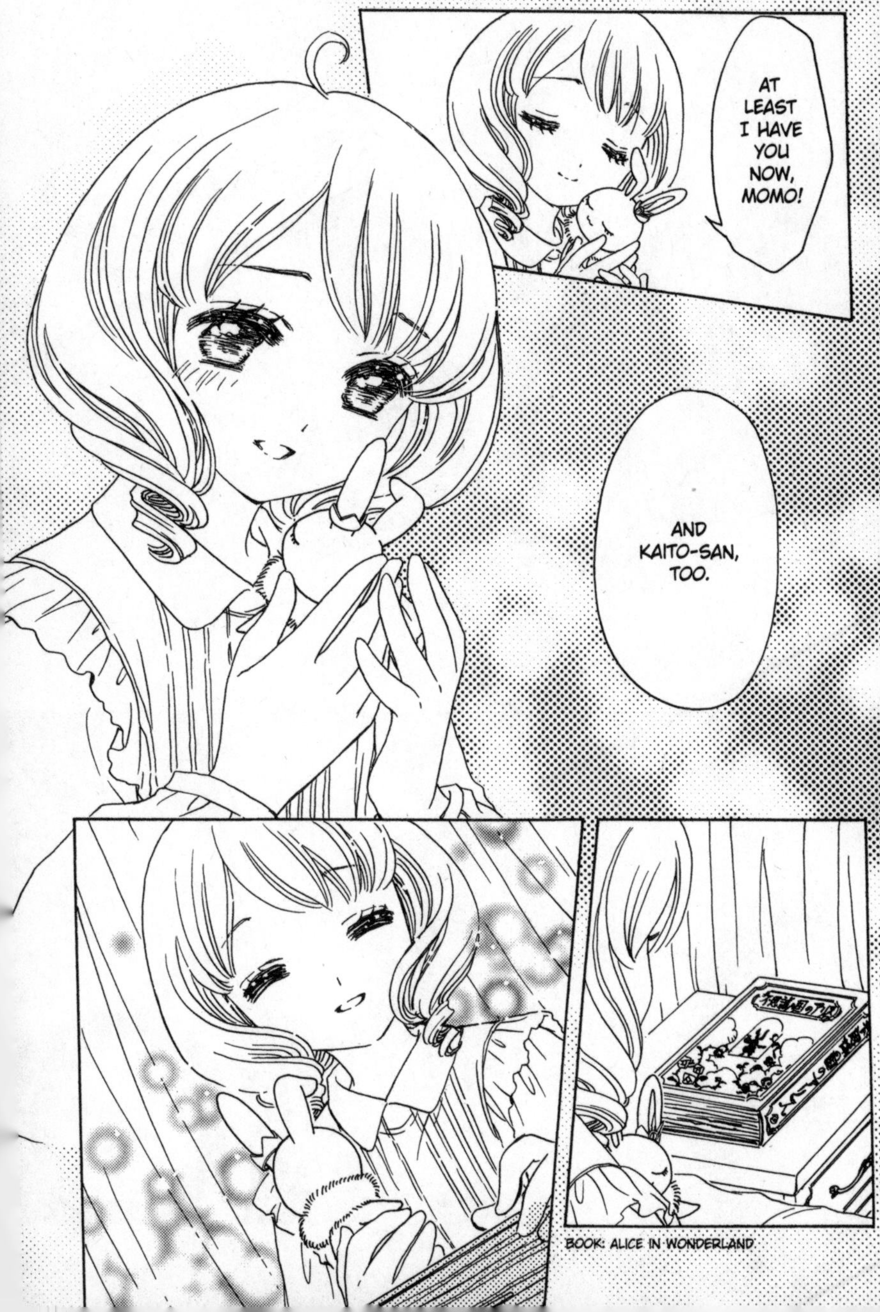
AT LEAST I HAVE YOU NOW, MOMO!
AND KAITO-SAN, TOO.
BOOK: ALICE IN WONDERLAND

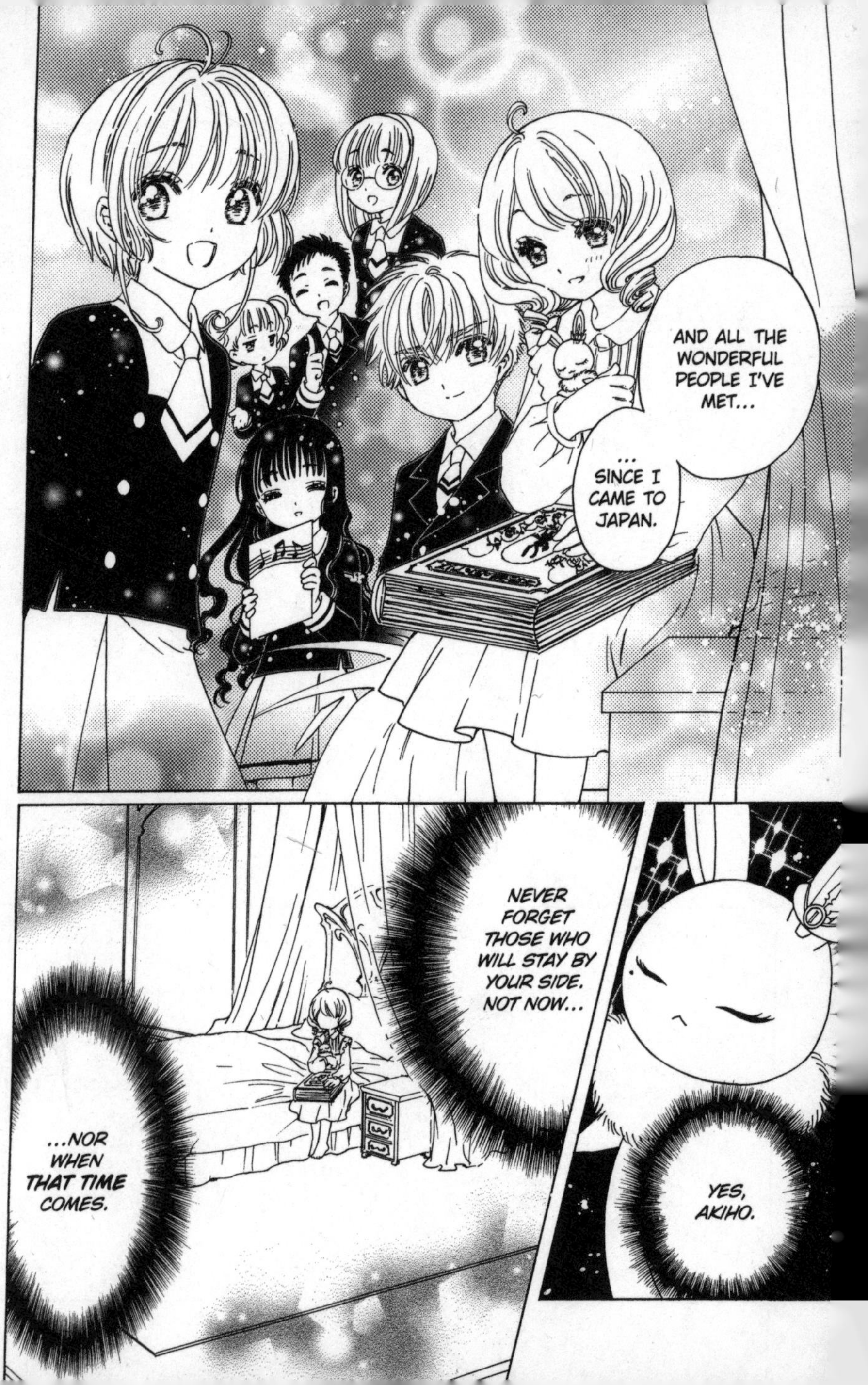
AND ALL THE WONDERFUL PEOPLE I'VE MET...
...SINCE I CAME TO JAPAN.
NEVER FORGET THOSE WHO WILL STAY BY YOUR SIDE. NOT NOW...
...NOR WHEN THAT TIME COMES.
YES, AKIHO.

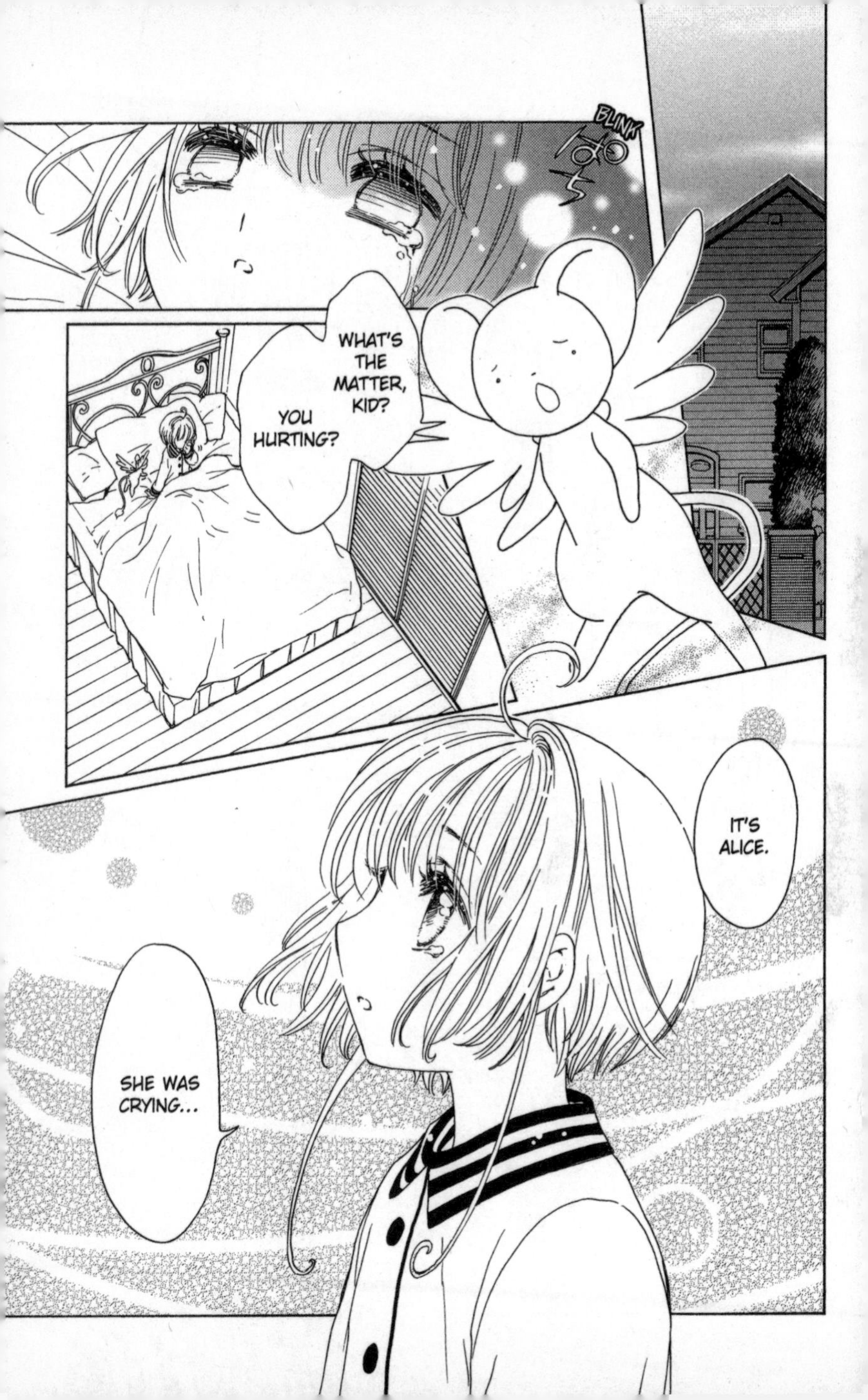
BLINK
WHAT'S THE MATTER, KID?
YOU HURTING?
IT'S ALICE.
SHE WAS CRYING...

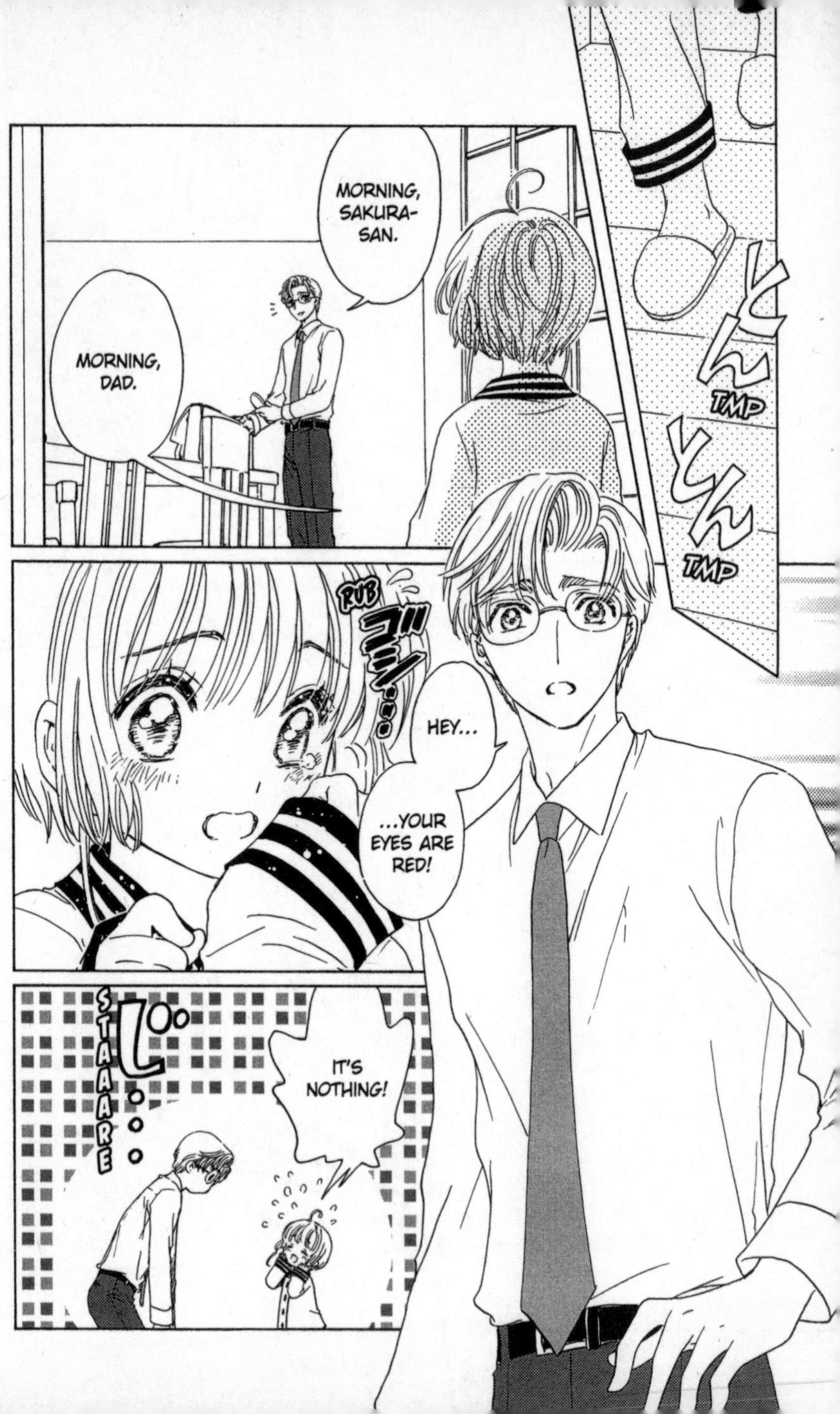
とん
TMP
とん
TMP
MORNING, SAKURA-SAN.
MORNING, DAD.
HEY...
...YOUR EYES ARE RED!
RUB
ゴシ...
STAAAARE
じー
IT'S NOTHING!

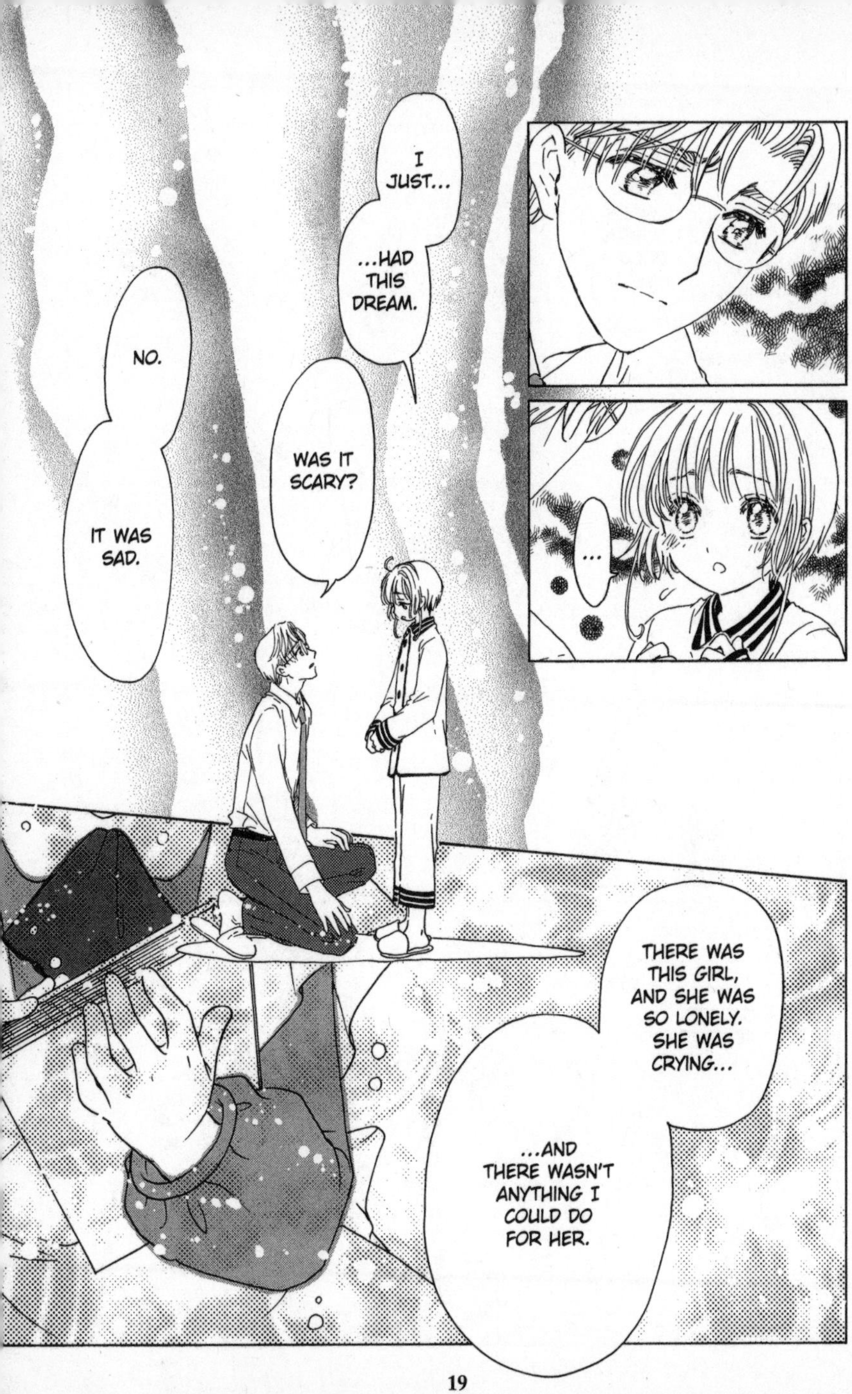
...
I JUST...
...HAD THIS DREAM.
WAS IT SCARY?
NO.
IT WAS SAD.
THERE WAS THIS GIRL, AND SHE WAS SO LONELY. SHE WAS CRYING...
...AND THERE WASN'T ANYTHING I COULD DO FOR HER.

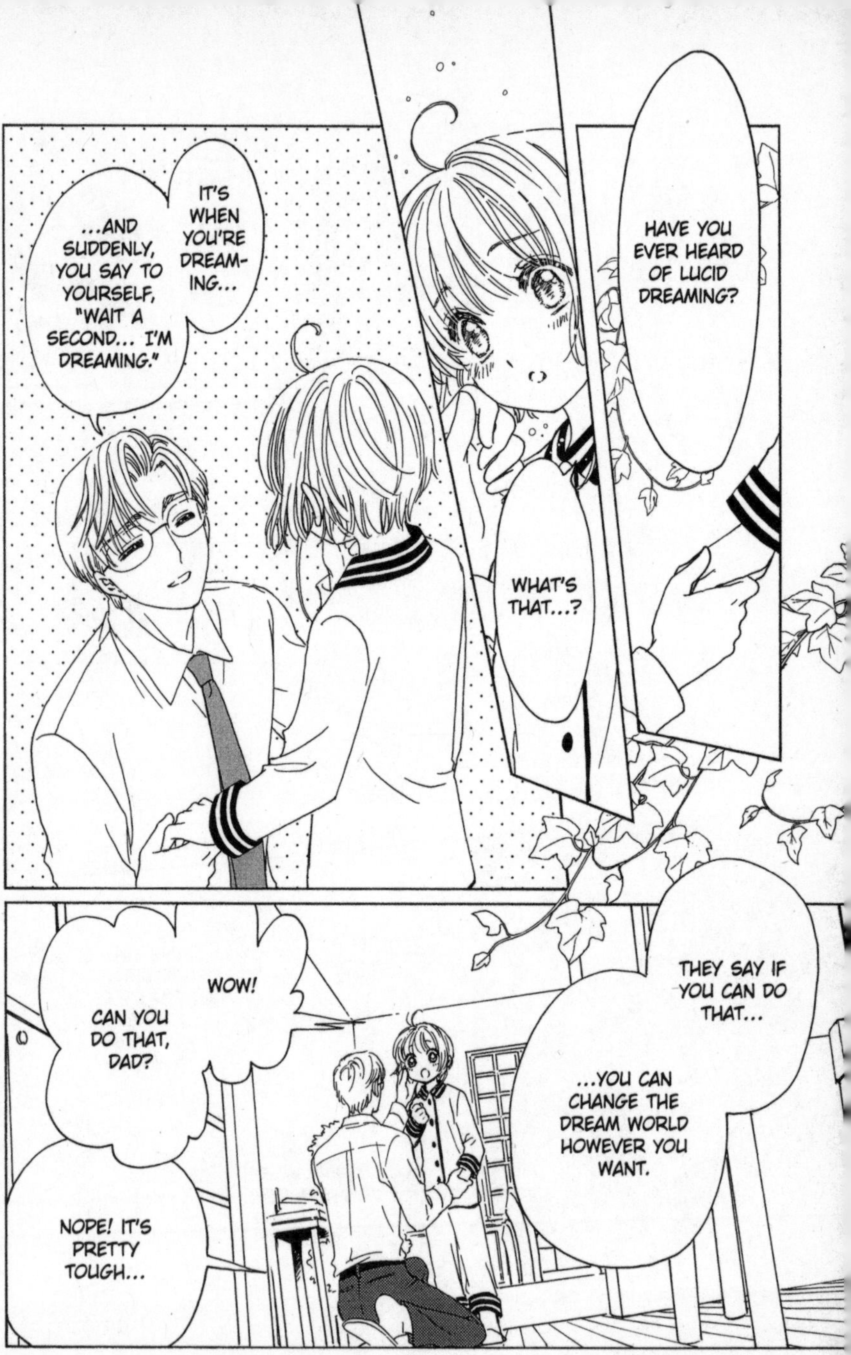
HAVE YOU EVER HEARD OF LUCID DREAMING?
WHAT'S THAT...?
IT'S WHEN YOU'RE DREAMING...
...AND SUDDENLY, YOU SAY TO YOURSELF, "WAIT A SECOND... I'M DREAMING."
THEY SAY IF YOU CAN DO THAT...
...YOU CAN CHANGE THE DREAM WORLD HOWEVER YOU WANT.
WOW!
CAN YOU DO THAT, DAD?
NOPE! IT'S PRETTY TOUGH...

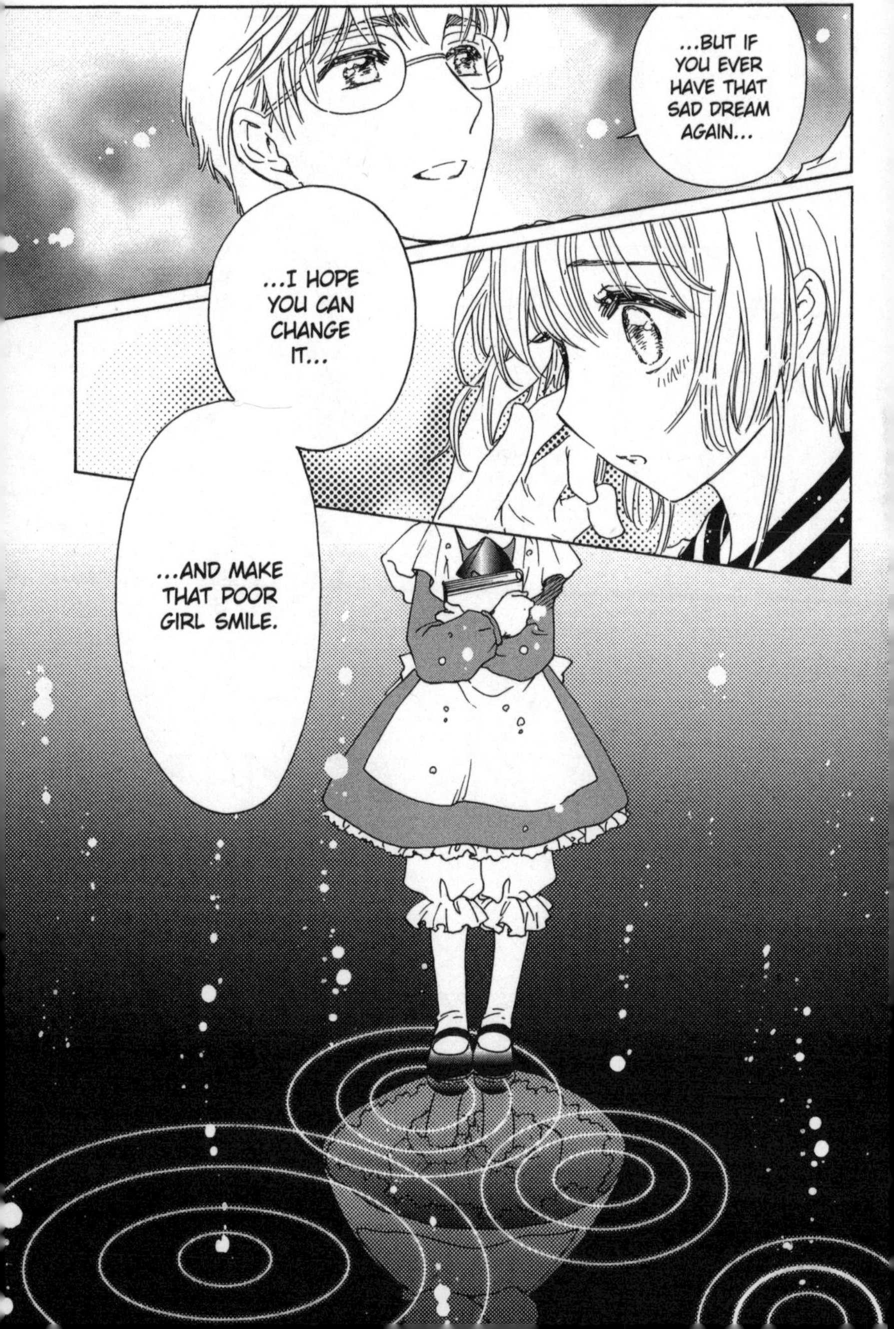
...BUT IF YOU EVER HAVE THAT SAD DREAM AGAIN...
...I HOPE YOU CAN CHANGE IT...
...AND MAKE THAT POOR GIRL SMILE.

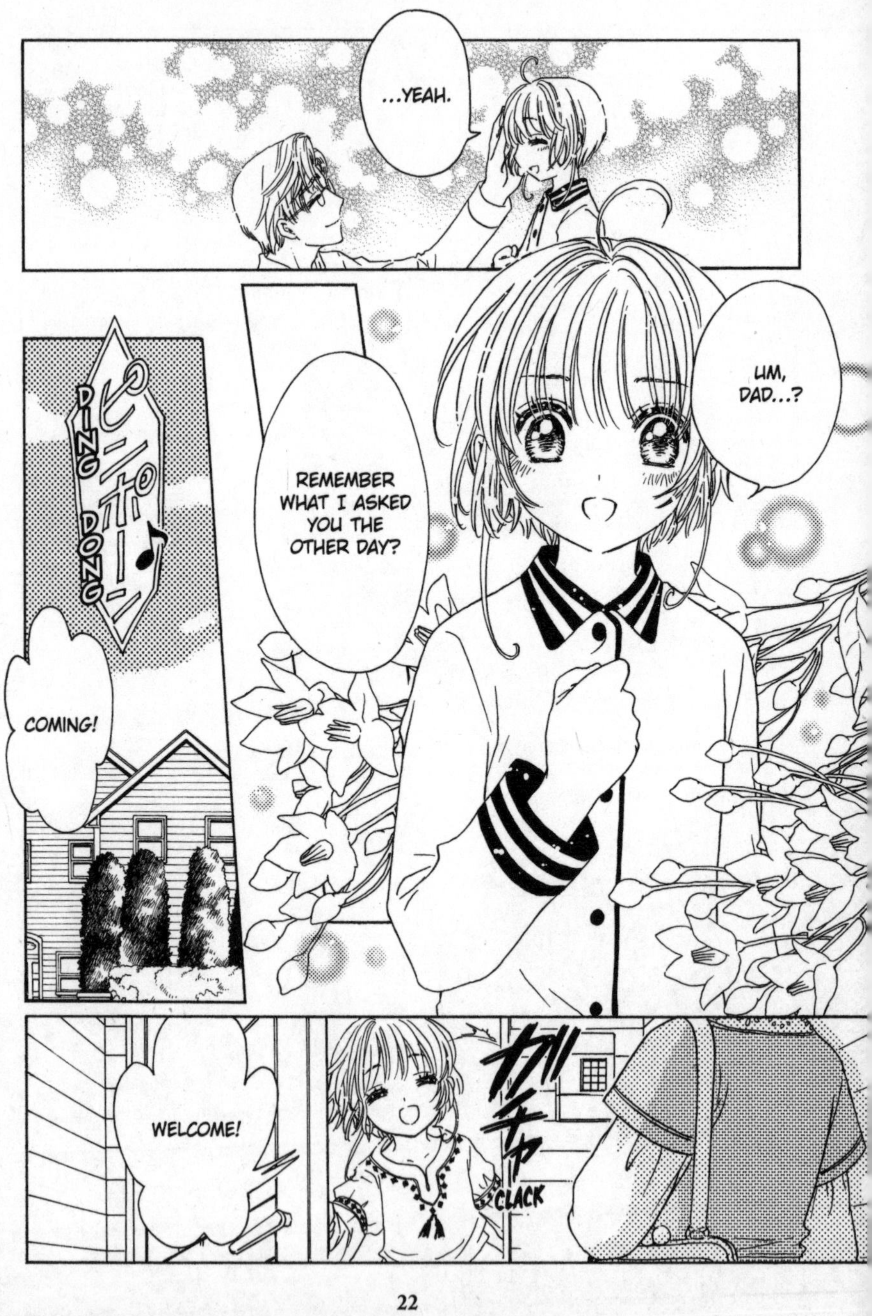
...YEAH.
UM, DAD...?
REMEMBER WHAT I ASKED YOU THE OTHER DAY?
ピンポーン
DING DONG
COMING!
ガチャ
CLACK
WELCOME!

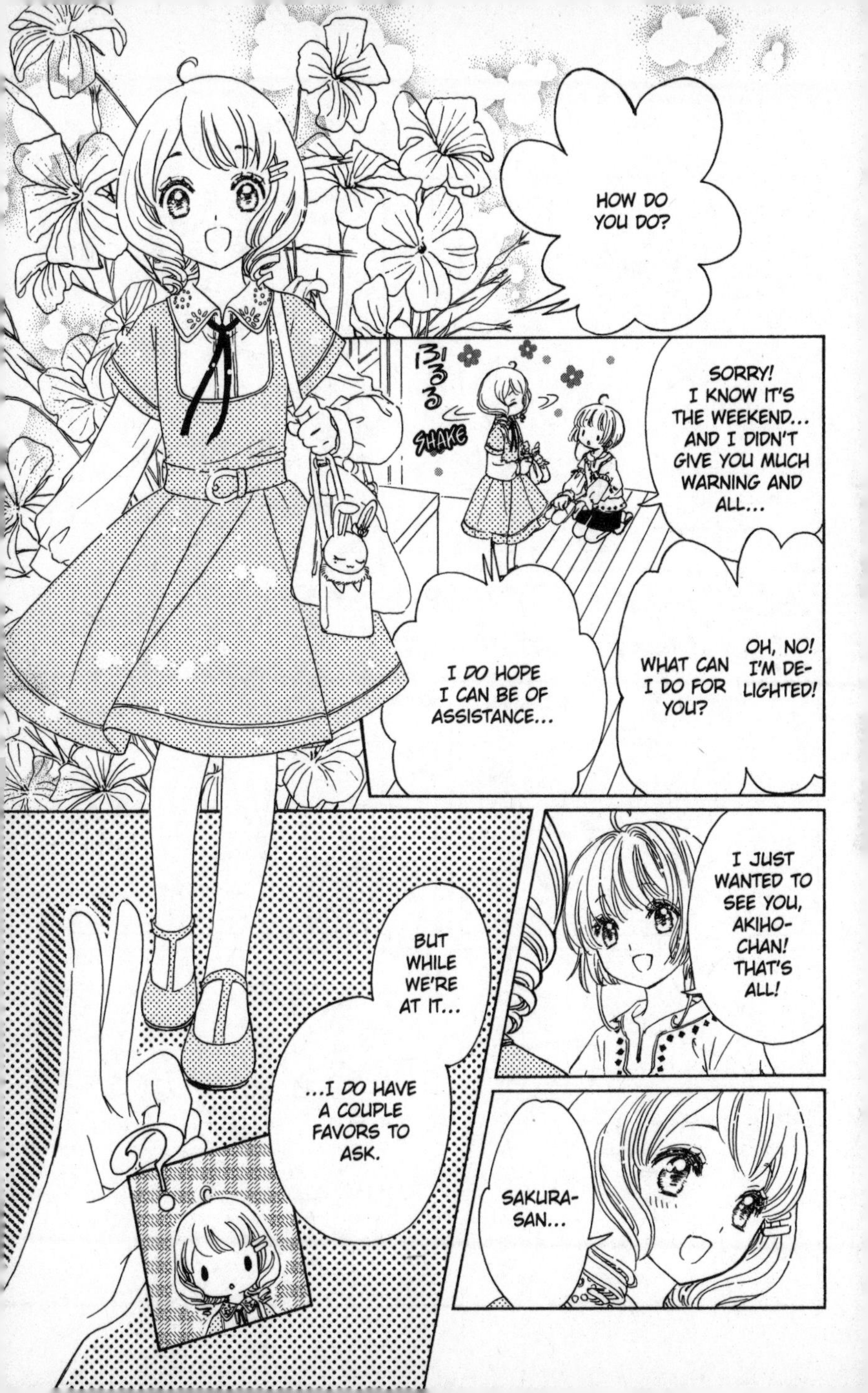
HOW DO YOU DO?
SORRY! I KNOW IT'S THE WEEKEND... AND I DIDN'T GIVE YOU MUCH WARNING AND ALL...
ぷるるる
SHAKE
OH, NO! I'M DE-LIGHTED!
WHAT CAN I DO FOR YOU?
I *DO* HOPE I CAN BE OF ASSISTANCE...
I JUST WANTED TO SEE YOU, AKIHO-CHAN! THAT'S ALL!
SAKURA-SAN...
BUT WHILE WE'RE AT IT...
...I DO HAVE A COUPLE FAVORS TO ASK.

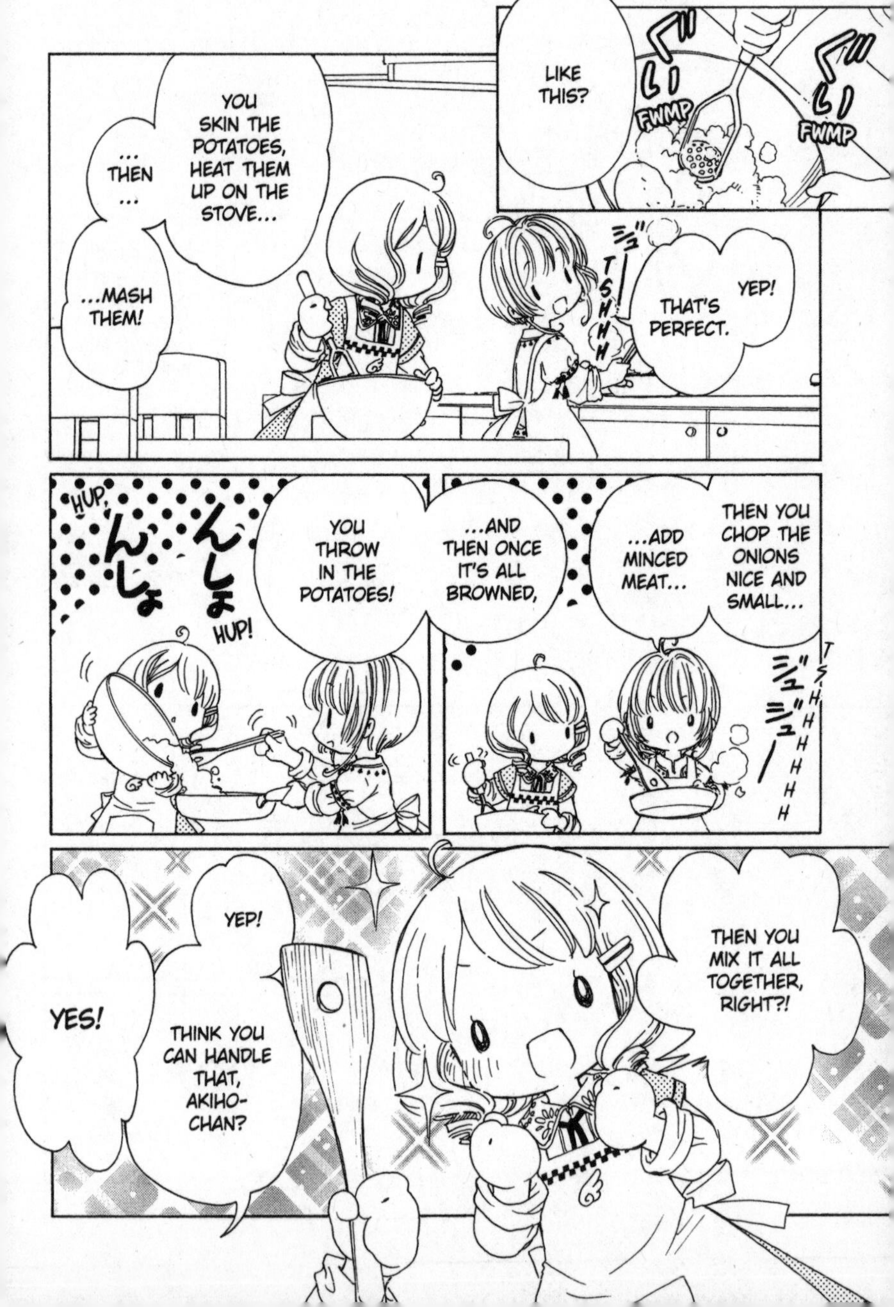
LIKE THIS?
FWMP
FWMP
TSHHH
YEP! THAT'S PERFECT.
YOU SKIN THE POTATOES, HEAT THEM UP ON THE STOVE...
... THEN ...
...MASH THEM!
TSHHHHHHH
THEN YOU CHOP THE ONIONS NICE AND SMALL...
...ADD MINCED MEAT...
...AND THEN ONCE IT'S ALL BROWNED,
YOU THROW IN THE POTATOES!
HUP,
HUP!
THEN YOU MIX IT ALL TOGETHER, RIGHT?!
YEP!
THINK YOU CAN HANDLE THAT, AKIHO-CHAN?
YES!

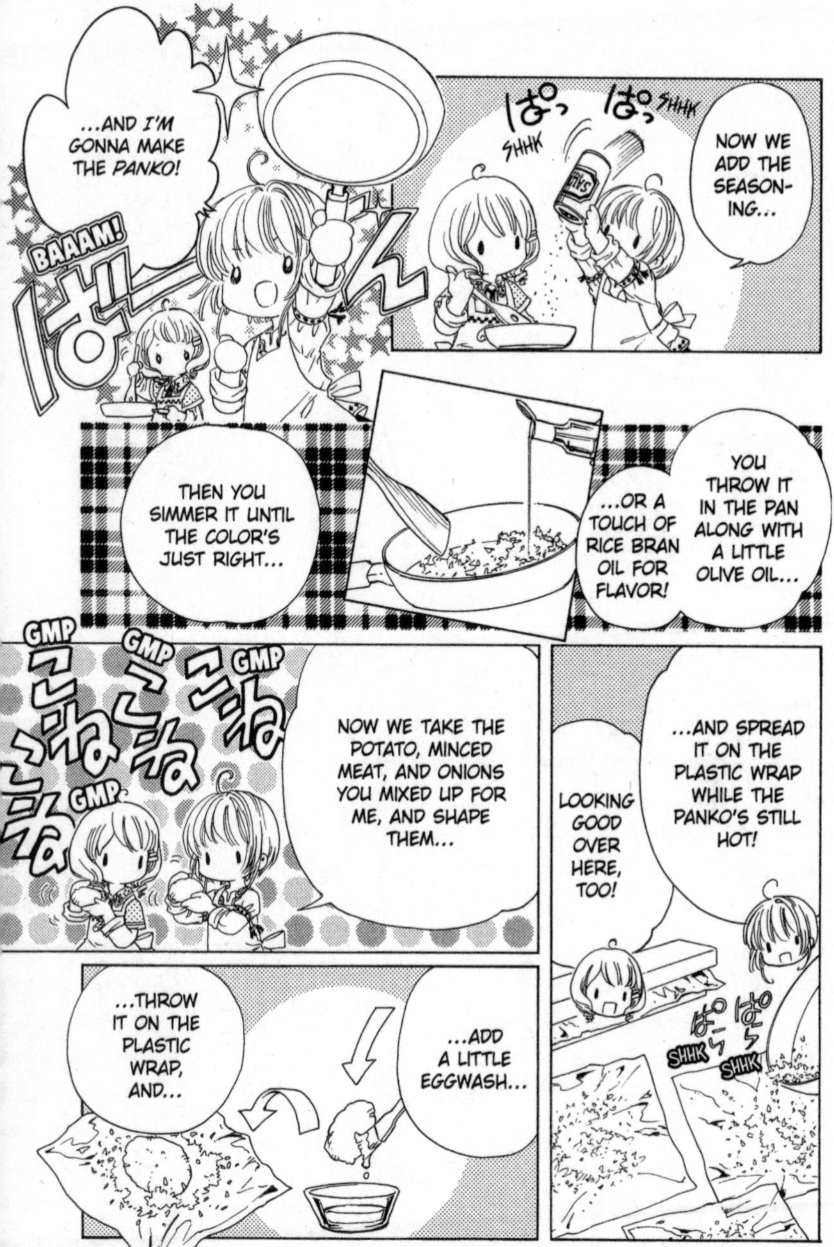
ぱっ ぱっ
SHHK SHHK
NOW WE ADD THE SEASON-ING...
...AND I'M GONNA MAKE THE PANKO!
BAAAM!
ばーん
YOU THROW IT IN THE PAN ALONG WITH A LITTLE OLIVE OIL...
...OR A TOUCH OF RICE BRAN OIL FOR FLAVOR!
THEN YOU SIMMER IT UNTIL THE COLOR'S JUST RIGHT...
...AND SPREAD IT ON THE PLASTIC WRAP WHILE THE PANKO'S STILL HOT!
LOOKING GOOD OVER HERE, TOO!
ぱら ぱら
SHHK SHHK
NOW WE TAKE THE POTATO, MINCED MEAT, AND ONIONS YOU MIXED UP FOR ME, AND SHAPE THEM...
こね こね こね こね
GMP GMP GMP GMP
...ADD A LITTLE EGGWASH...
...THROW IT ON THE PLASTIC WRAP, AND...

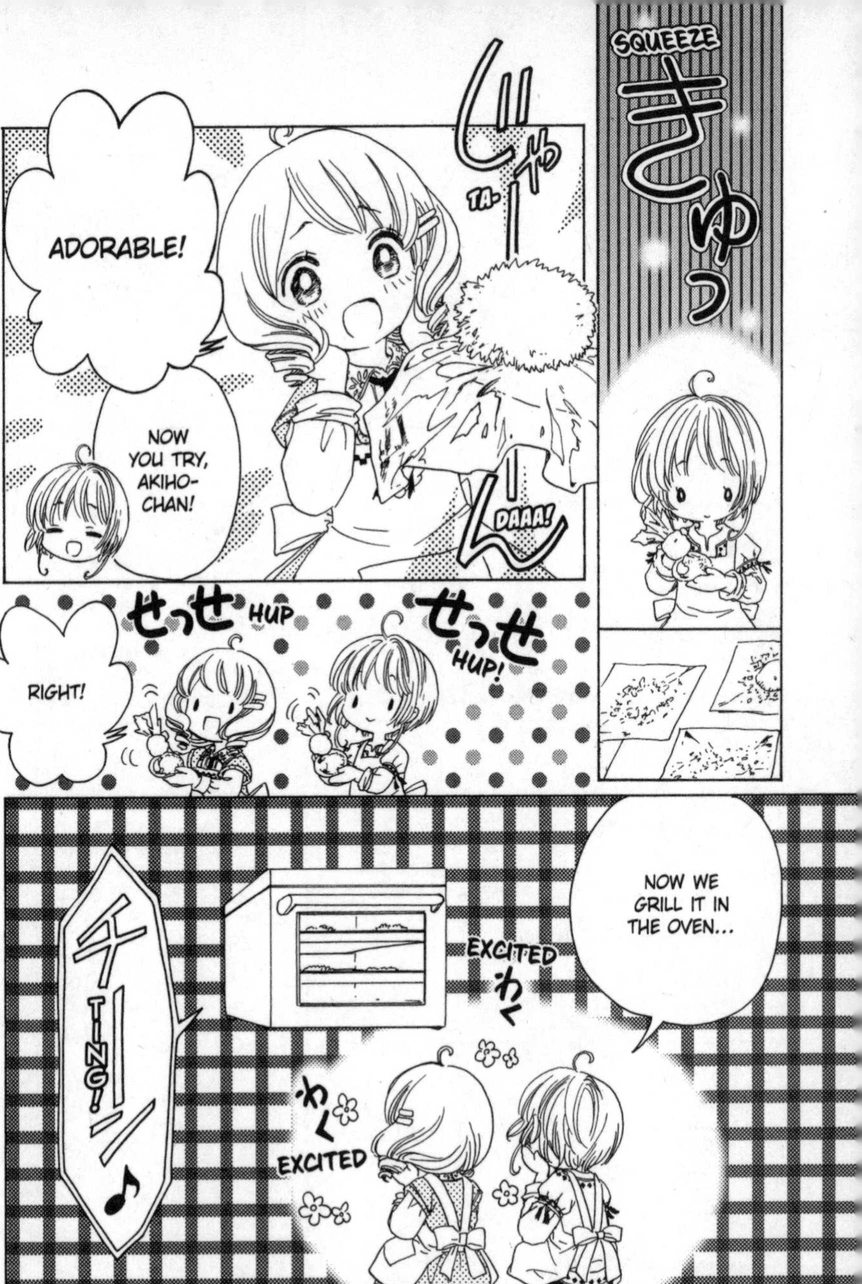
SQUEEZE
きゅっ
じゅーん
TA-DAAA!
ADORABLE!
NOW YOU TRY, AKIHO-CHAN!
せっせ
HUP!
せっせ
HUP
RIGHT!
NOW WE GRILL IT IN THE OVEN...
EXCITED
わく
わく
EXCITED
チーン
TING!
♪

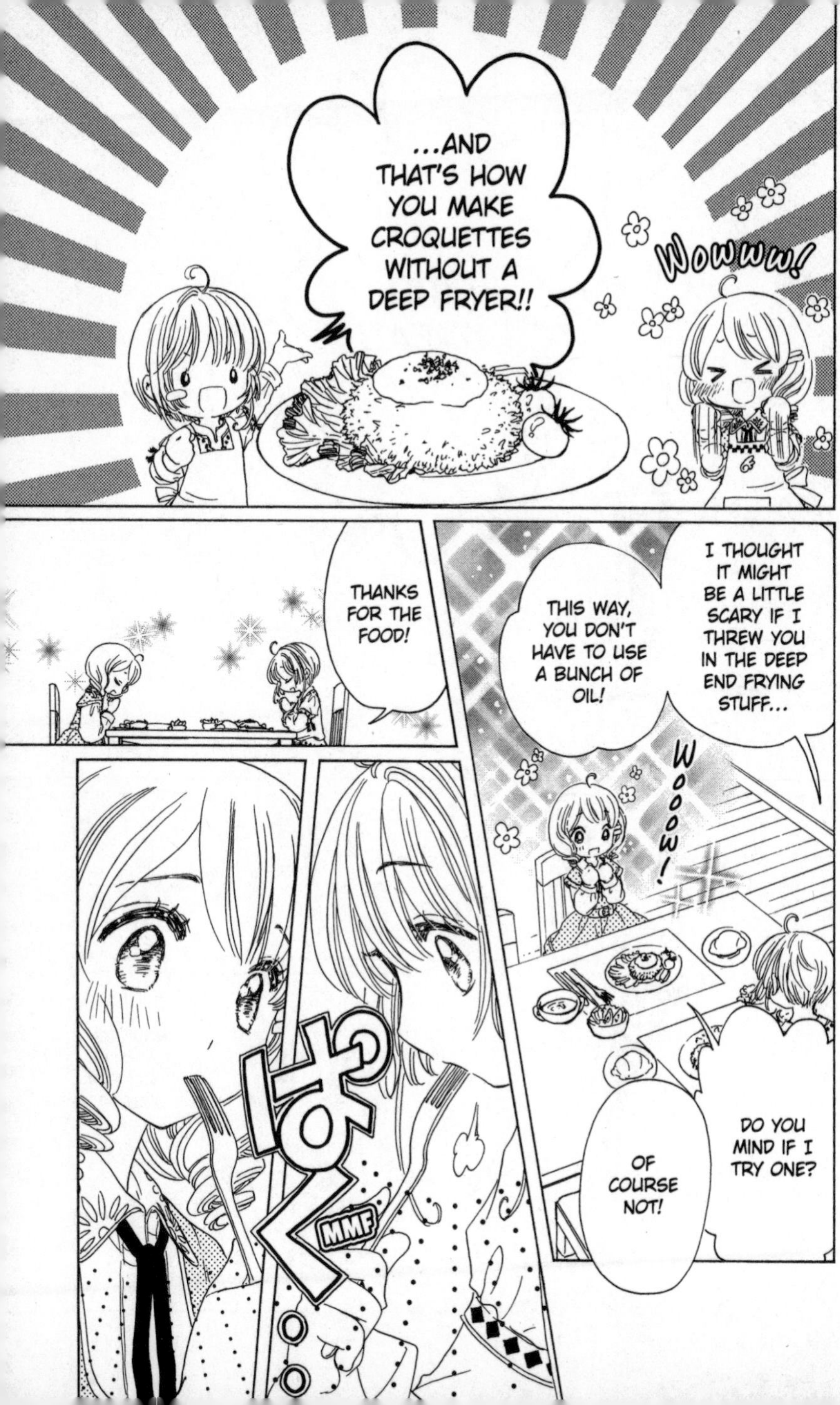
...AND THAT'S HOW YOU MAKE CROQUETTES WITHOUT A DEEP FRYER!!
Wowww!
I THOUGHT IT MIGHT BE A LITTLE SCARY IF I THREW YOU IN THE DEEP END FRYING STUFF...
THIS WAY, YOU DON'T HAVE TO USE A BUNCH OF OIL!
Wooow!
DO YOU MIND IF I TRY ONE?
OF COURSE NOT!
THANKS FOR THE FOOD!
ぱく
MMF

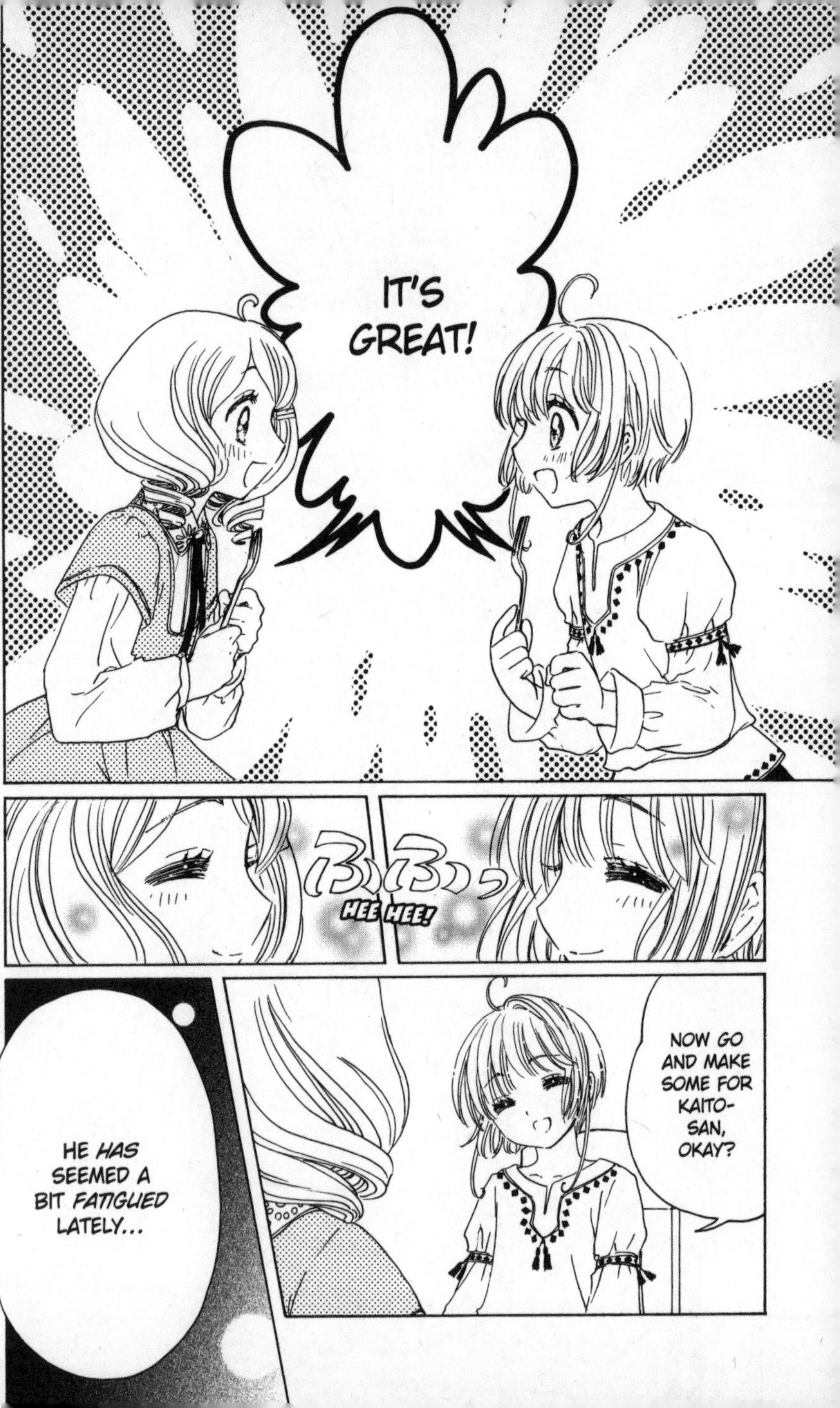
IT'S GREAT!
HEE HEE!
NOW GO AND MAKE SOME FOR KAITO-SAN, OKAY?
HE *HAS* SEEMED A BIT *FATIGUED* LATELY...

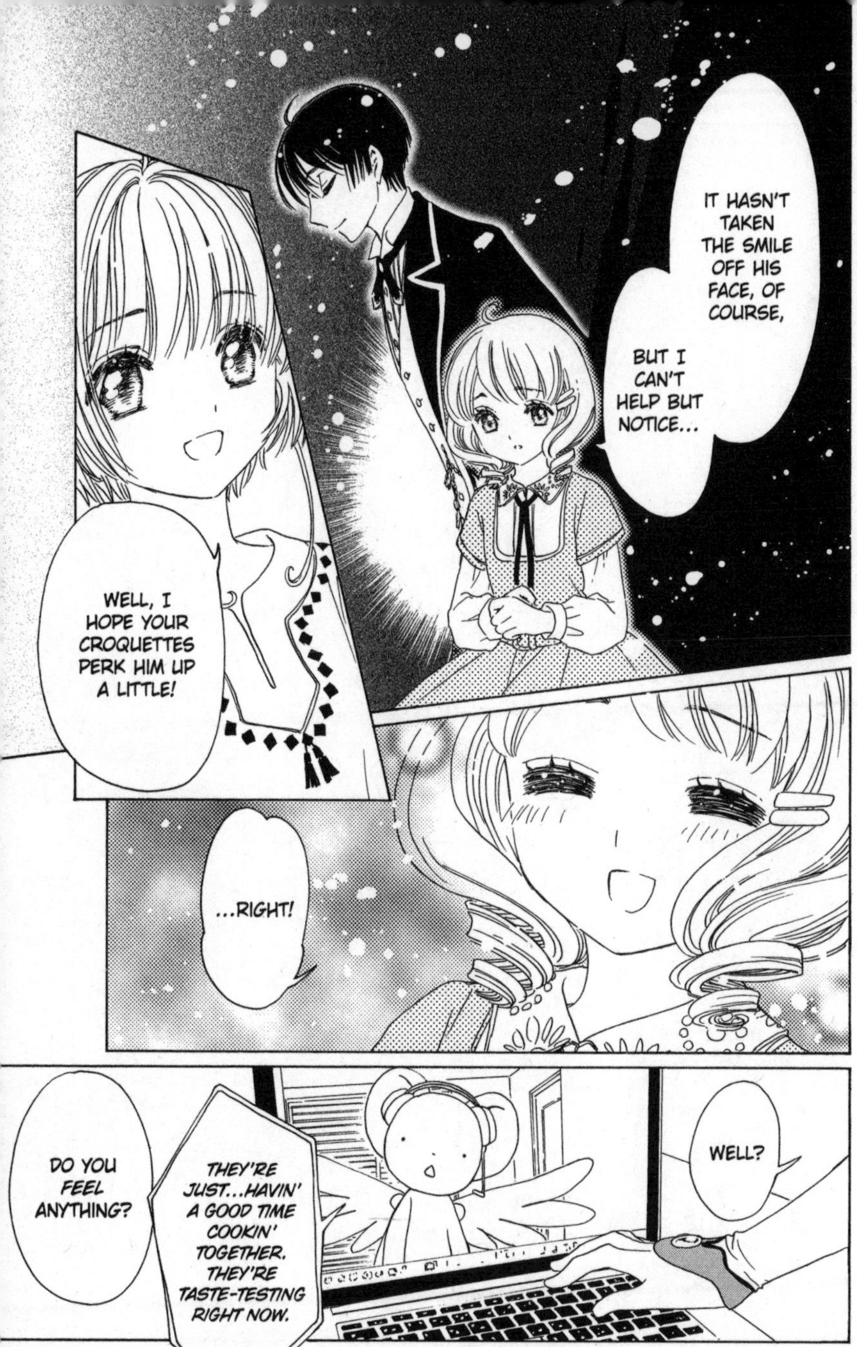
IT HASN'T TAKEN THE SMILE OFF HIS FACE, OF COURSE,
BUT I CAN'T HELP BUT NOTICE...
WELL, I HOPE YOUR CROQUETTES PERK HIM UP A LITTLE!
...RIGHT!
WELL?
DO YOU FEEL ANYTHING?
THEY'RE JUST...HAVIN' A GOOD TIME COOKIN' TOGETHER. THEY'RE TASTE-TESTING RIGHT NOW.

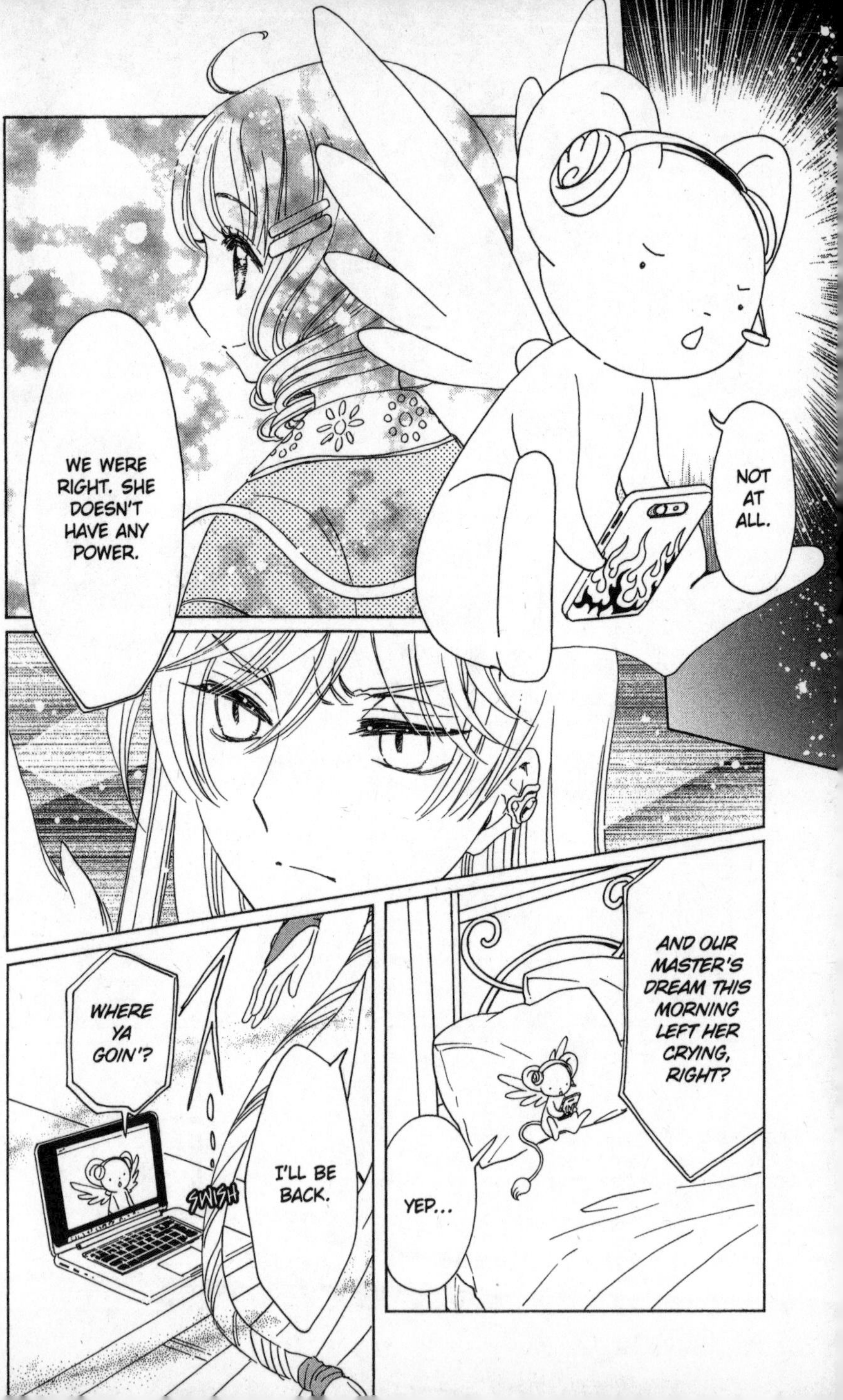
WE WERE RIGHT. SHE DOESN'T HAVE ANY POWER.
NOT AT ALL.
AND OUR MASTER'S DREAM THIS MORNING LEFT HER CRYING, RIGHT?
YEP...
WHERE YA GOIN'?
SWISH
I'LL BE BACK.

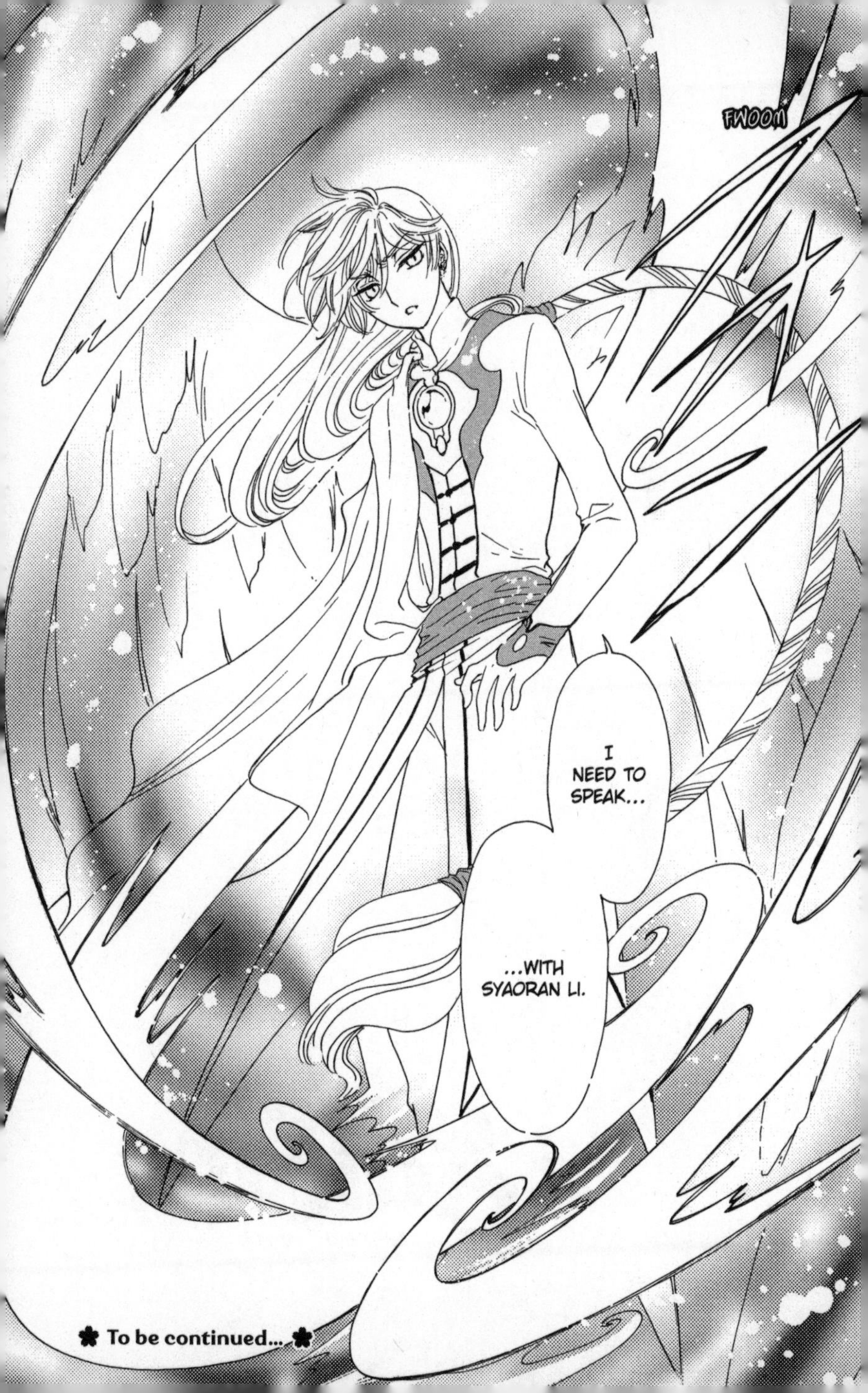
FWOOM
I NEED TO SPEAK...
...WITH SYAORAN LI.

✿ To be continued... ✿

Cardcaptor Sakura
CLEAR CARD

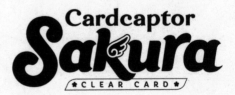

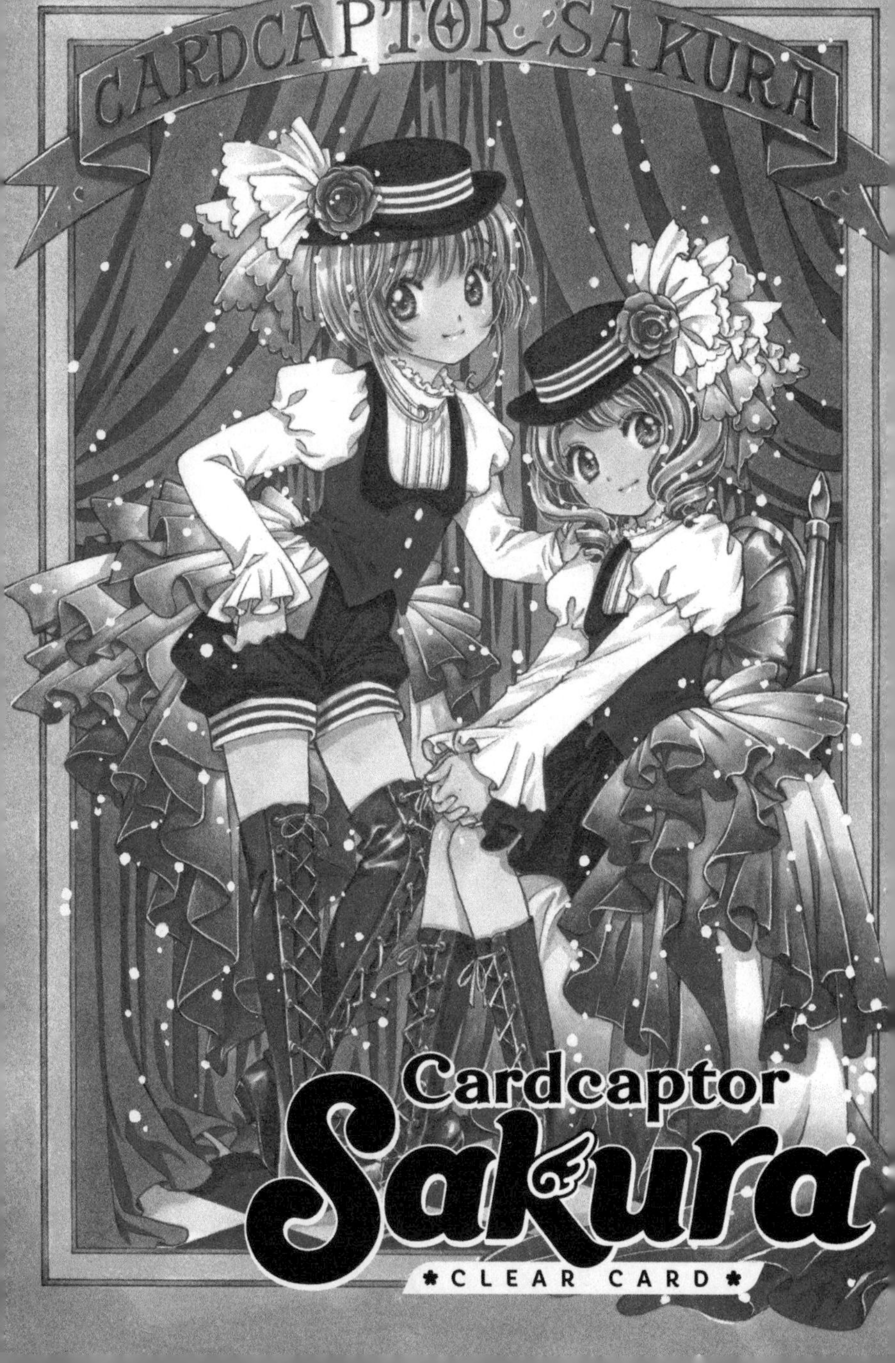
CARDCAPTOR SAKURA
Cardcaptor
Sakura
CLEAR CARD

Cardcaptor Sakura

CLEAR CARD

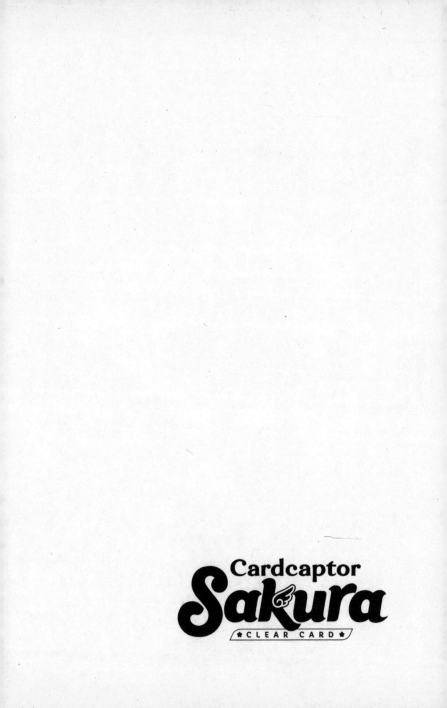

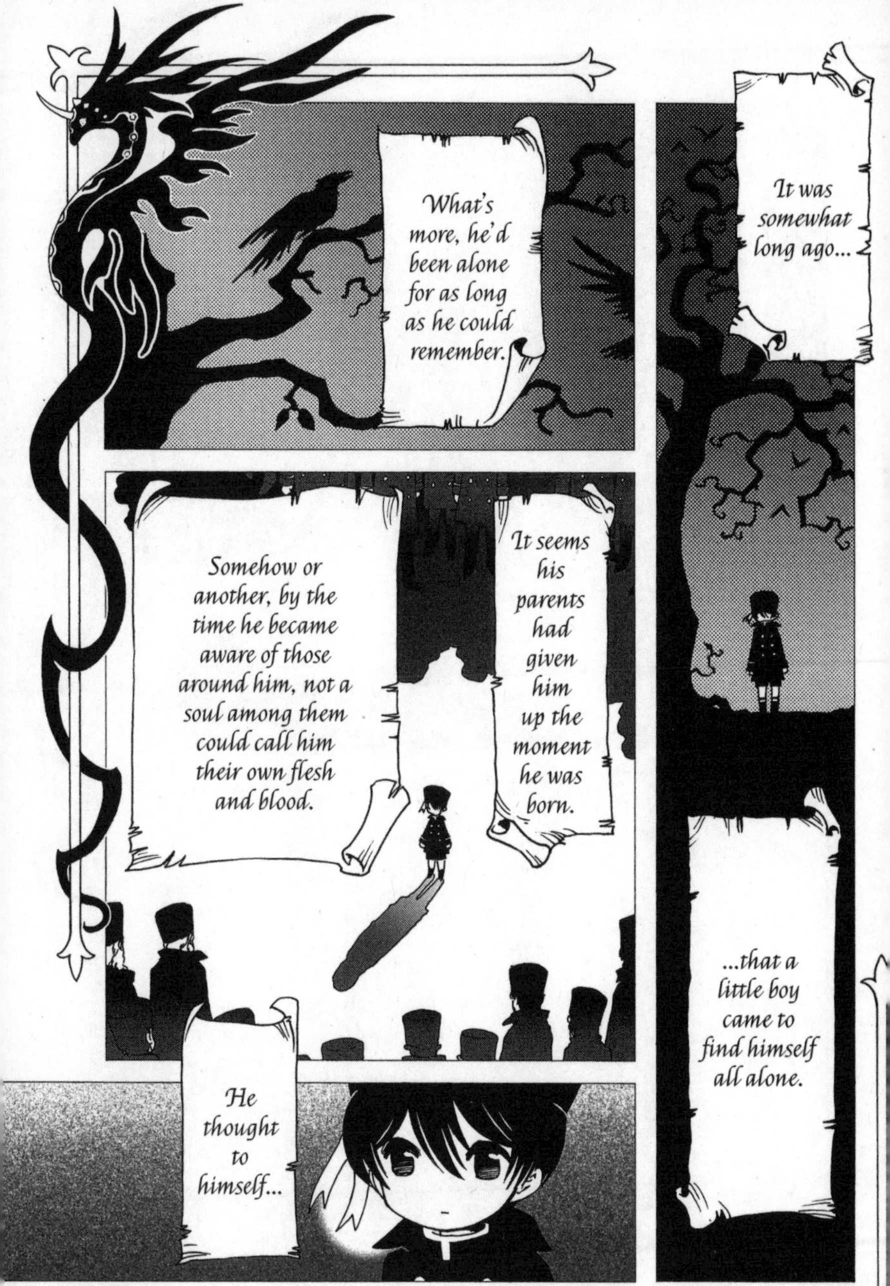
It was somewhat long ago...
...that a little boy came to find himself all alone.
What's more, he'd been alone for as long as he could remember.
It seems his parents had given him up the moment he was born.
Somehow or another, by the time he became aware of those around him, not a soul among them could call him their own flesh and blood.
He thought to himself...

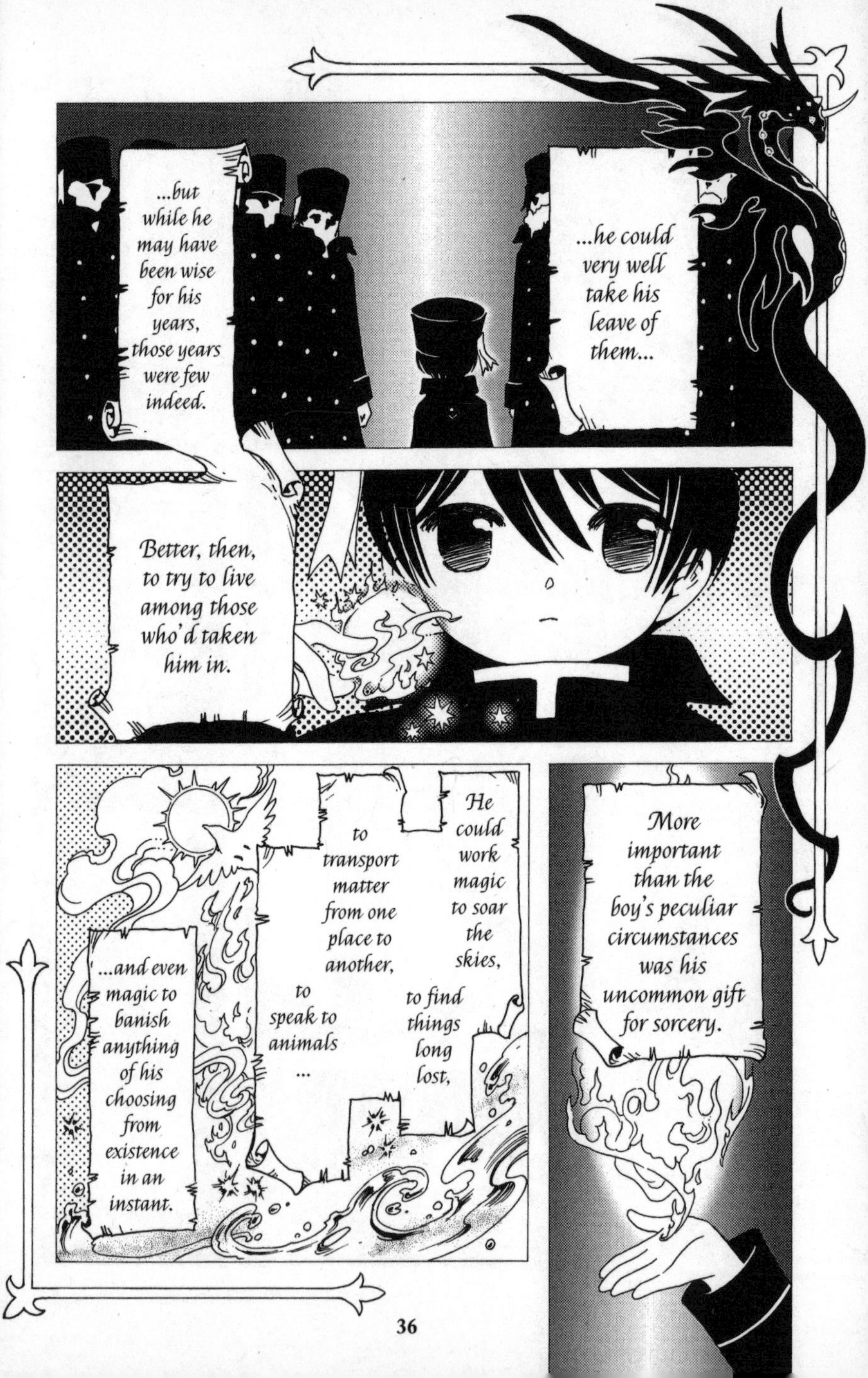
...he could very well take his leave of them...
...but while he may have been wise for his years, those years were few indeed.
Better, then, to try to live among those who'd taken him in.
More important than the boy's peculiar circumstances was his uncommon gift for sorcery.
He could work magic to soar the skies,
to transport matter from one place to another,
to find things long lost,
to speak to animals ...
...and even magic to banish anything of his choosing from existence in an instant.

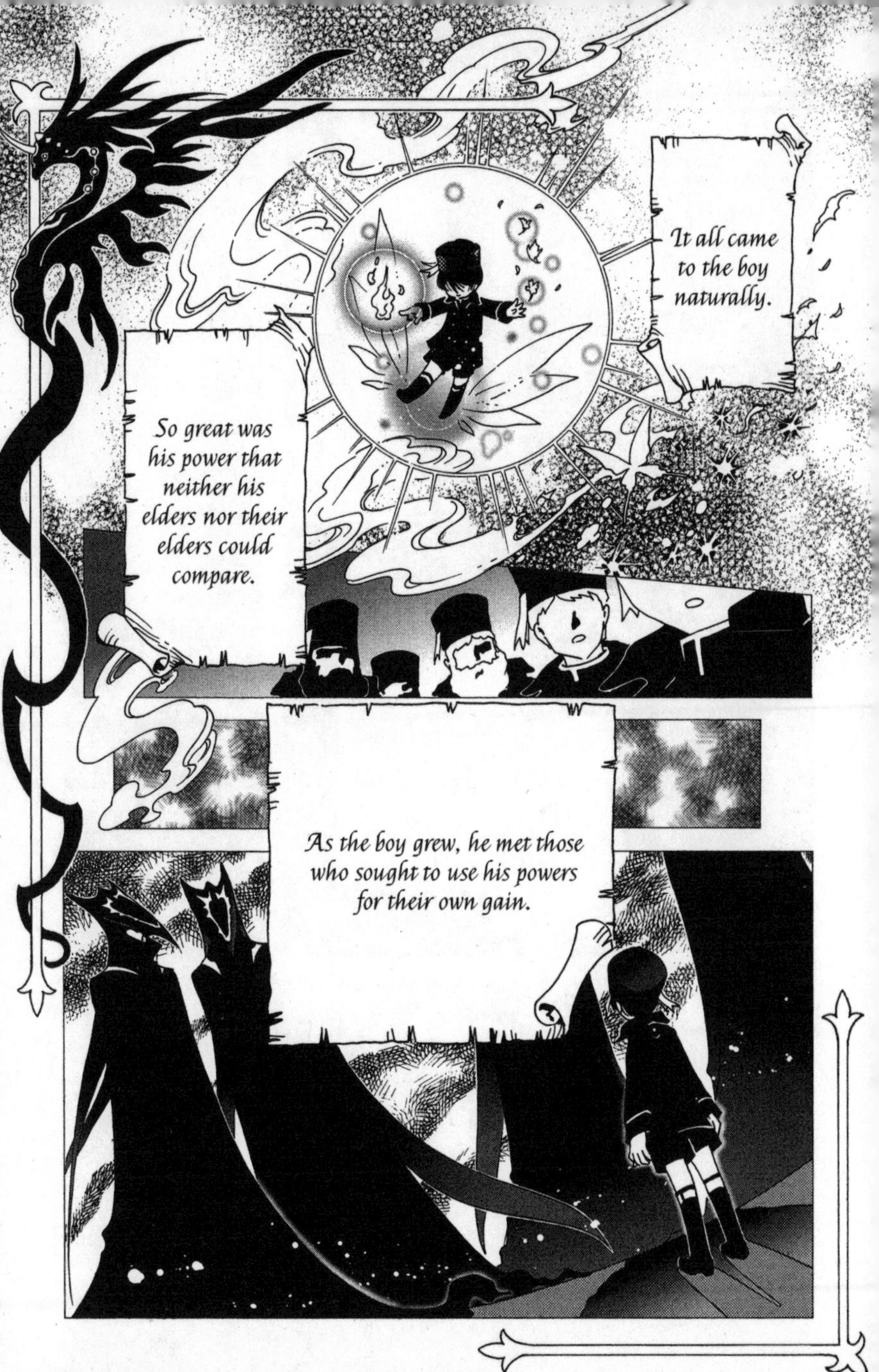
It all came to the boy naturally.
So great was his power that neither his elders nor their elders could compare.
As the boy grew, he met those who sought to use his powers for their own gain.

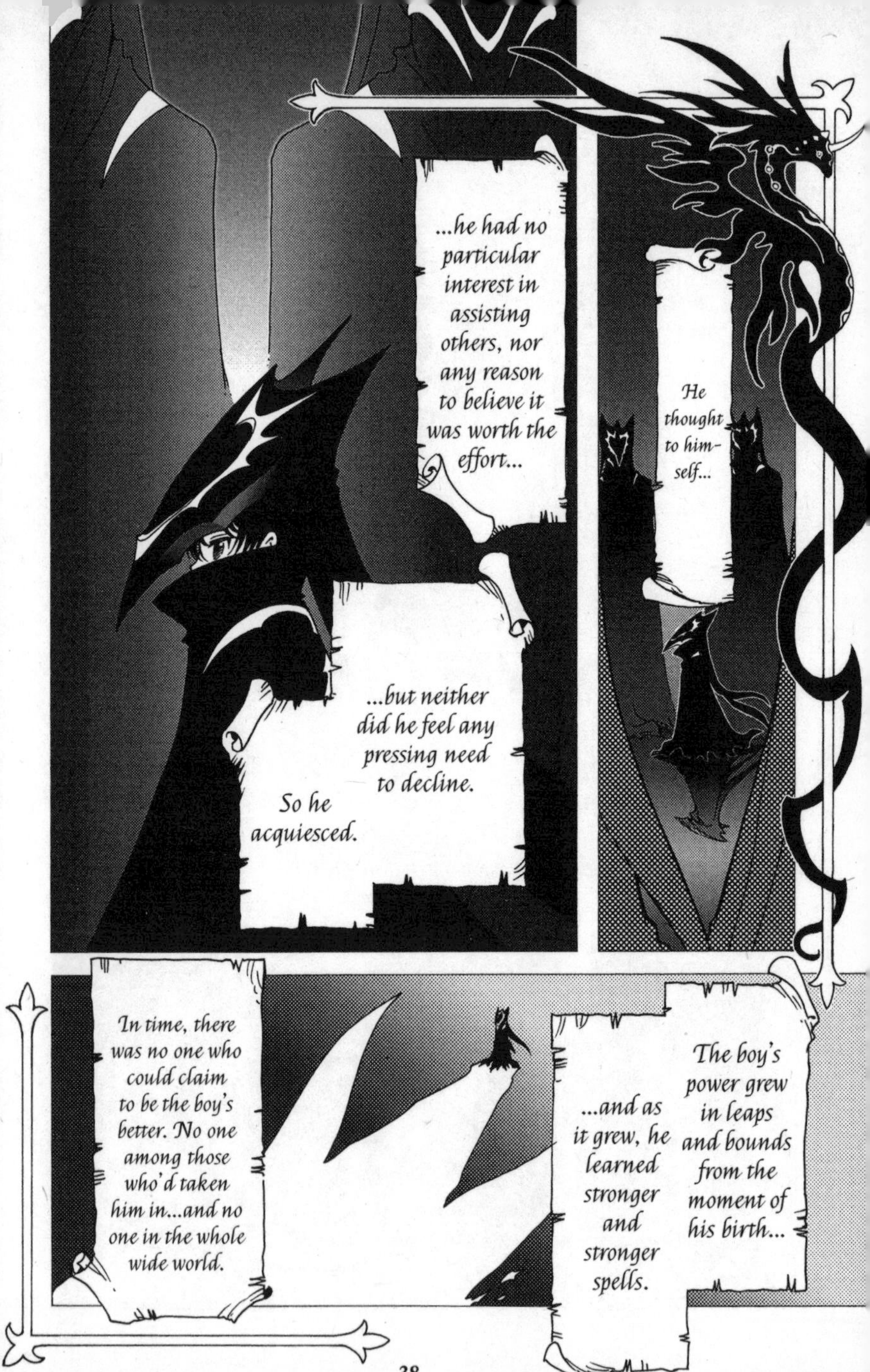
He thought to himself...
...he had no particular interest in assisting others, nor any reason to believe it was worth the effort...
...but neither did he feel any pressing need to decline.
So he acquiesced.
The boy's power grew in leaps and bounds from the moment of his birth...
...and as it grew, he learned stronger and stronger spells.
In time, there was no one who could claim to be the boy's better. No one among those who'd taken him in...and no one in the whole wide world.

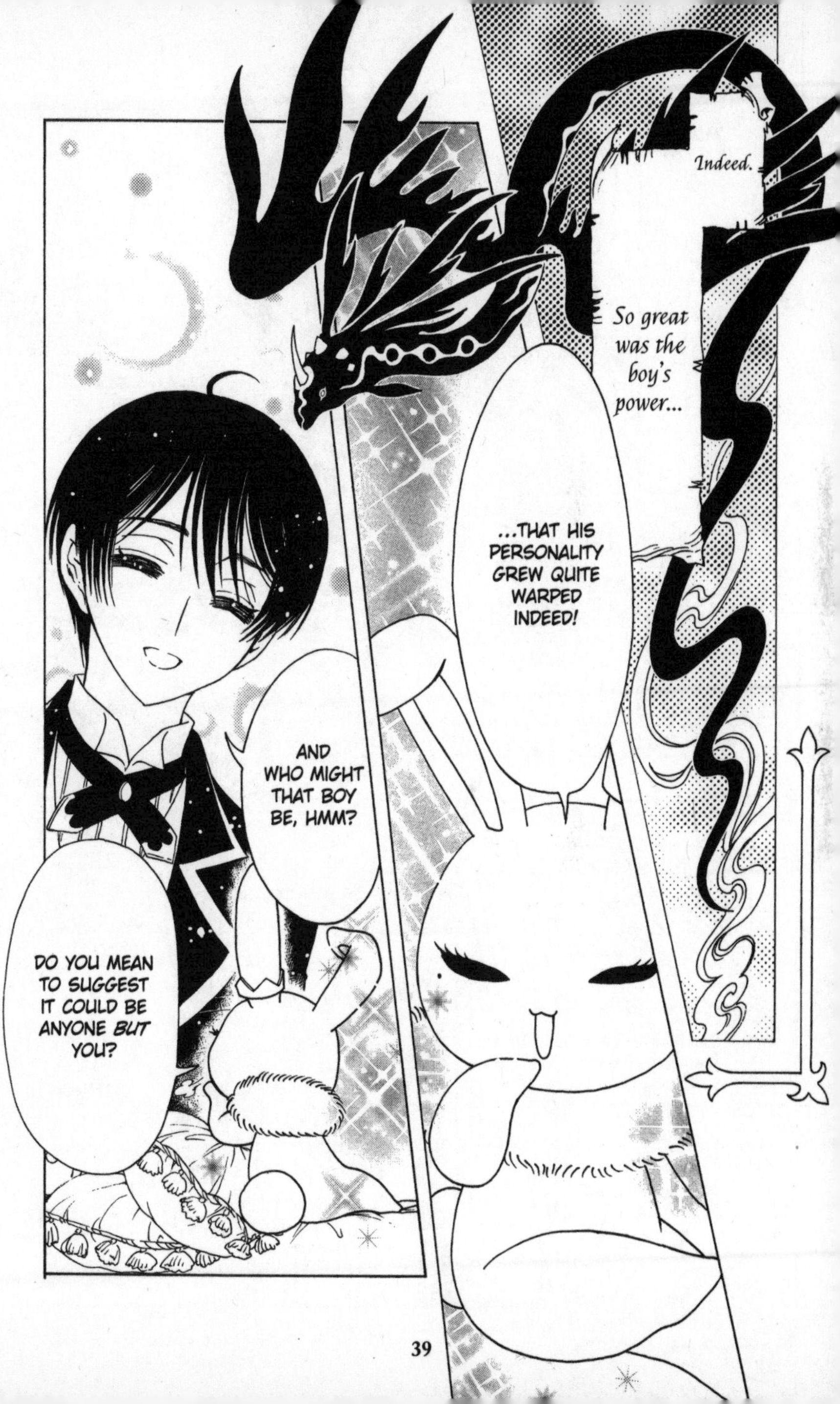
Indeed.
So great was the boy's power...
...THAT HIS PERSONALITY GREW QUITE WARPED INDEED!
AND WHO MIGHT THAT BOY BE, HMM?
DO YOU MEAN TO SUGGEST IT COULD BE ANYONE *BUT* YOU?

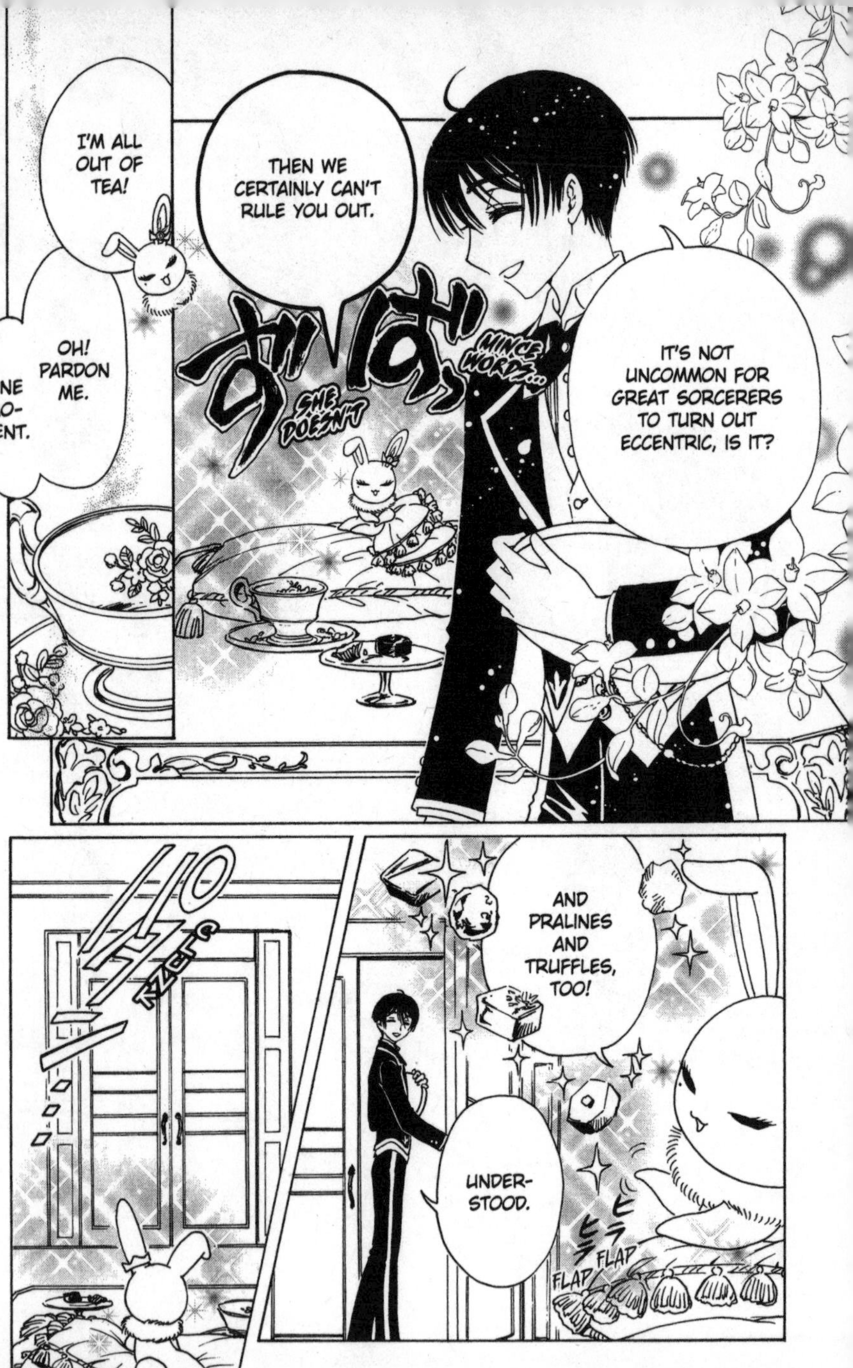
IT'S NOT UNCOMMON FOR GREAT SORCERERS TO TURN OUT ECCENTRIC, IS IT?
SHE DOESN'T MINCE WORDS...
THEN WE CERTAINLY CAN'T RULE YOU OUT.
I'M ALL OUT OF TEA!
OH! PARDON ME.
ONE MOMENT.
AND PRALINES AND TRUFFLES, TOO!
UNDERSTOOD.
FLAP FLAP

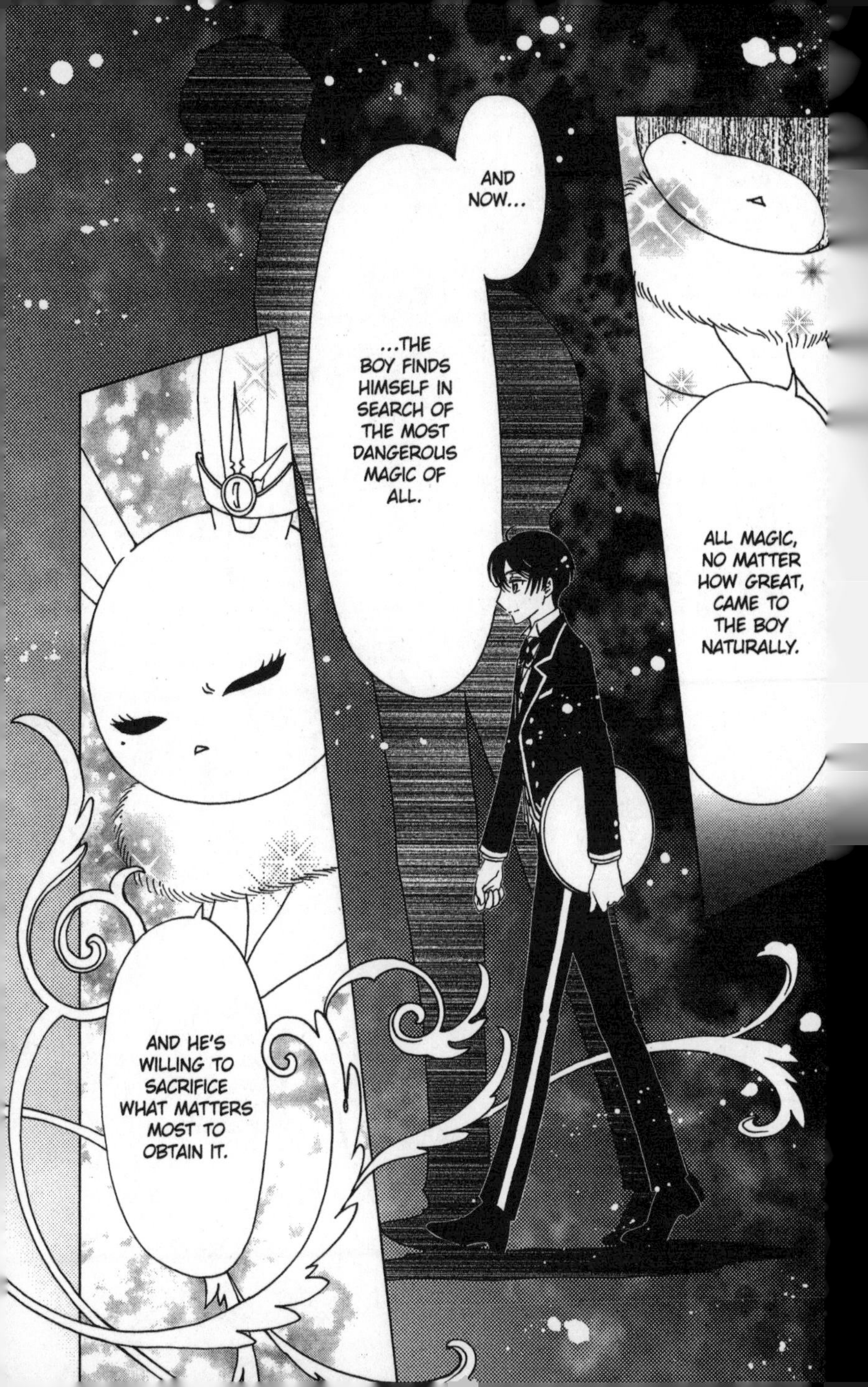
ALL MAGIC, NO MATTER HOW GREAT, CAME TO THE BOY NATURALLY.
AND NOW...
...THE BOY FINDS HIMSELF IN SEARCH OF THE MOST DANGEROUS MAGIC OF ALL.
AND HE'S WILLING TO SACRIFICE WHAT MATTERS MOST TO OBTAIN IT.

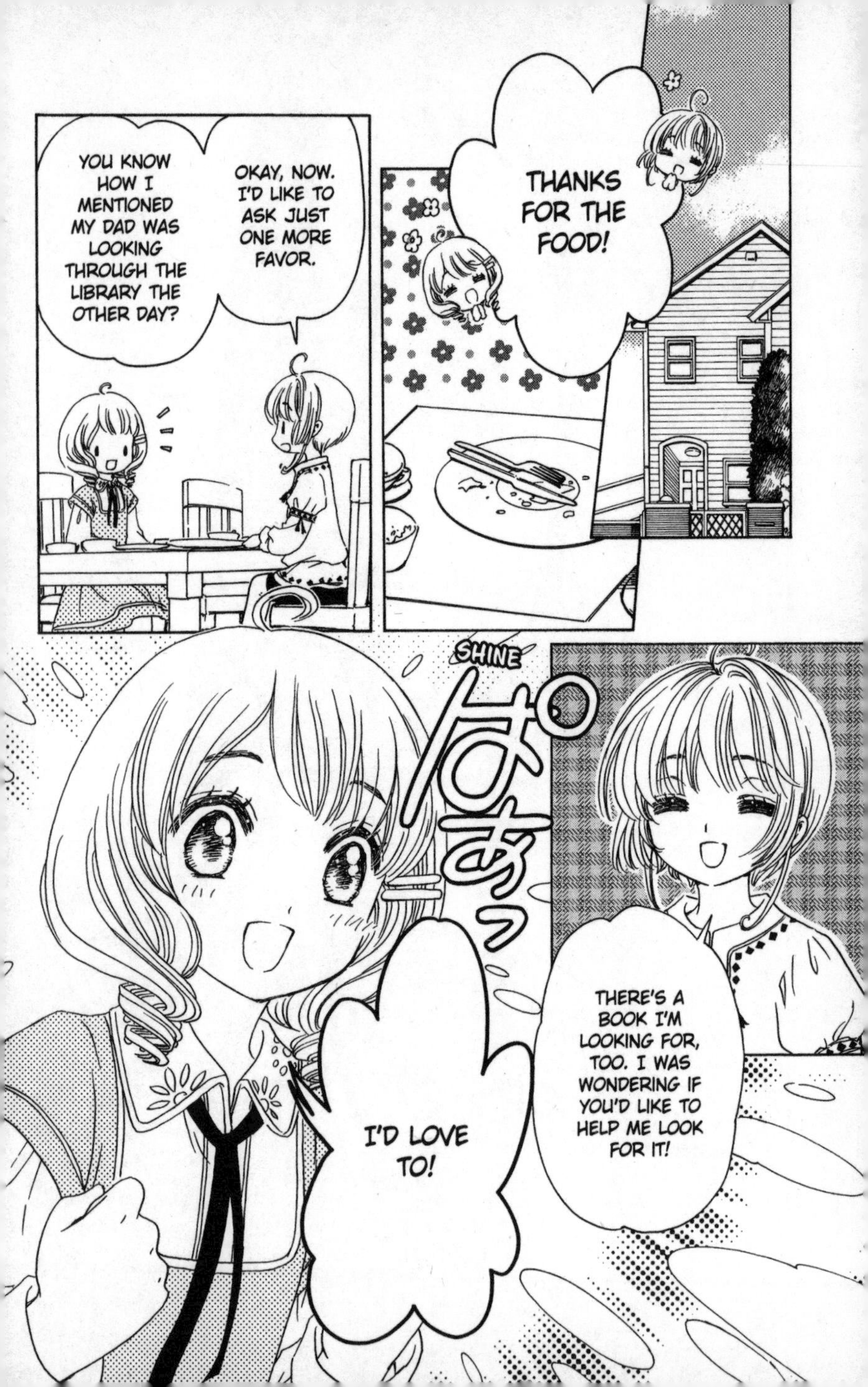
THANKS FOR THE FOOD!
OKAY, NOW. I'D LIKE TO ASK JUST ONE MORE FAVOR.
YOU KNOW HOW I MENTIONED MY DAD WAS LOOKING THROUGH THE LIBRARY THE OTHER DAY?
THERE'S A BOOK I'M LOOKING FOR, TOO. I WAS WONDERING IF YOU'D LIKE TO HELP ME LOOK FOR IT!
SHINE
ぱあっ
I'D LOVE TO!

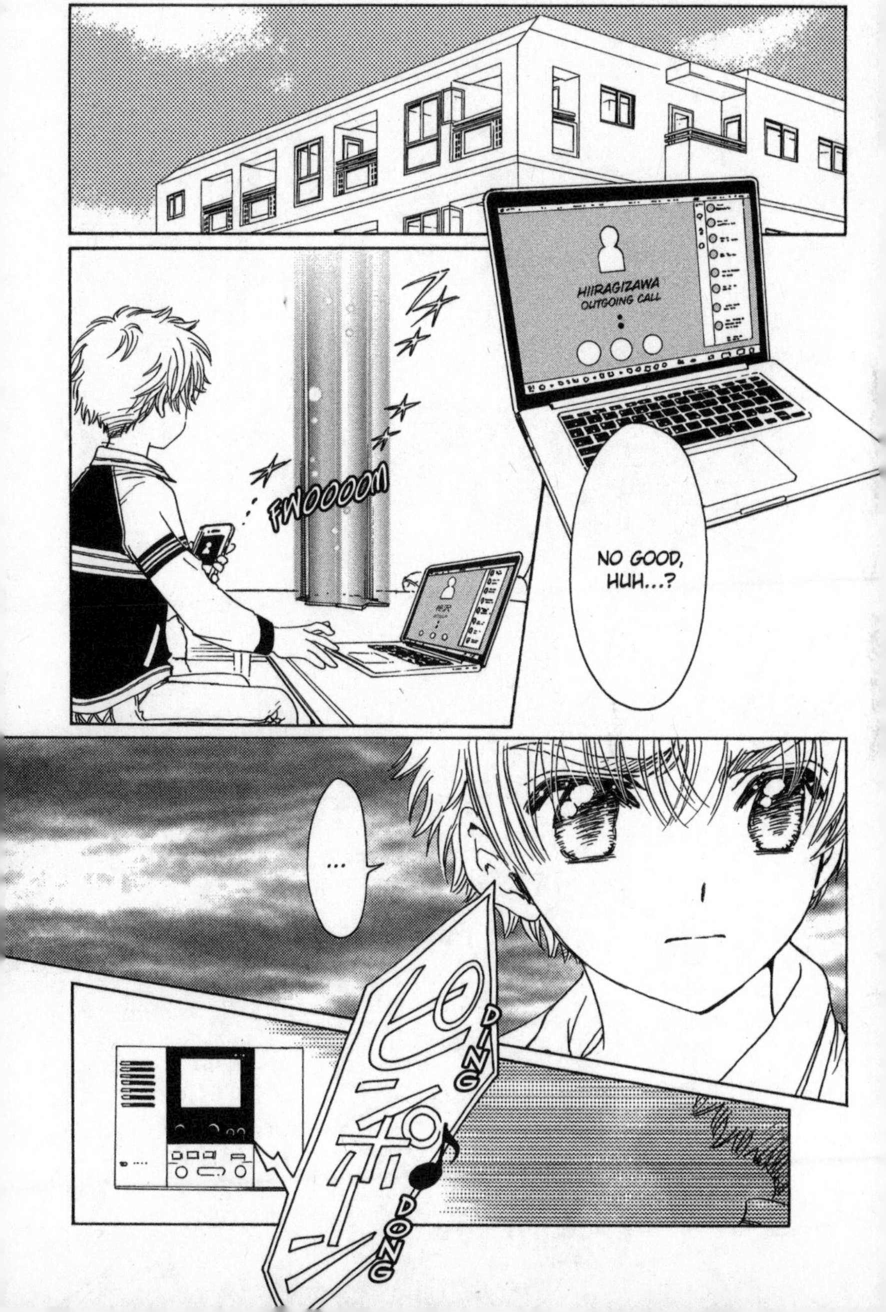
HIIRAGIZAWA
OUTGOING CALL
FWOOOOM
NO GOOD, HUH...?
...
DING
DONG

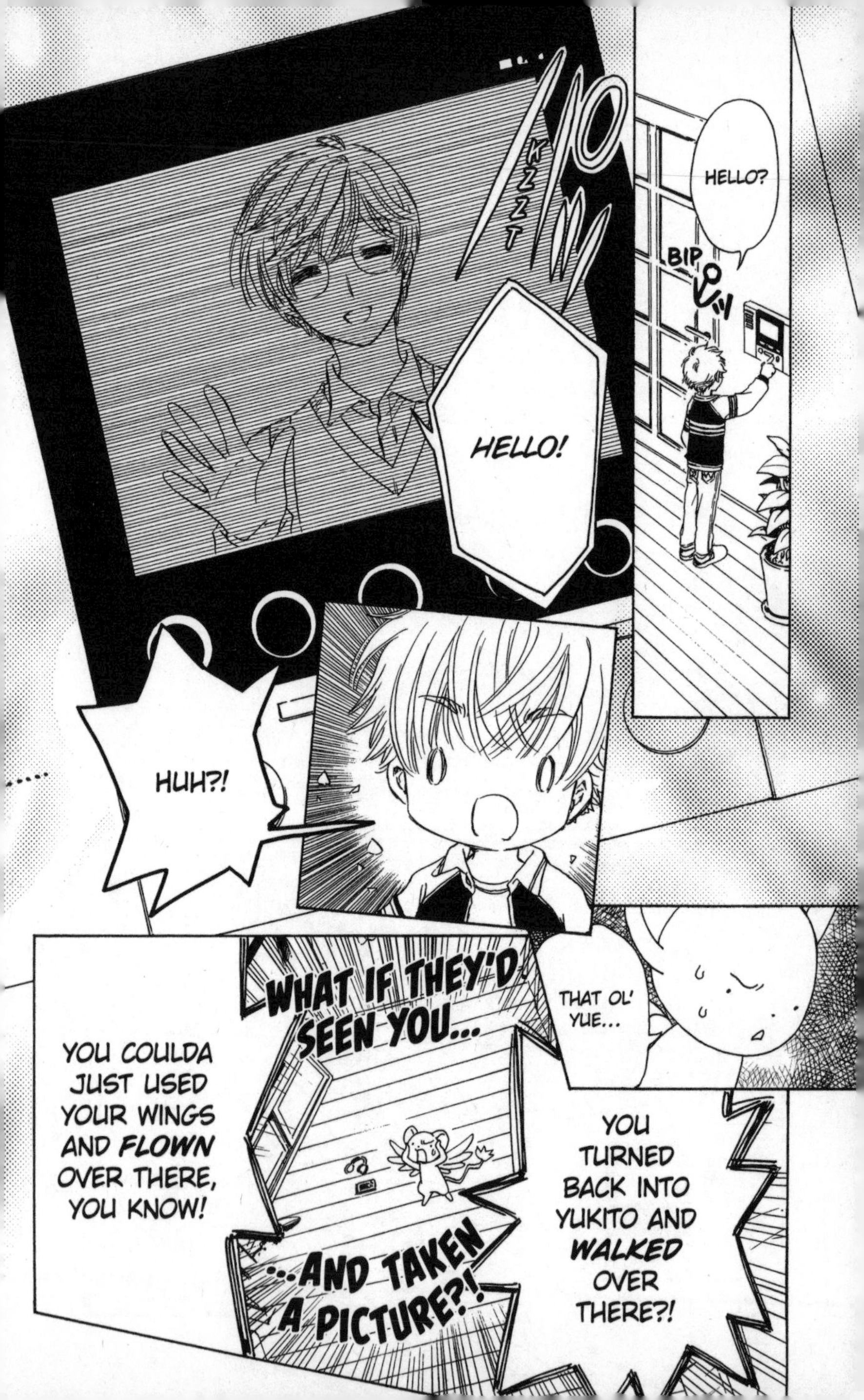
HELLO?
BIP
KZZZT
HELLO!
HUH?!
THAT OL' YUE...
YOU TURNED BACK INTO YUKITO AND *WALKED* OVER THERE?!
WHAT IF THEY'D SEEN YOU...
...AND TAKEN A PICTURE?!
YOU COULDA JUST USED YOUR WINGS AND *FLOWN* OVER THERE, YOU KNOW!

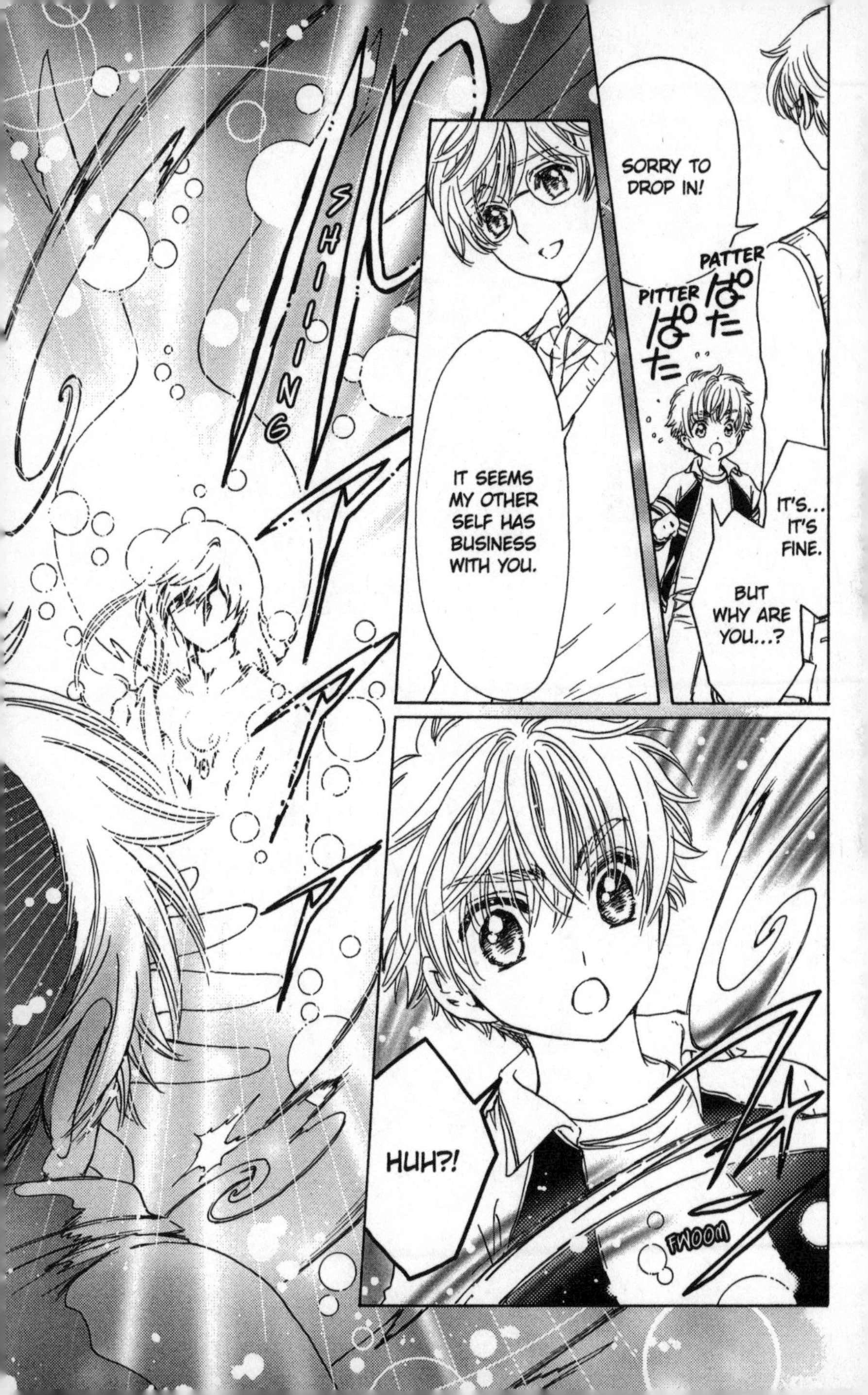
SORRY TO DROP IN!
PATTER ぱた
PITTER ぱた
IT'S... IT'S FINE.
BUT WHY ARE YOU...?
IT SEEMS MY OTHER SELF HAS BUSINESS WITH YOU.
SHIIIING
FWOOM
HUH?!

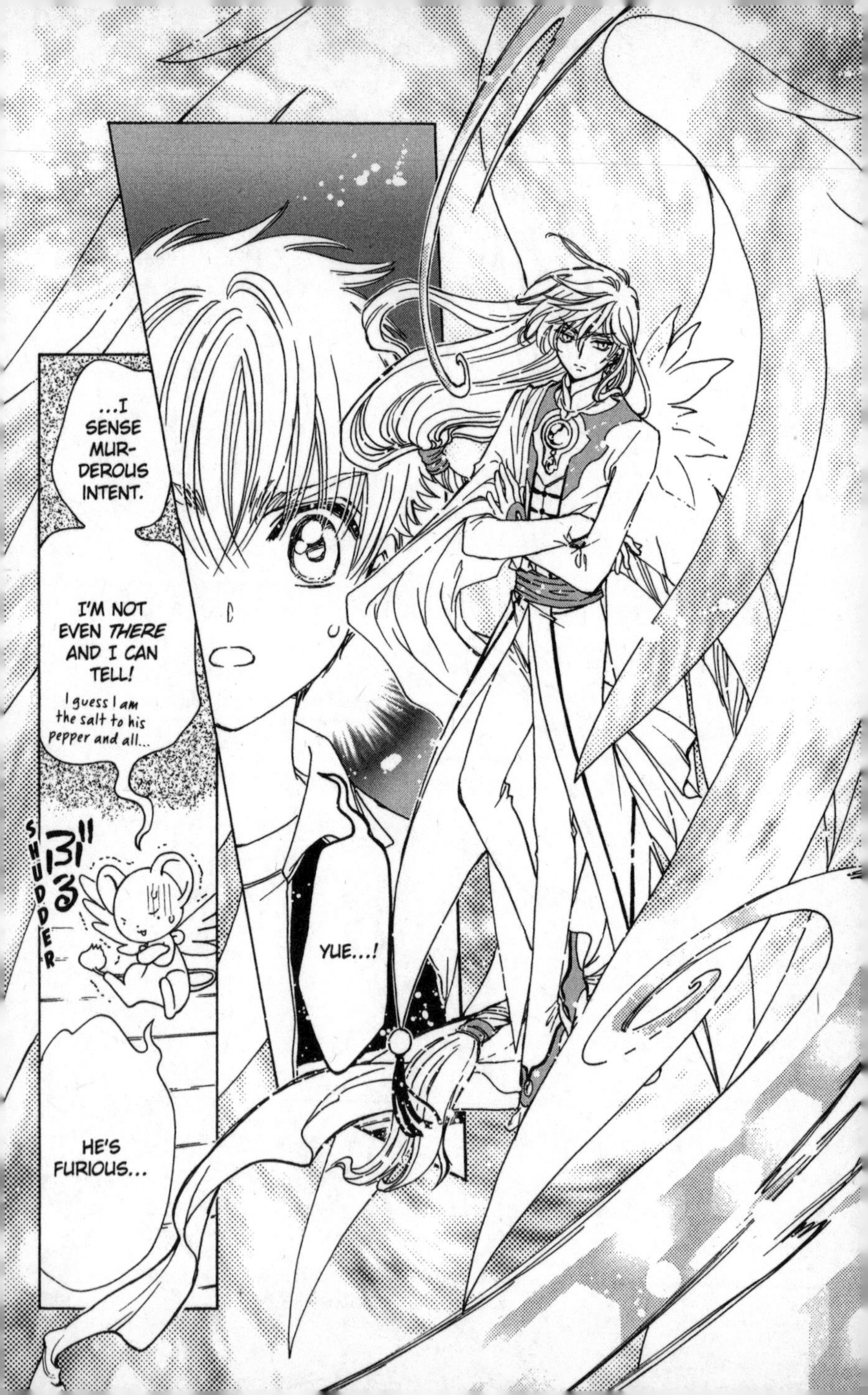
...I SENSE MURDEROUS INTENT.
I'M NOT EVEN *THERE* AND I CAN TELL!
I guess I am the salt to his pepper and all...
SHUDDER
YUE...!
HE'S FURIOUS...

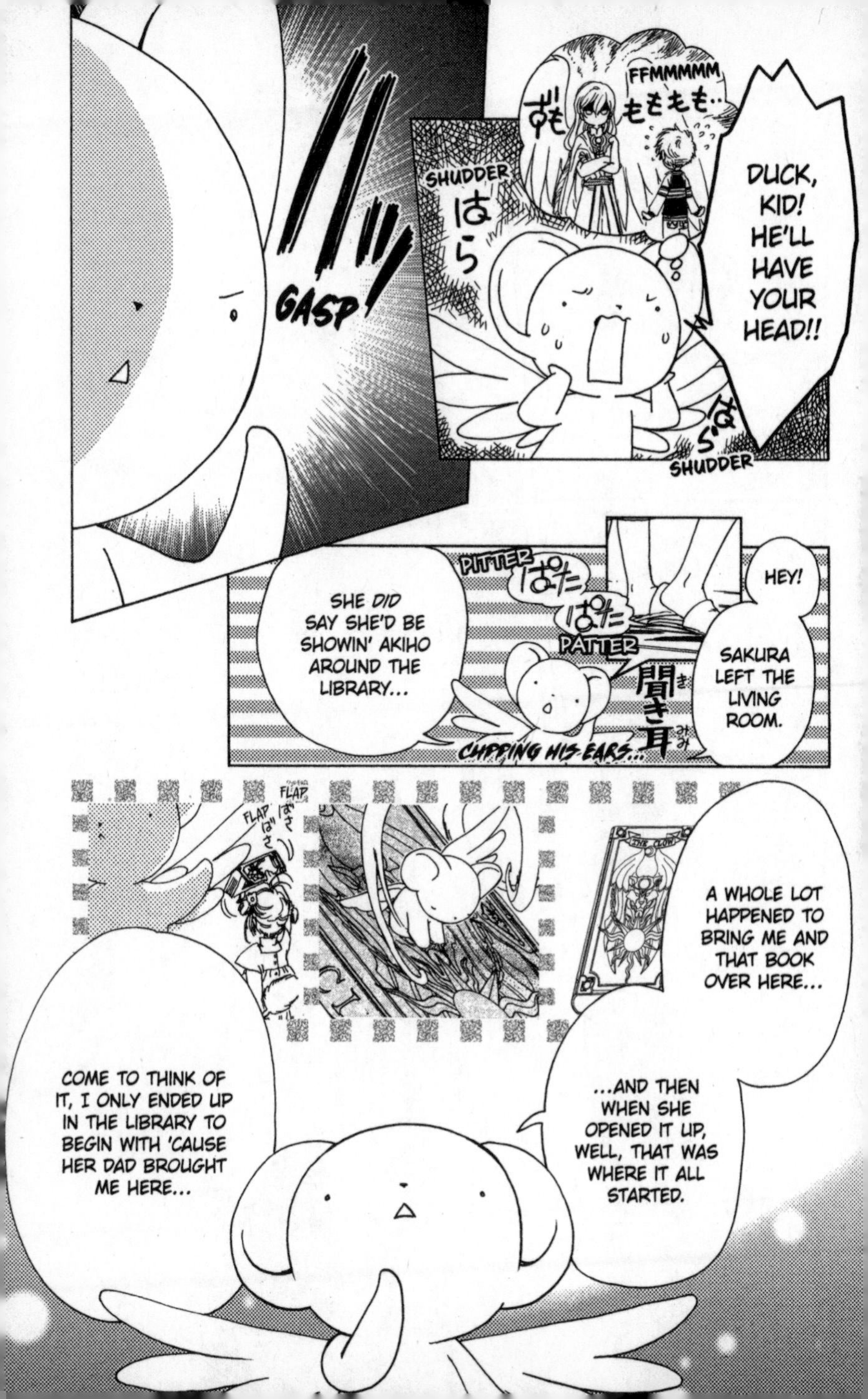
FFMMMMM
もももも…
ずも
SHUDDER
はら
DUCK, KID! HE'LL HAVE YOUR HEAD!!
はら
SHUDDER
GASP
HEY!
SAKURA LEFT THE LIVING ROOM.
聞き耳
CUPPING HIS EARS...
PITTER
ぱた
ぱた
PATTER
SHE *DID* SAY SHE'D BE SHOWIN' AKIHO AROUND THE LIBRARY...
A WHOLE LOT HAPPENED TO BRING ME AND THAT BOOK OVER HERE...
THE CLOW
FLAP
ばさ
FLAP
ばさ
...AND THEN WHEN SHE OPENED IT UP, WELL, THAT WAS WHERE IT ALL STARTED.
COME TO THINK OF IT, I ONLY ENDED UP IN THE LIBRARY TO BEGIN WITH 'CAUSE HER DAD BROUGHT ME HERE...

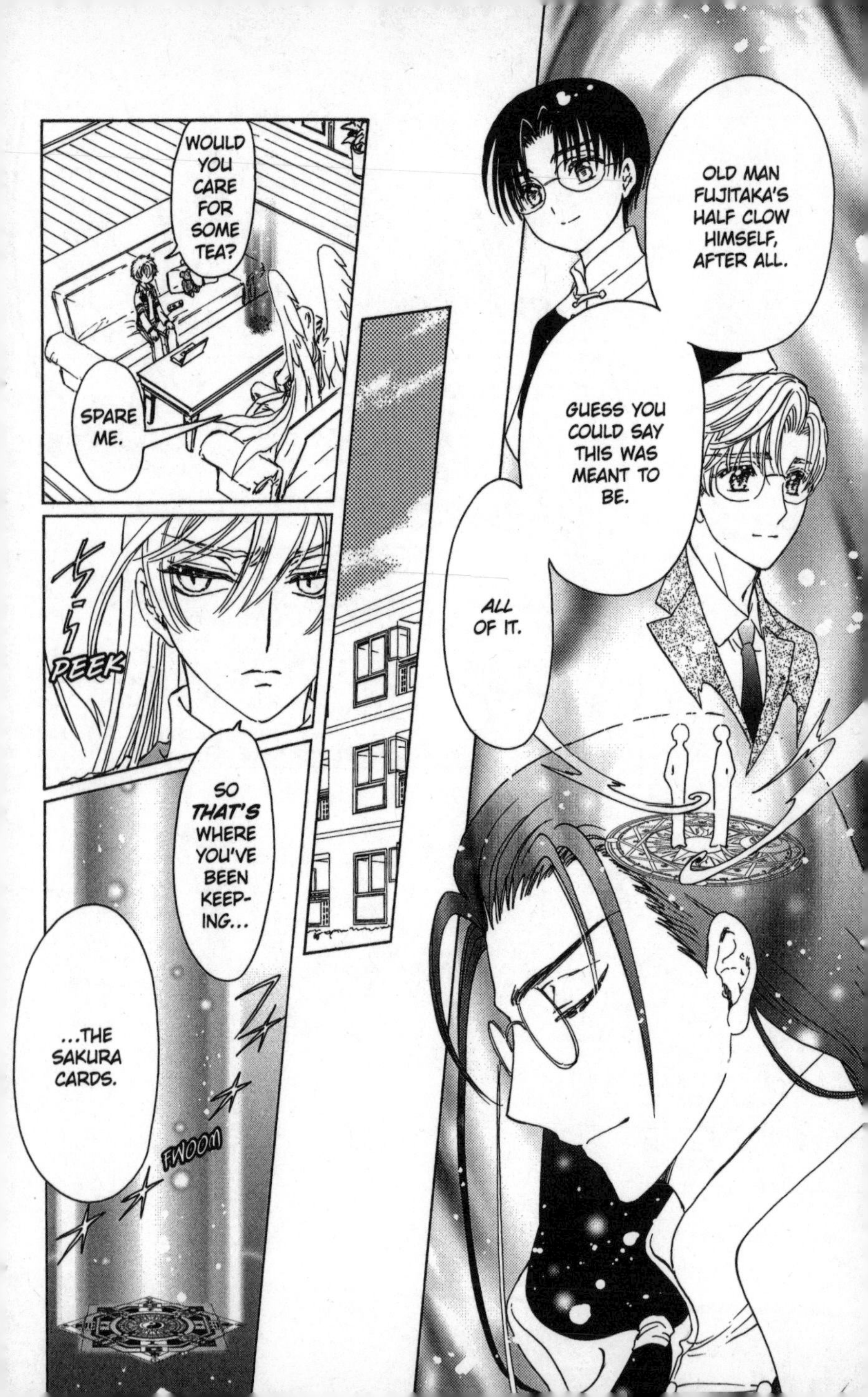
OLD MAN FUJITAKA'S HALF CLOW HIMSELF, AFTER ALL.
GUESS YOU COULD SAY THIS WAS MEANT TO BE.
ALL OF IT.
WOULD YOU CARE FOR SOME TEA?
SPARE ME.
PEEK
SO THAT'S WHERE YOU'VE BEEN KEEP-ING...
...THE SAKURA CARDS.
FWOOM

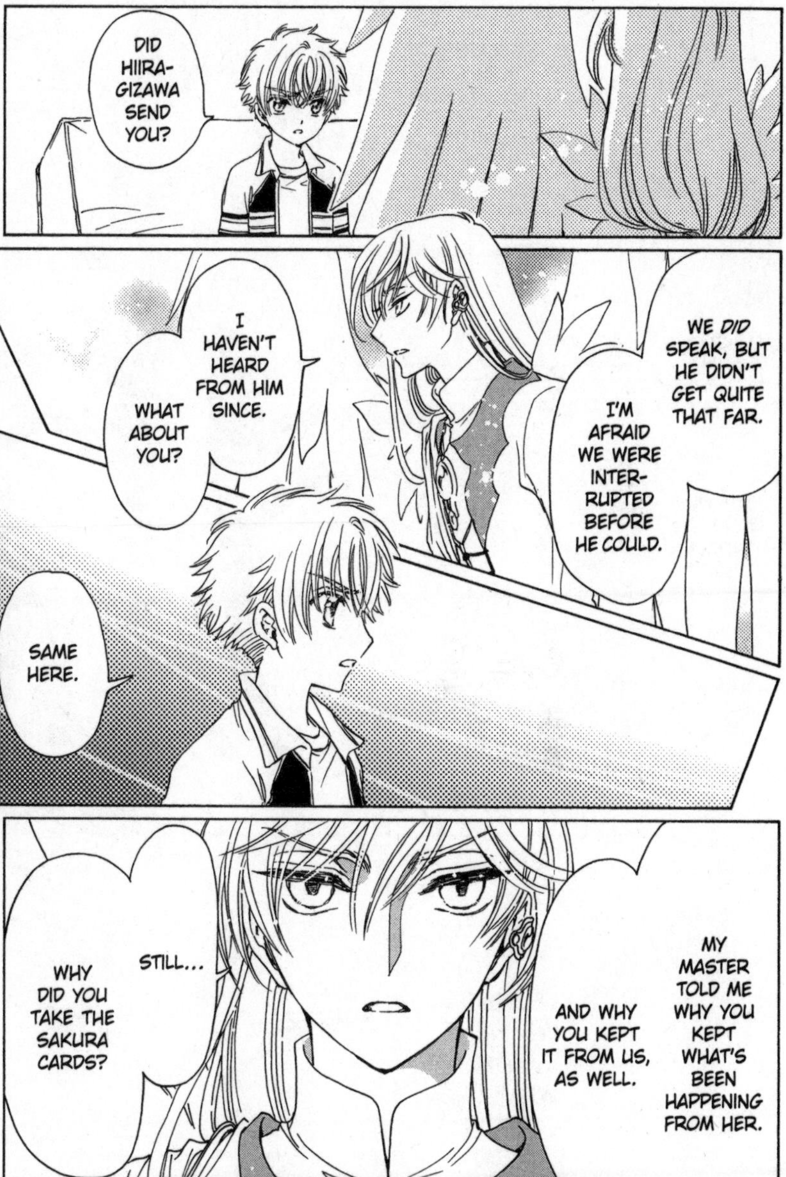
DID HIIRA-GIZAWA SEND YOU?
WE *DID* SPEAK, BUT HE DIDN'T GET QUITE THAT FAR.
I'M AFRAID WE WERE INTER-RUPTED BEFORE HE COULD.
I HAVEN'T HEARD FROM HIM SINCE.
WHAT ABOUT YOU?
SAME HERE.
MY MASTER TOLD ME WHY YOU KEPT WHAT'S BEEN HAPPENING FROM HER.
AND WHY YOU KEPT IT FROM US, AS WELL.
STILL...
WHY DID YOU TAKE THE SAKURA CARDS?

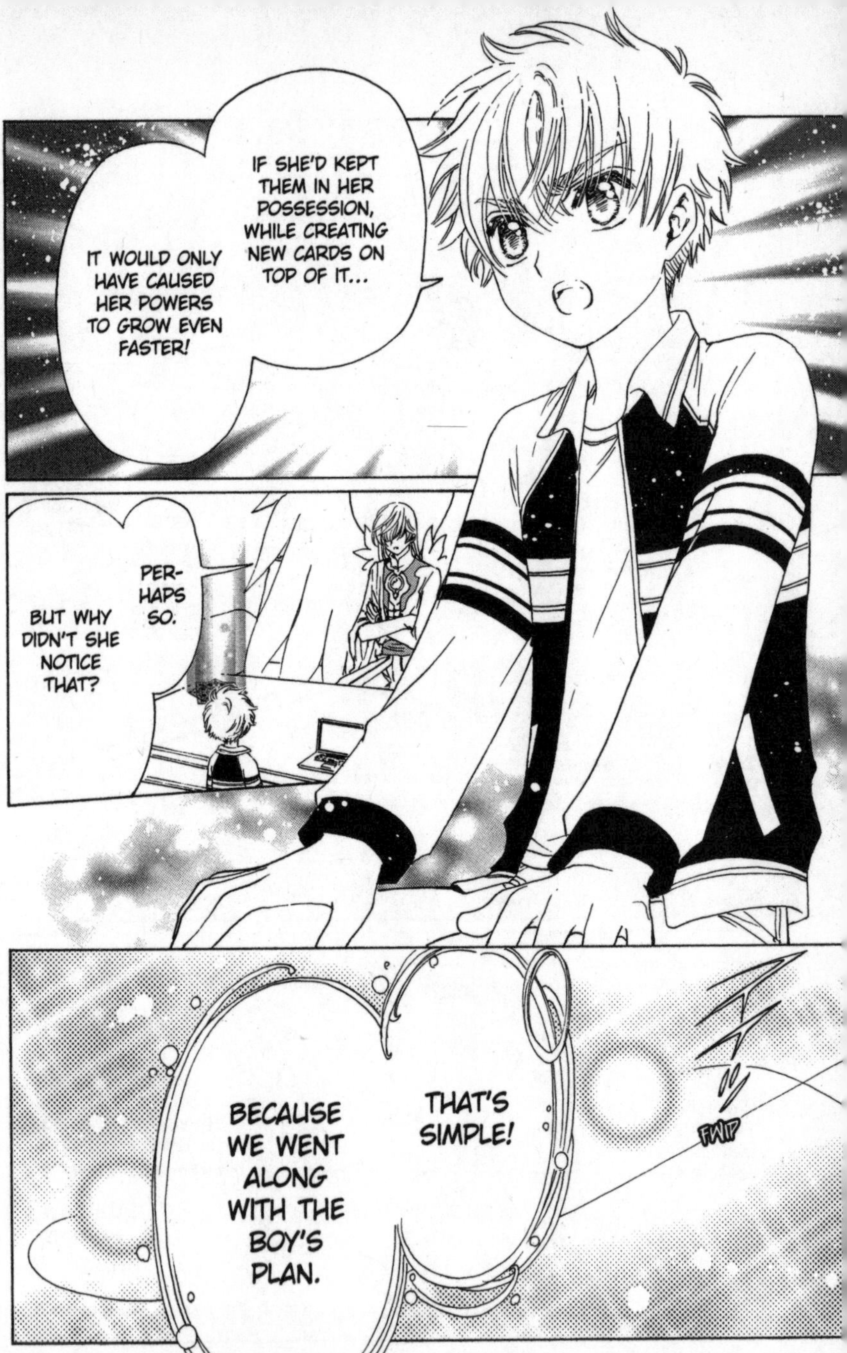
IF SHE'D KEPT THEM IN HER POSSESSION, WHILE CREATING NEW CARDS ON TOP OF IT...
IT WOULD ONLY HAVE CAUSED HER POWERS TO GROW EVEN FASTER!
PER-HAPS SO.
BUT WHY DIDN'T SHE NOTICE THAT?
FWIP
THAT'S SIMPLE!
BECAUSE WE WENT ALONG WITH THE BOY'S PLAN.

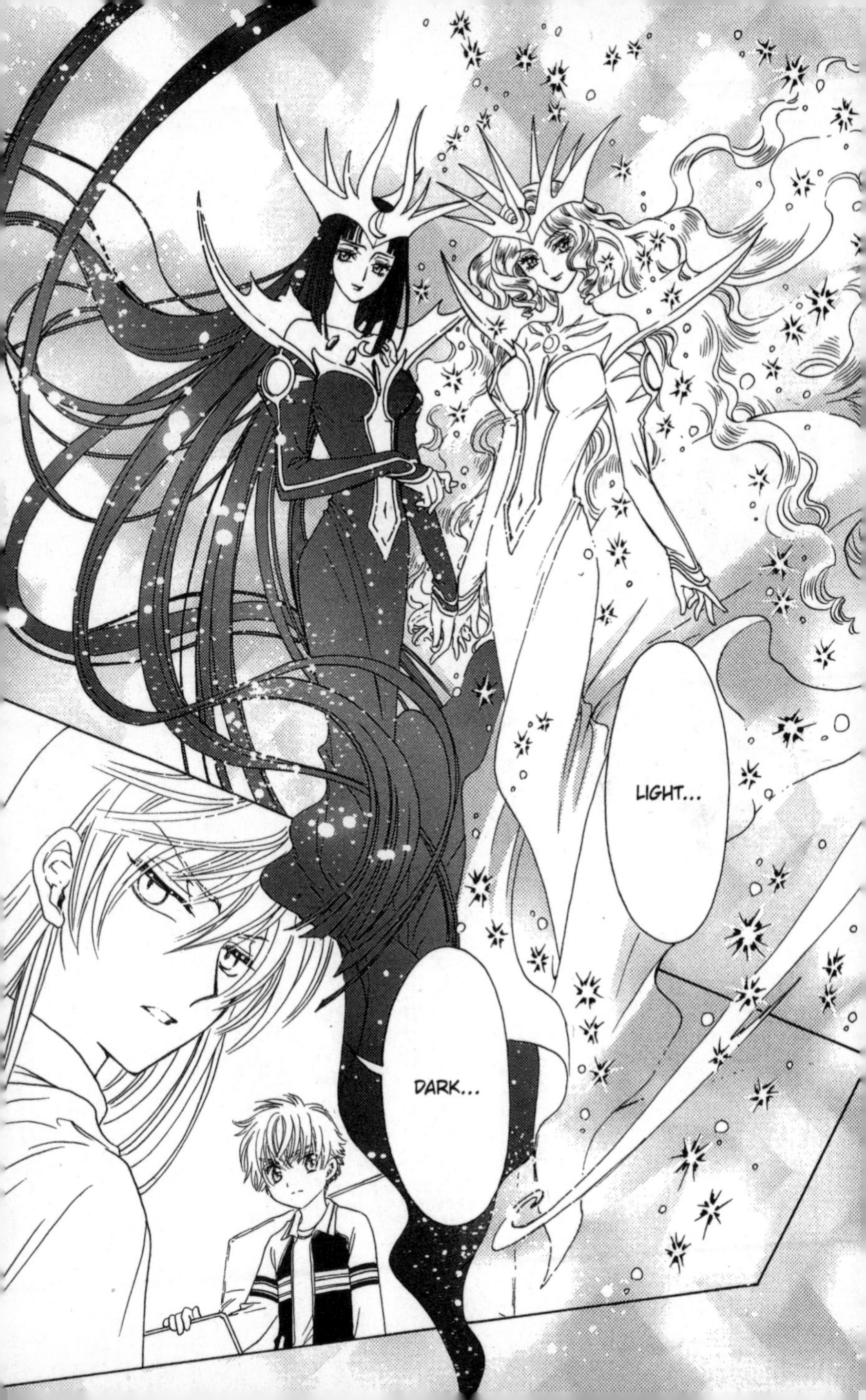
LIGHT...
DARK...

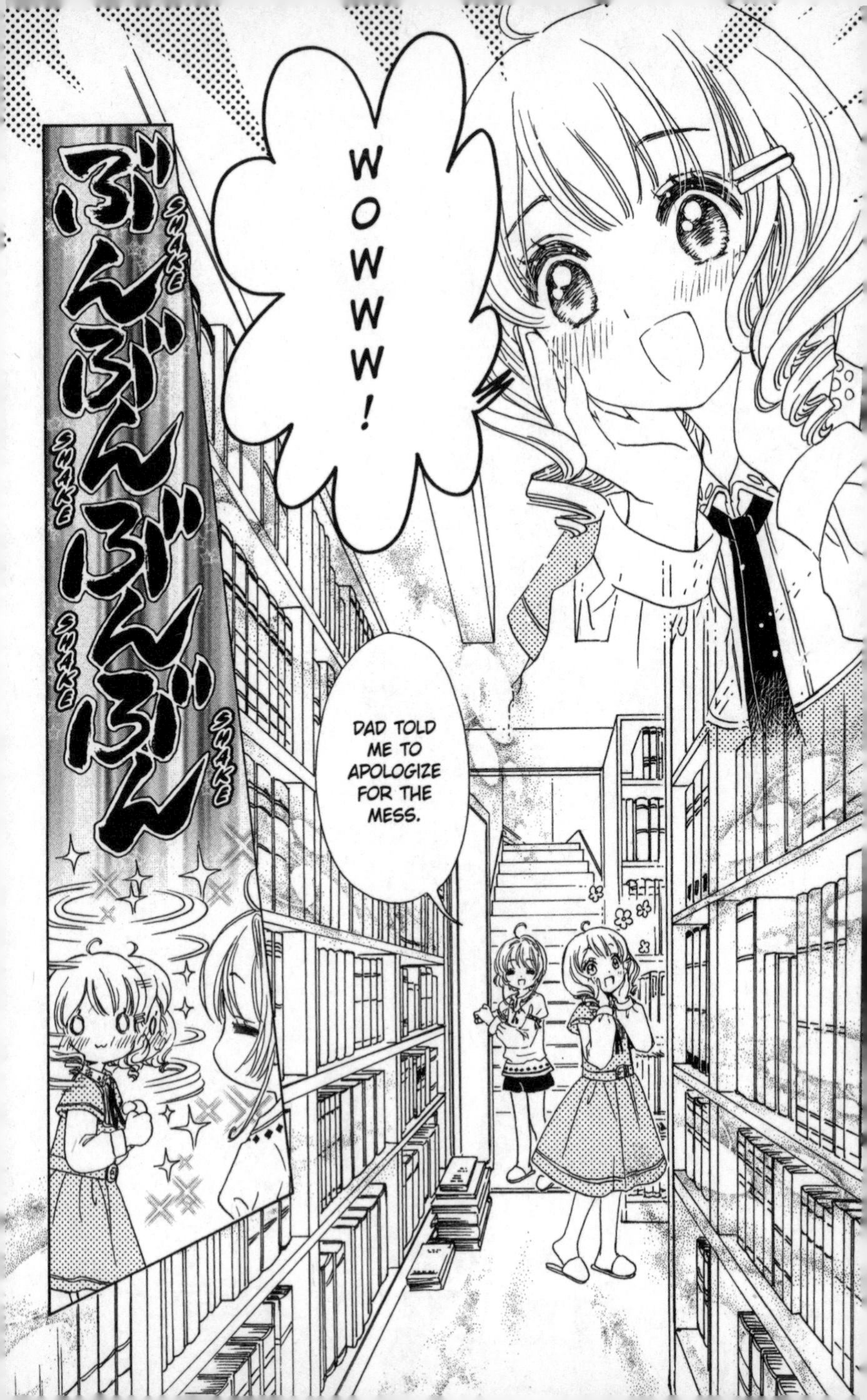
WOWWW!
DAD TOLD ME TO APOLOGIZE FOR THE MESS.
ぶんぶんぶんぶん
SHAKE SHAKE SHAKE SHAKE

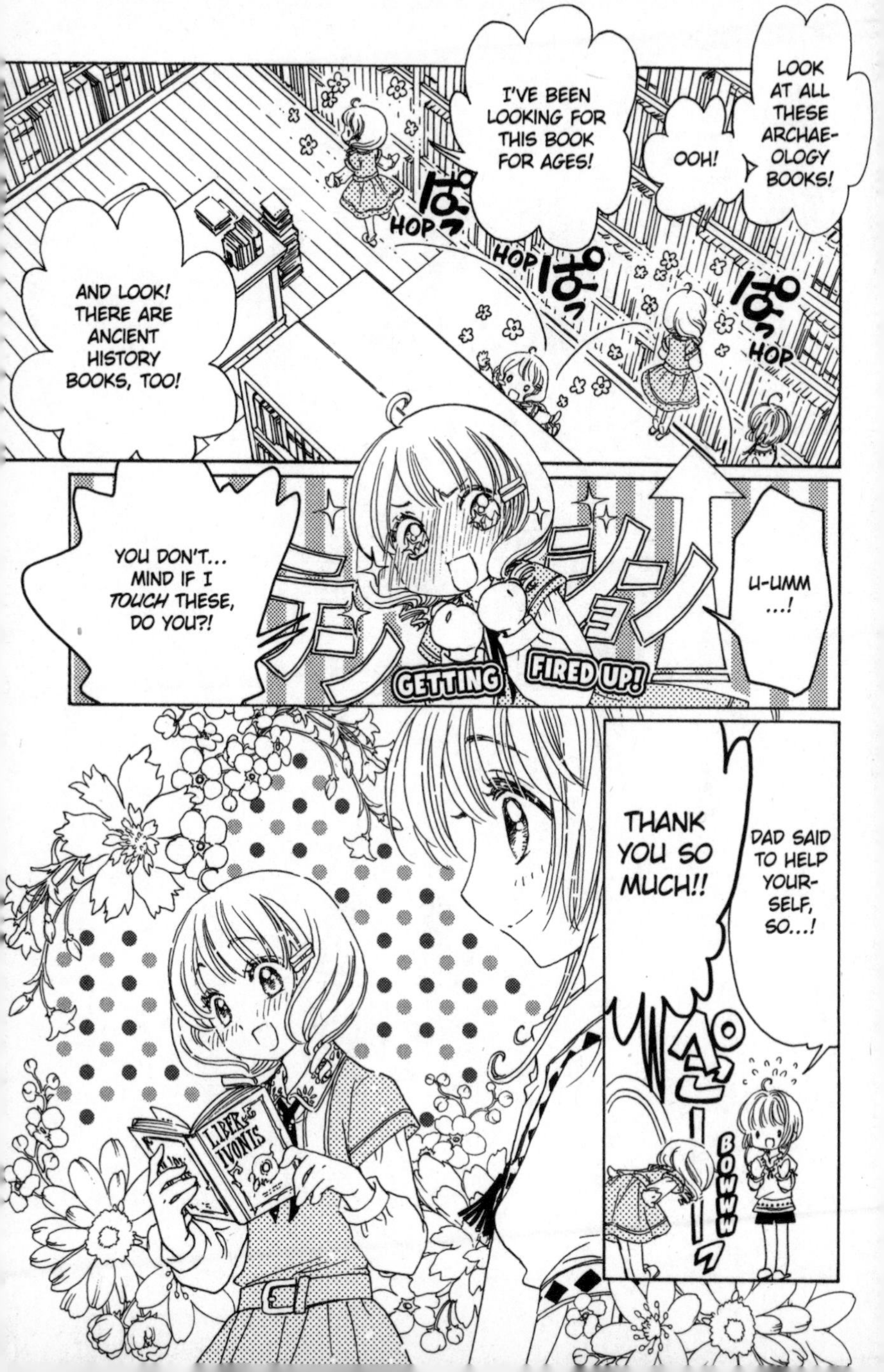
LOOK AT ALL THESE ARCHAEOLOGY BOOKS!
OOH!
I'VE BEEN LOOKING FOR THIS BOOK FOR AGES!
HOP
HOP
HOP
AND LOOK! THERE ARE ANCIENT HISTORY BOOKS, TOO!
U-UMM ...!
YOU DON'T... MIND IF I TOUCH THESE, DO YOU?!
GETTING FIRED UP!
DAD SAID TO HELP YOURSELF, SO...!
THANK YOU SO MUCH!!
BOWWW
LIBER IVONIS

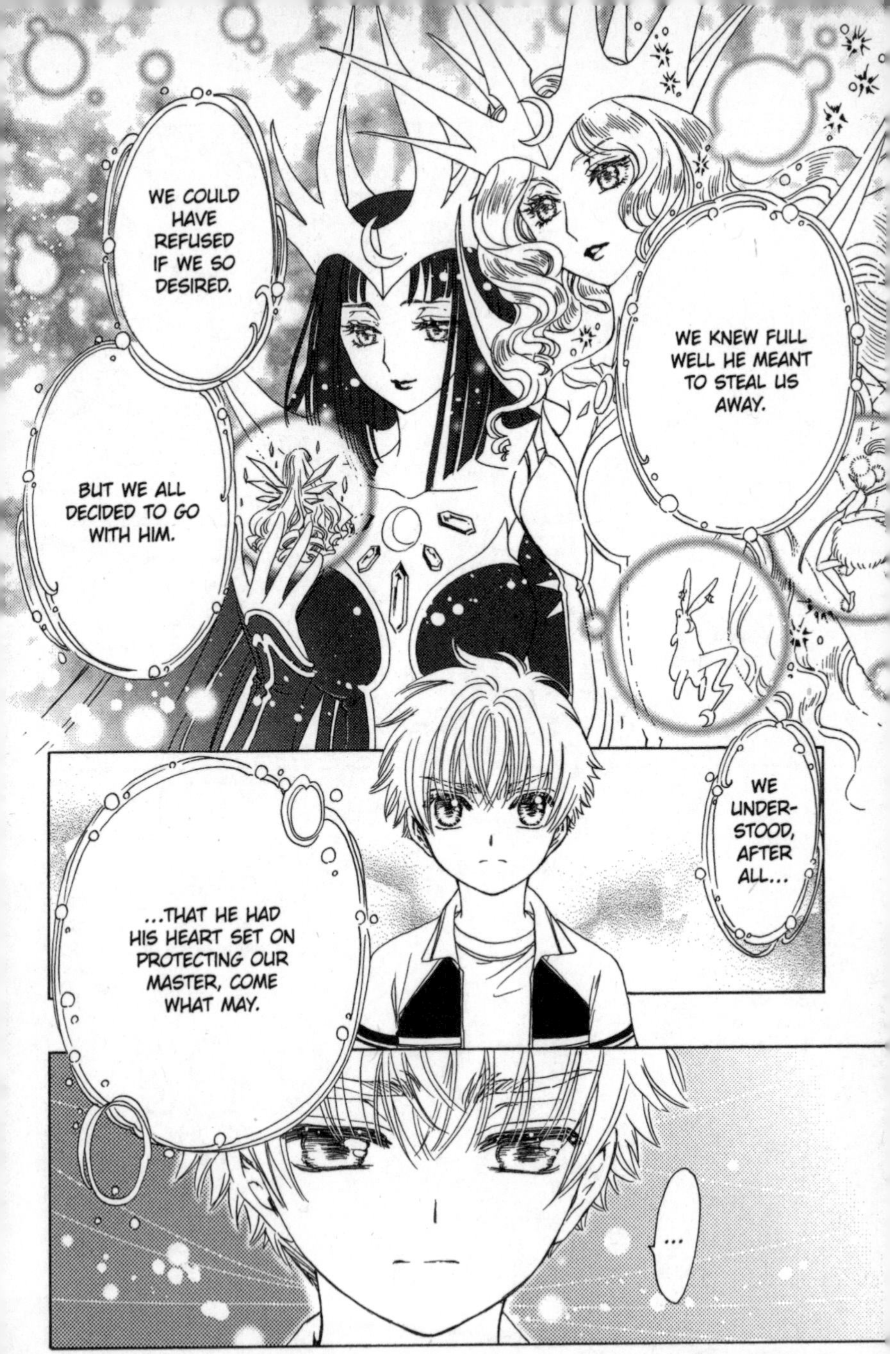
WE KNEW FULL WELL HE MEANT TO STEAL US AWAY.
WE COULD HAVE REFUSED IF WE SO DESIRED.
BUT WE ALL DECIDED TO GO WITH HIM.
WE UNDERSTOOD, AFTER ALL...
...THAT HE HAD HIS HEART SET ON PROTECTING OUR MASTER, COME WHAT MAY.
...

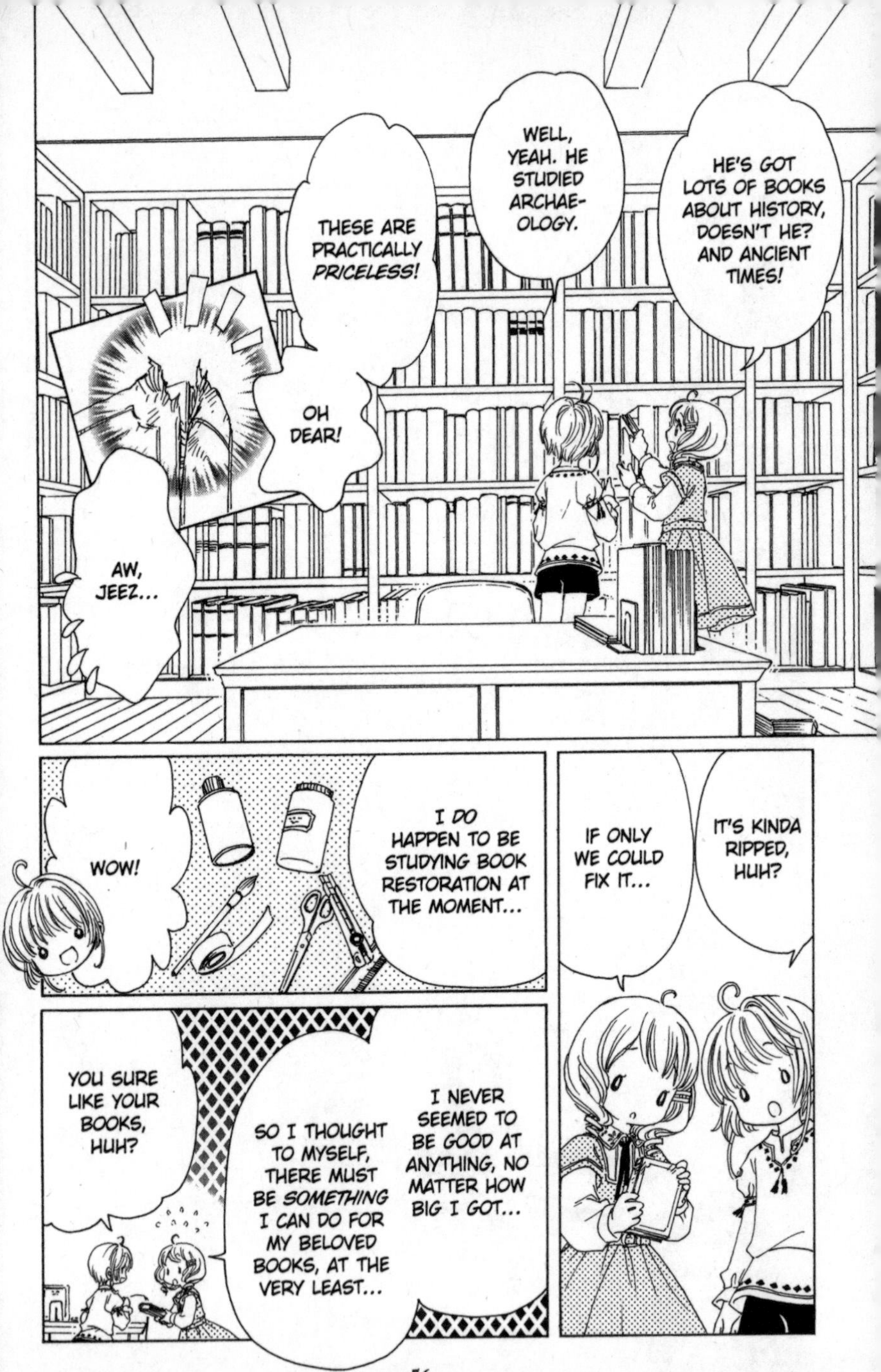
HE'S GOT LOTS OF BOOKS ABOUT HISTORY, DOESN'T HE? AND ANCIENT TIMES!
WELL, YEAH. HE STUDIED ARCHAE-OLOGY.
THESE ARE PRACTICALLY *PRICELESS!*
OH DEAR!
AW, JEEZ...
IT'S KINDA RIPPED, HUH?
IF ONLY WE COULD FIX IT...
I *DO* HAPPEN TO BE STUDYING BOOK RESTORATION AT THE MOMENT...
WOW!
I NEVER SEEMED TO BE GOOD AT ANYTHING, NO MATTER HOW BIG I GOT...
SO I THOUGHT TO MYSELF, THERE MUST BE *SOMETHING* I CAN DO FOR MY BELOVED BOOKS, AT THE VERY LEAST...
YOU SURE LIKE YOUR BOOKS, HUH?

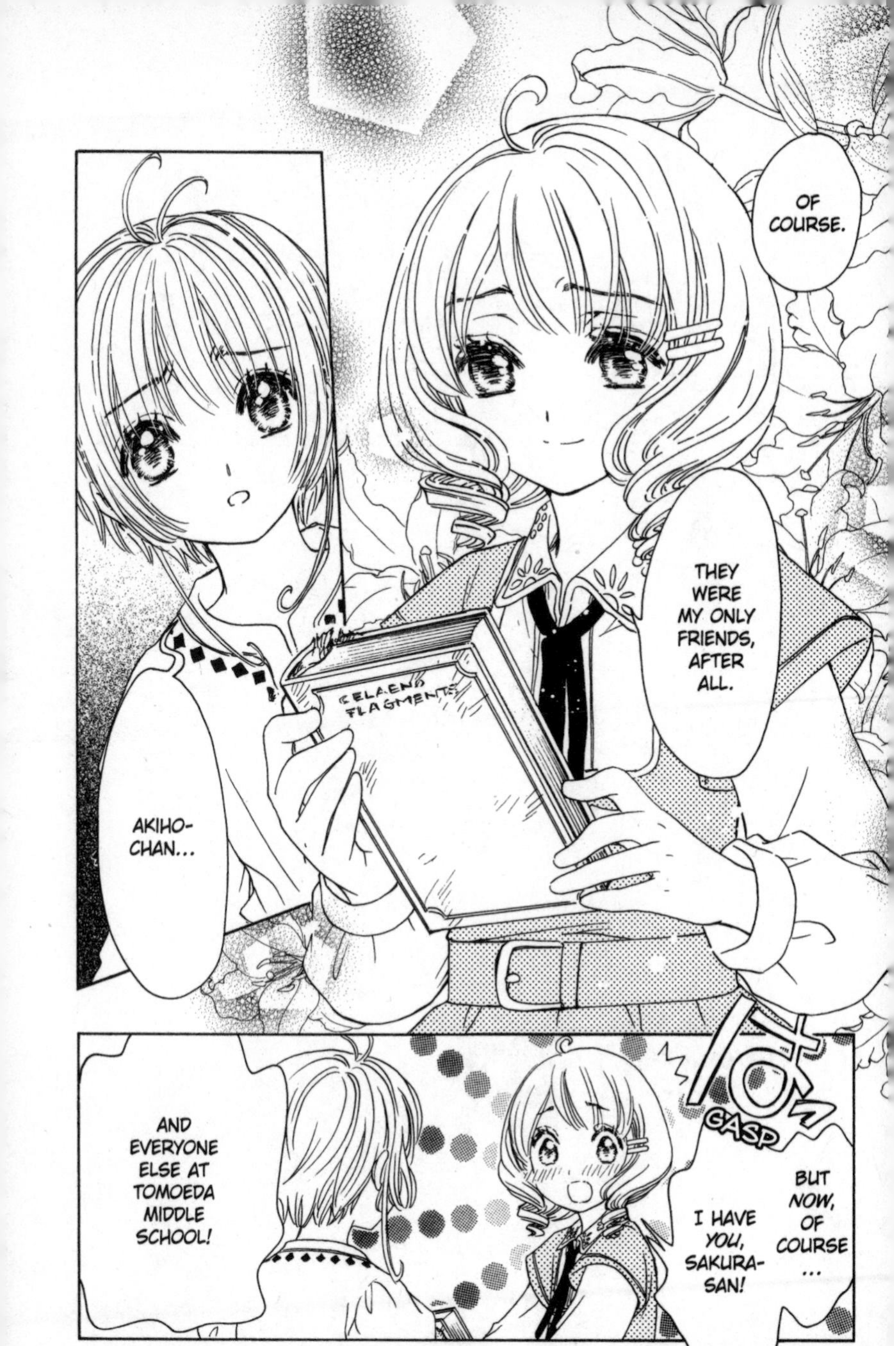

OF COURSE.
THEY WERE MY ONLY FRIENDS, AFTER ALL.
AKIHO-CHAN...
GASP
BUT NOW, OF COURSE ...
I HAVE *YOU*, SAKURA-SAN!
AND EVERYONE ELSE AT TOMOEDA MIDDLE SCHOOL!

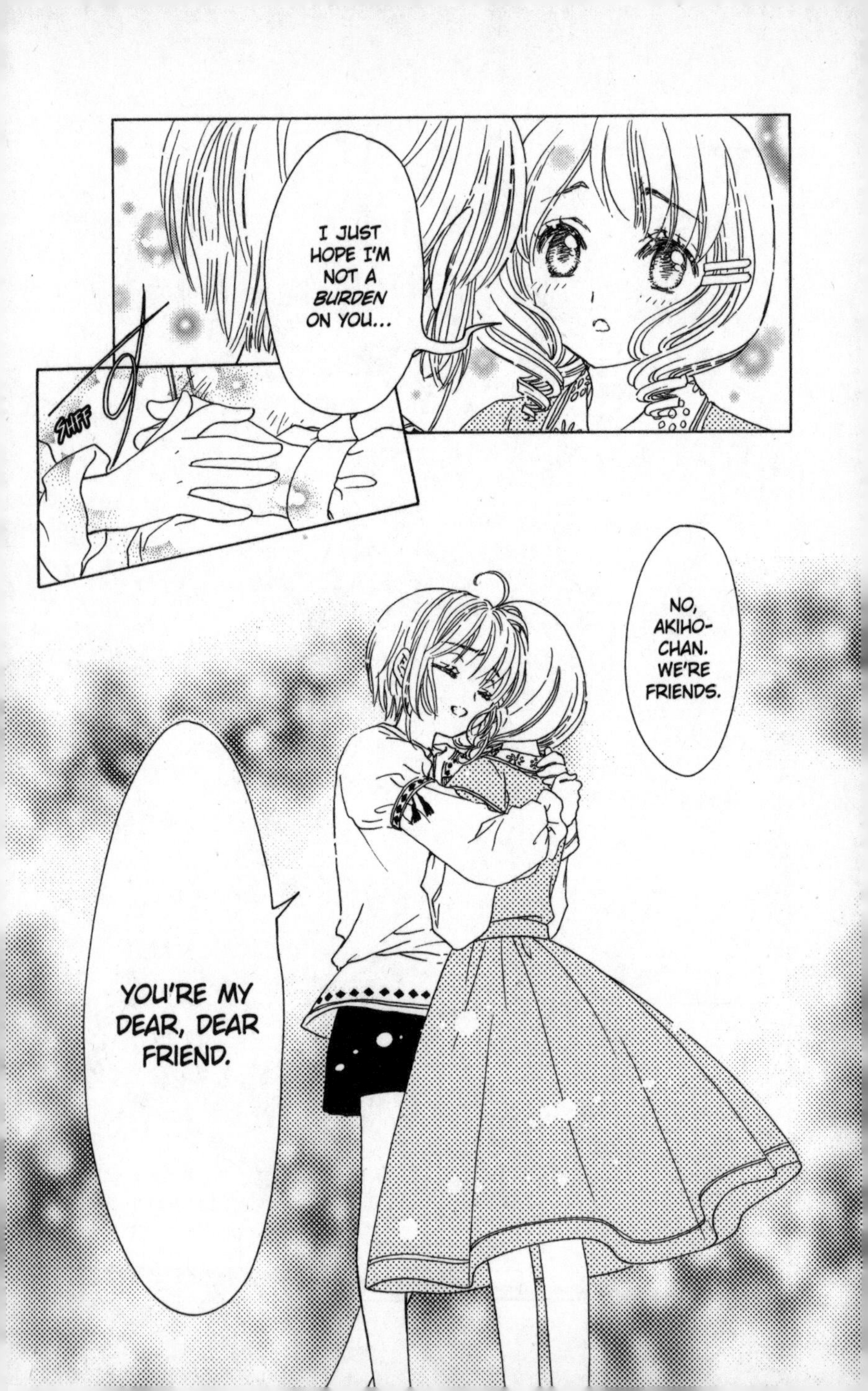
I JUST HOPE I'M NOT A BURDEN ON YOU...
SNIFF
NO, AKIHO-CHAN. WE'RE FRIENDS.
YOU'RE MY DEAR, DEAR FRIEND.

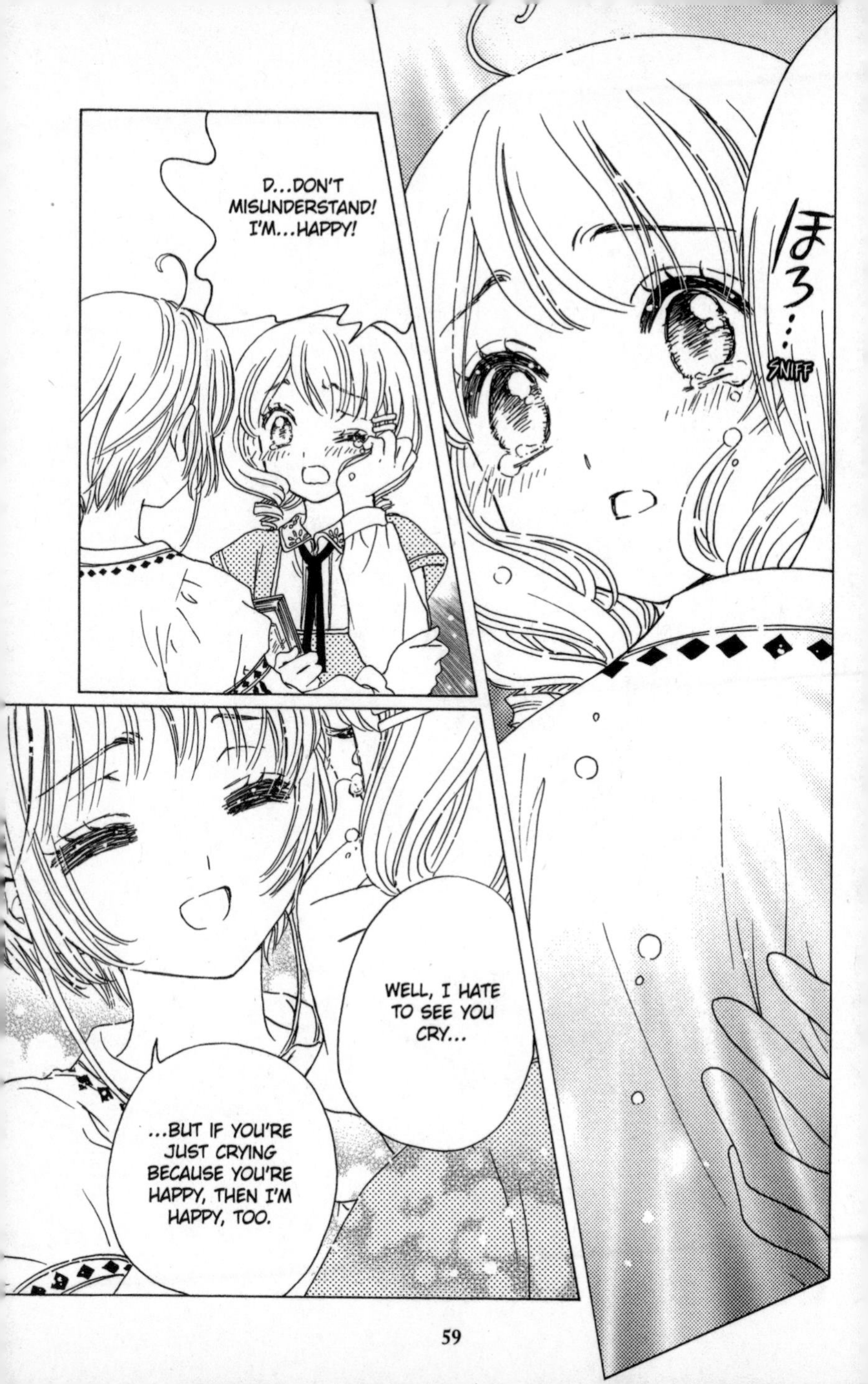
ほろ…
SNIFF
D...DON'T MISUNDERSTAND! I'M...HAPPY!
WELL, I HATE TO SEE YOU CRY...
...BUT IF YOU'RE JUST CRYING BECAUSE YOU'RE HAPPY, THEN I'M HAPPY, TOO.

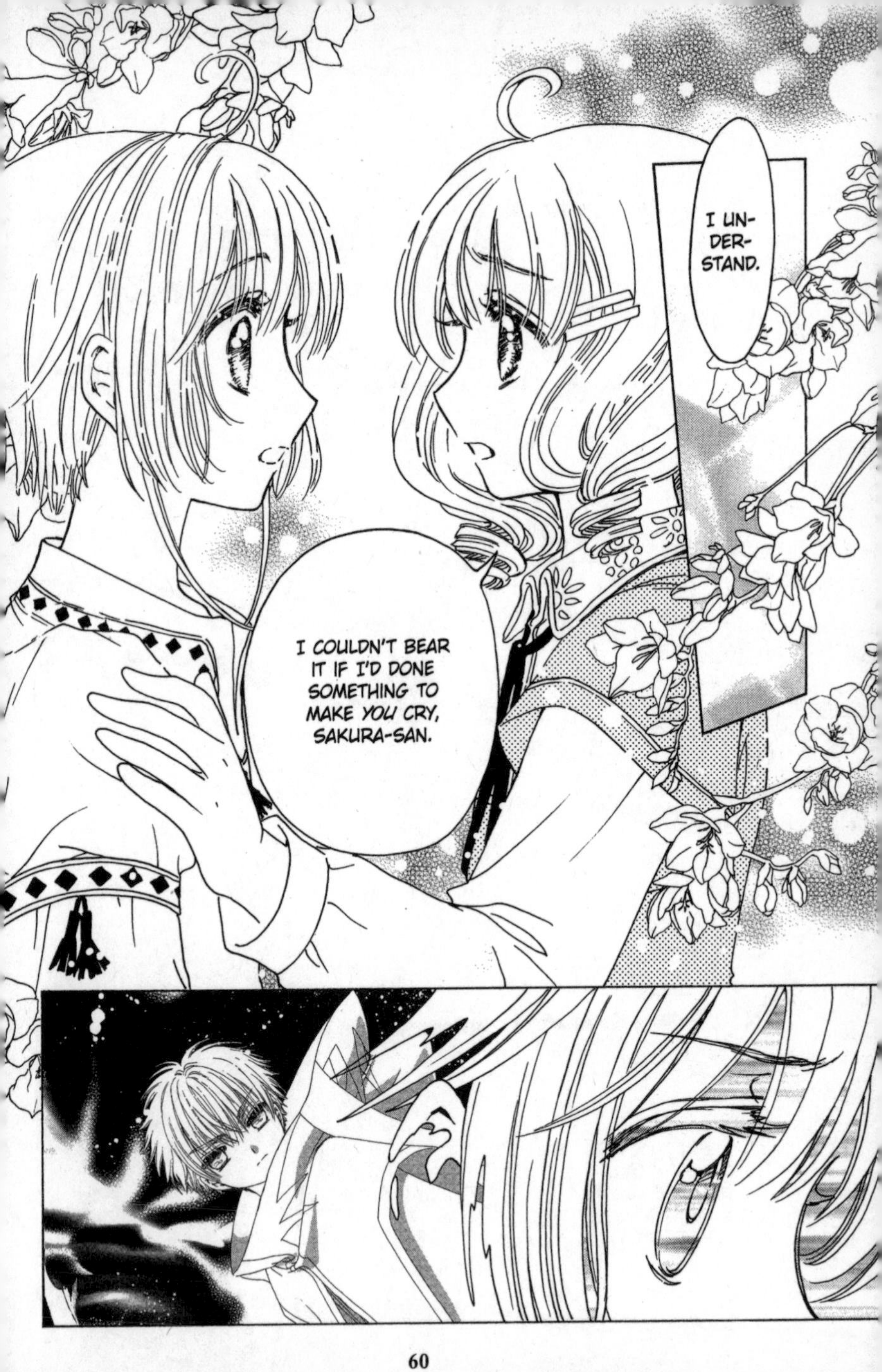
I UN-
DER-
STAND.
I COULDN'T BEAR IT IF I'D DONE SOMETHING TO MAKE *YOU* CRY, SAKURA-SAN.

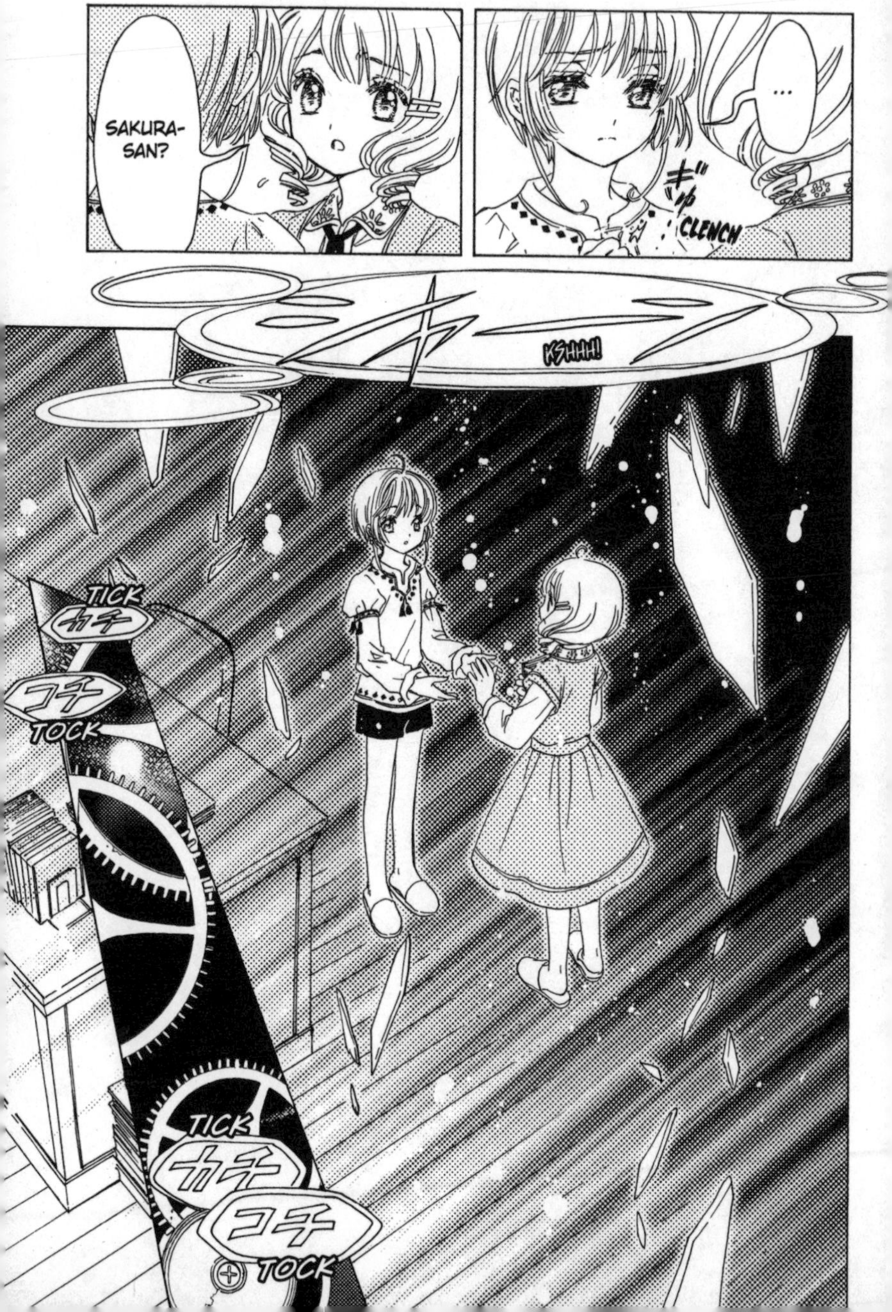
...
ギュ
CLENCH
SAKURA-SAN?
KSHHH!
TICK
カチ
コチ
TOCK
TICK
カチ
コチ
TOCK

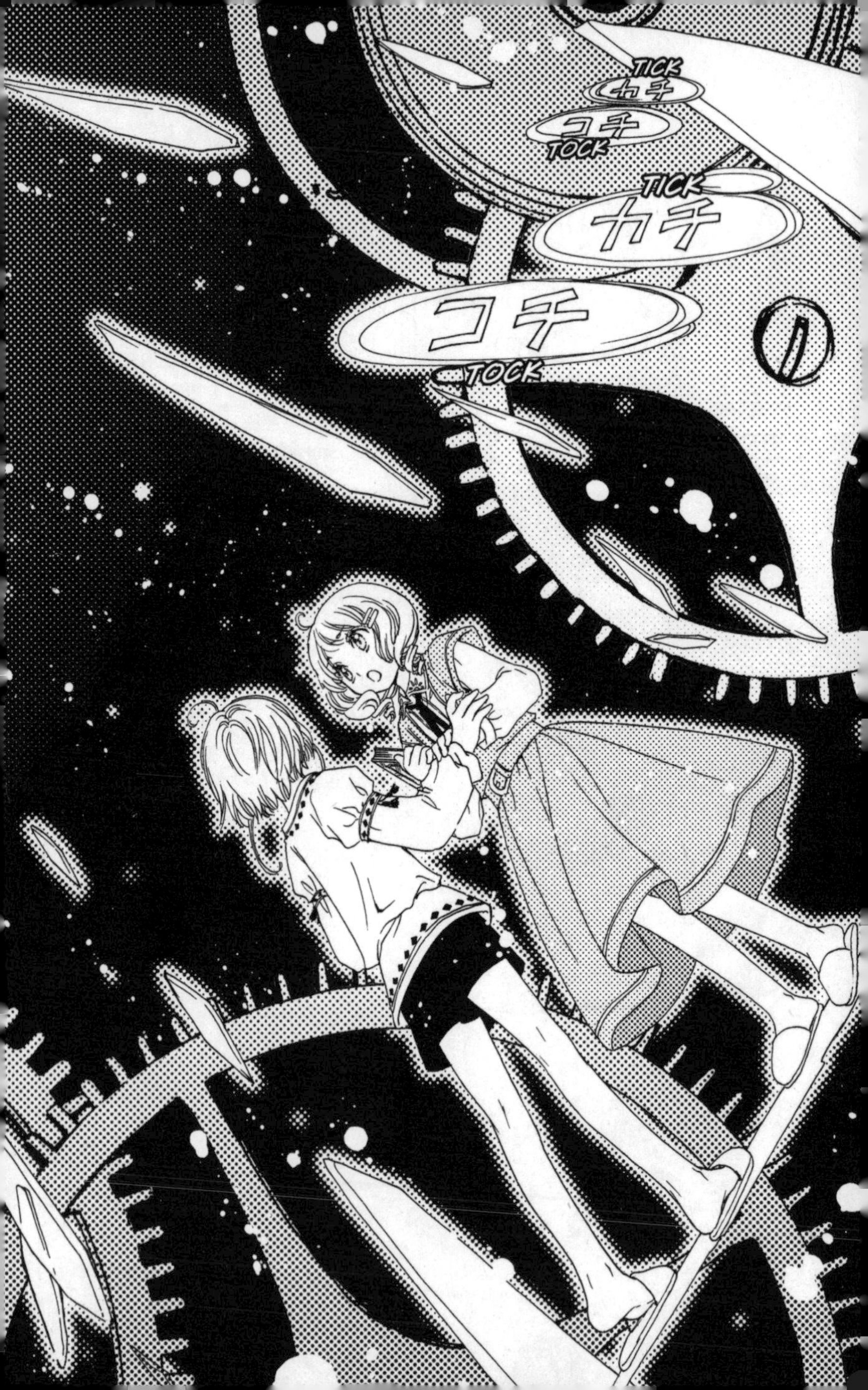
TICK
カチ
コチ
TOCK
TICK
カチ
コチ
TOCK

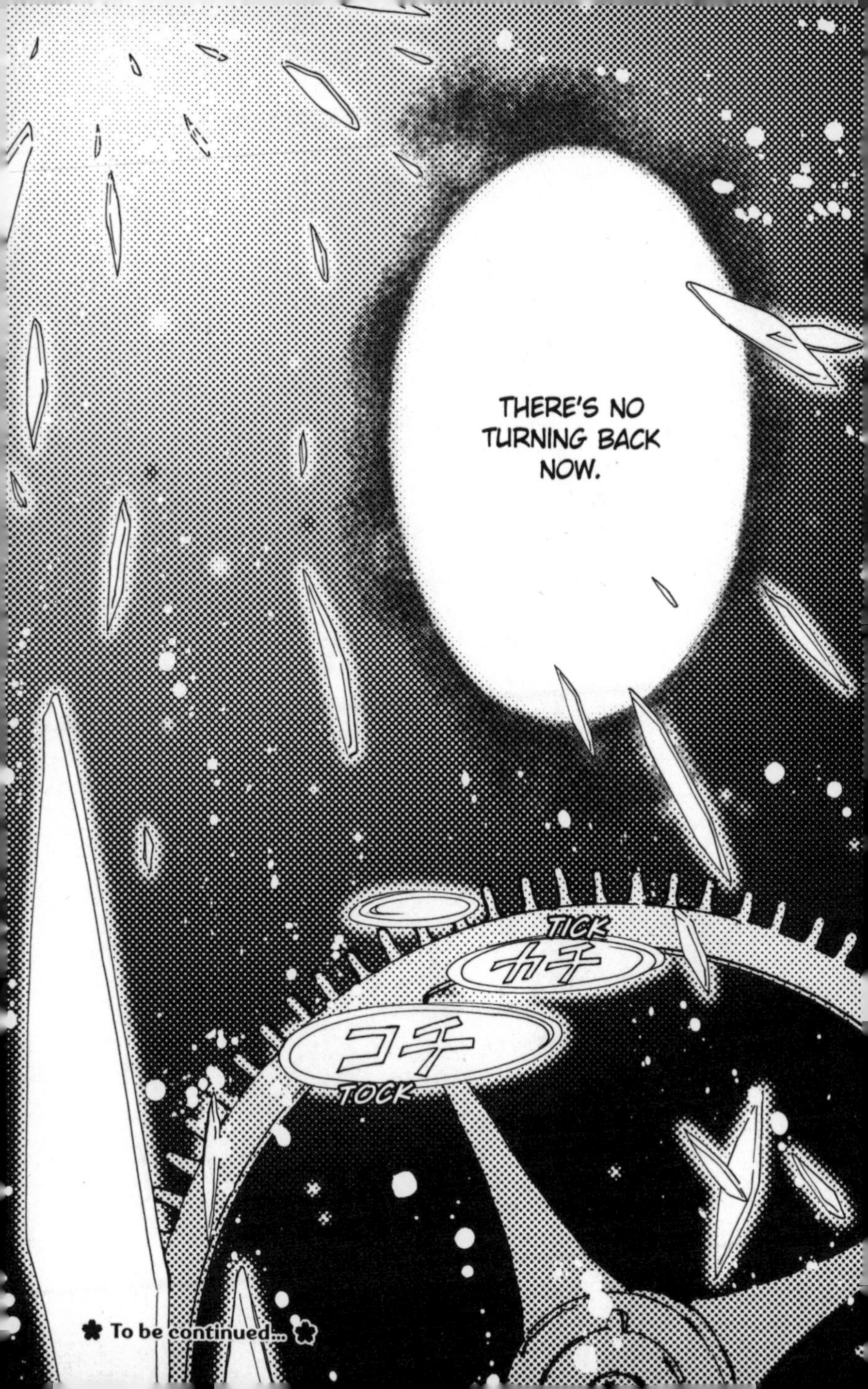
THERE'S NO TURNING BACK NOW.
TICK カチ
コチ TOCK

✿ To be continued... ✿

Cardcaptor Sakura

CLEAR CARD

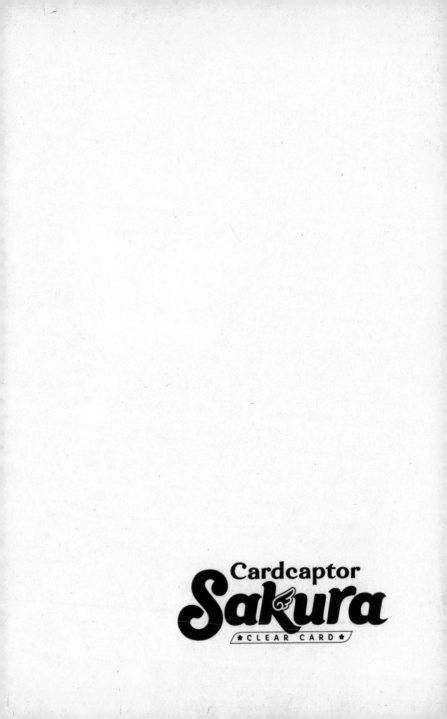

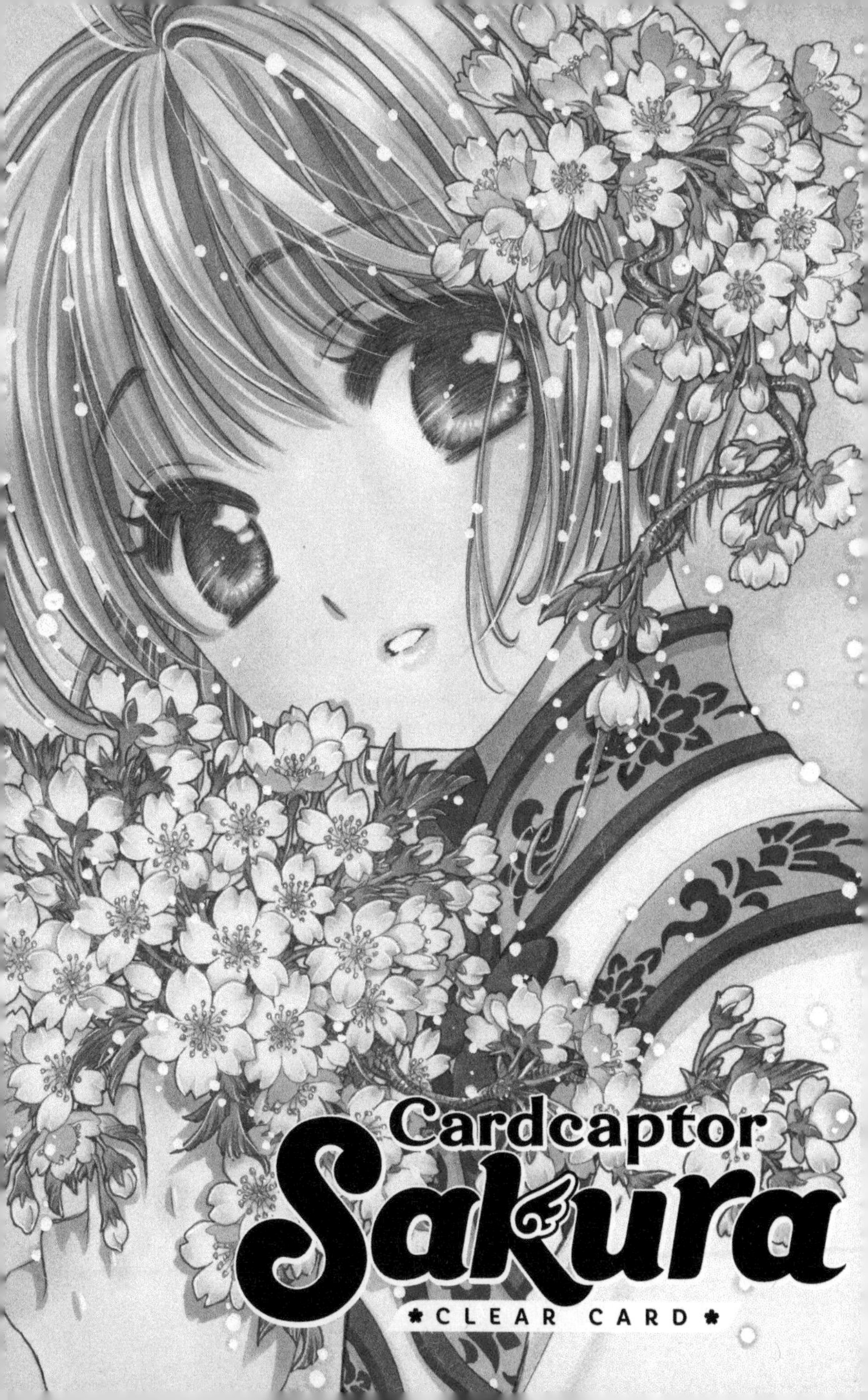
Cardcaptor
Sakura
CLEAR CARD

Cardcaptor Sakura
CLEAR CARD

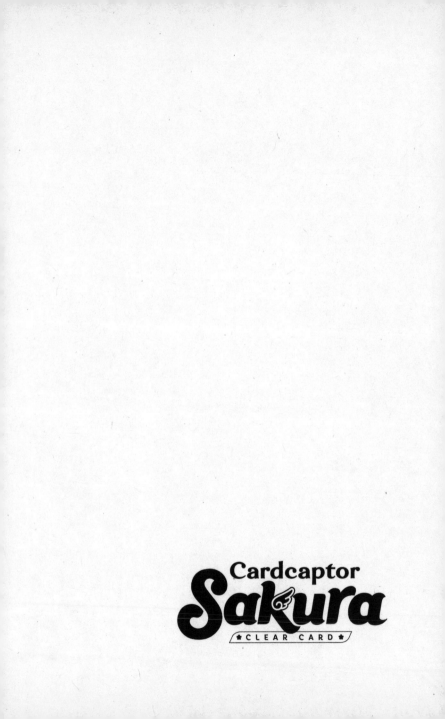

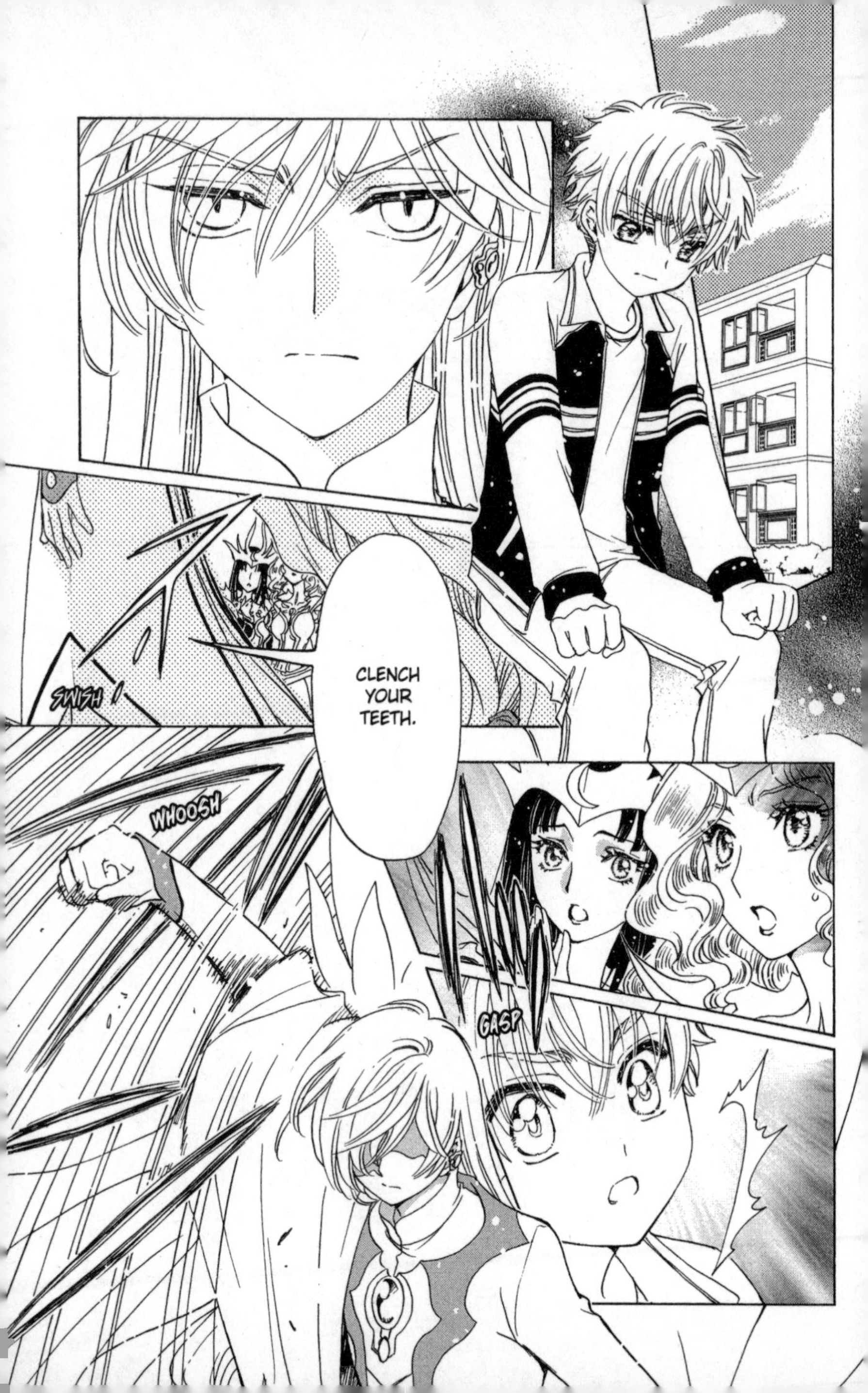
SWISH
CLENCH YOUR TEETH.
WHOOSH
GASP

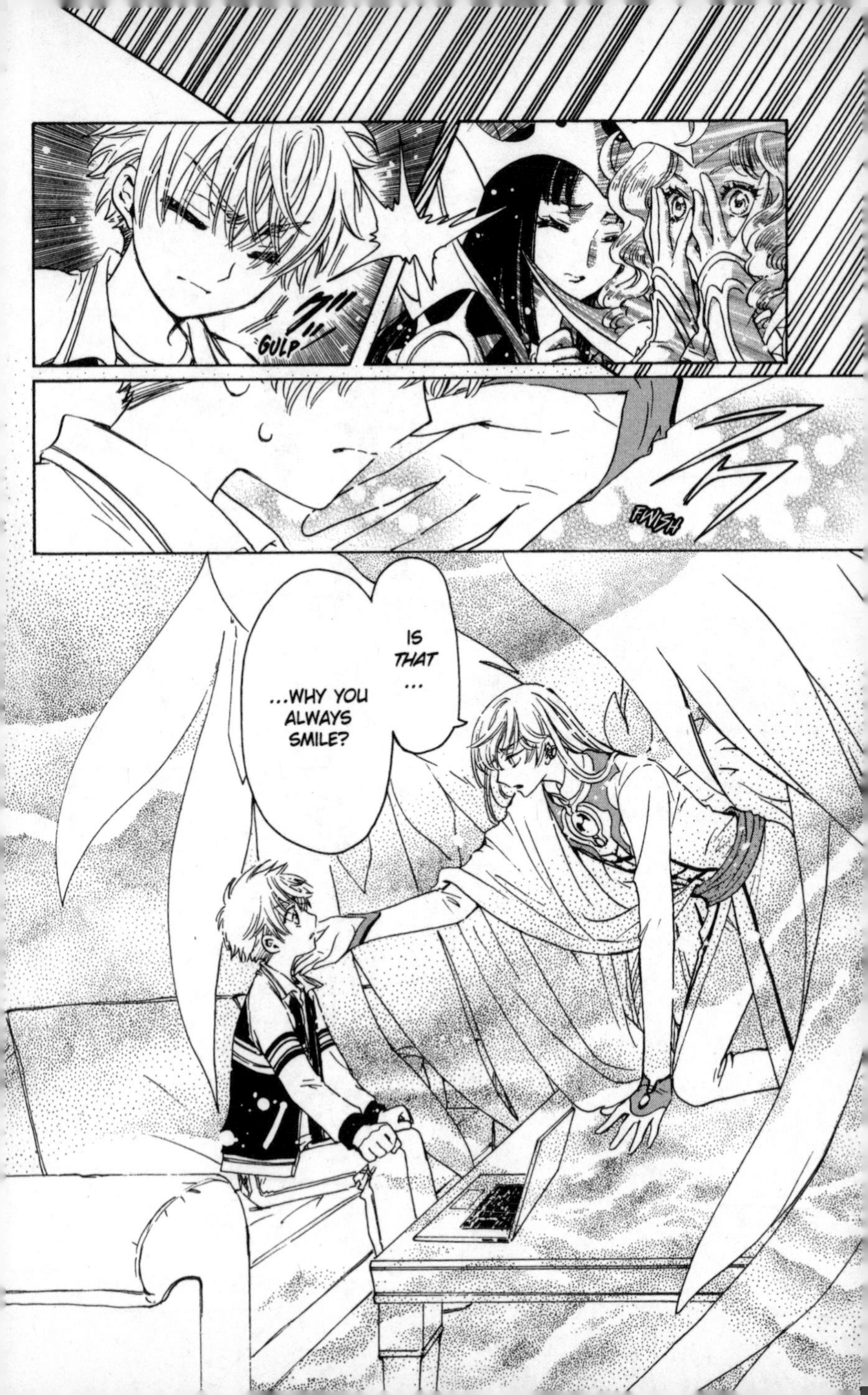
GULP
FWISH
IS THAT ...
...WHY YOU ALWAYS SMILE?

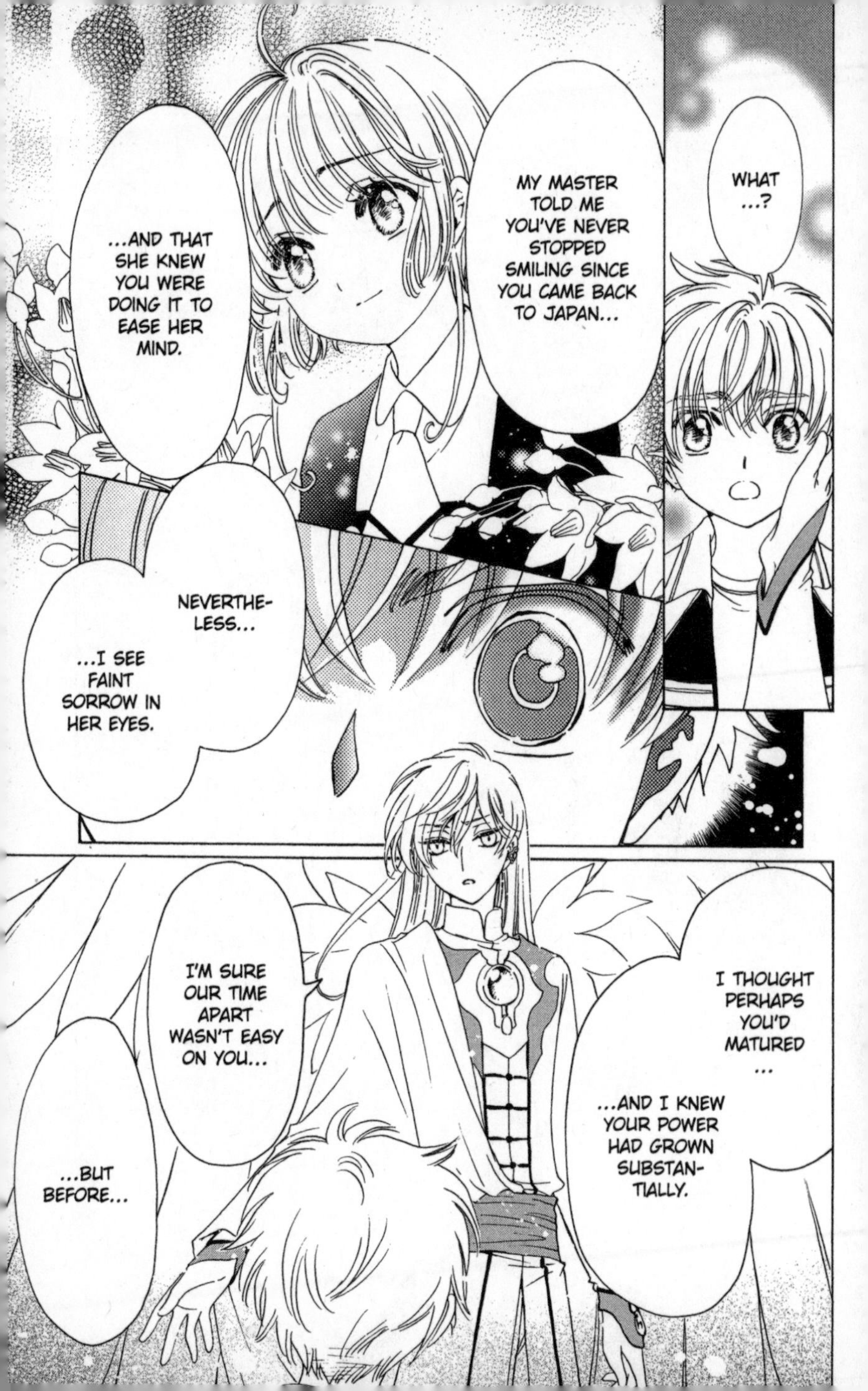
WHAT ...?
MY MASTER TOLD ME YOU'VE NEVER STOPPED SMILING SINCE YOU CAME BACK TO JAPAN...
...AND THAT SHE KNEW YOU WERE DOING IT TO EASE HER MIND.
NEVERTHE-LESS...
...I SEE FAINT SORROW IN HER EYES.
I THOUGHT PERHAPS YOU'D MATURED ...
...AND I KNEW YOUR POWER HAD GROWN SUBSTAN-TIALLY.
I'M SURE OUR TIME APART WASN'T EASY ON YOU...
...BUT BEFORE...

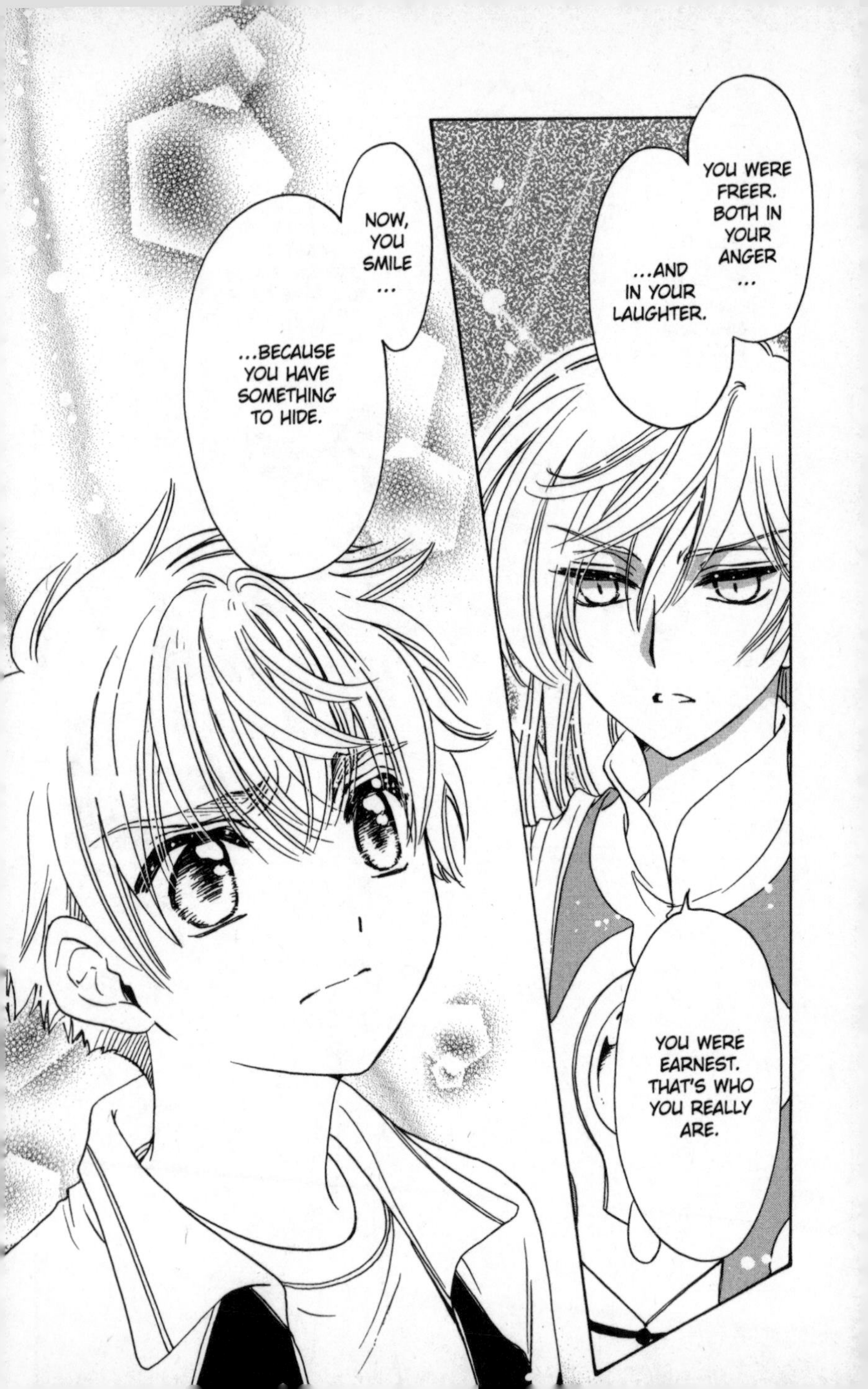
YOU WERE FREER. BOTH IN YOUR ANGER ...
...AND IN YOUR LAUGHTER.
NOW, YOU SMILE ...
...BECAUSE YOU HAVE SOMETHING TO HIDE.
YOU WERE EARNEST. THAT'S WHO YOU REALLY ARE.

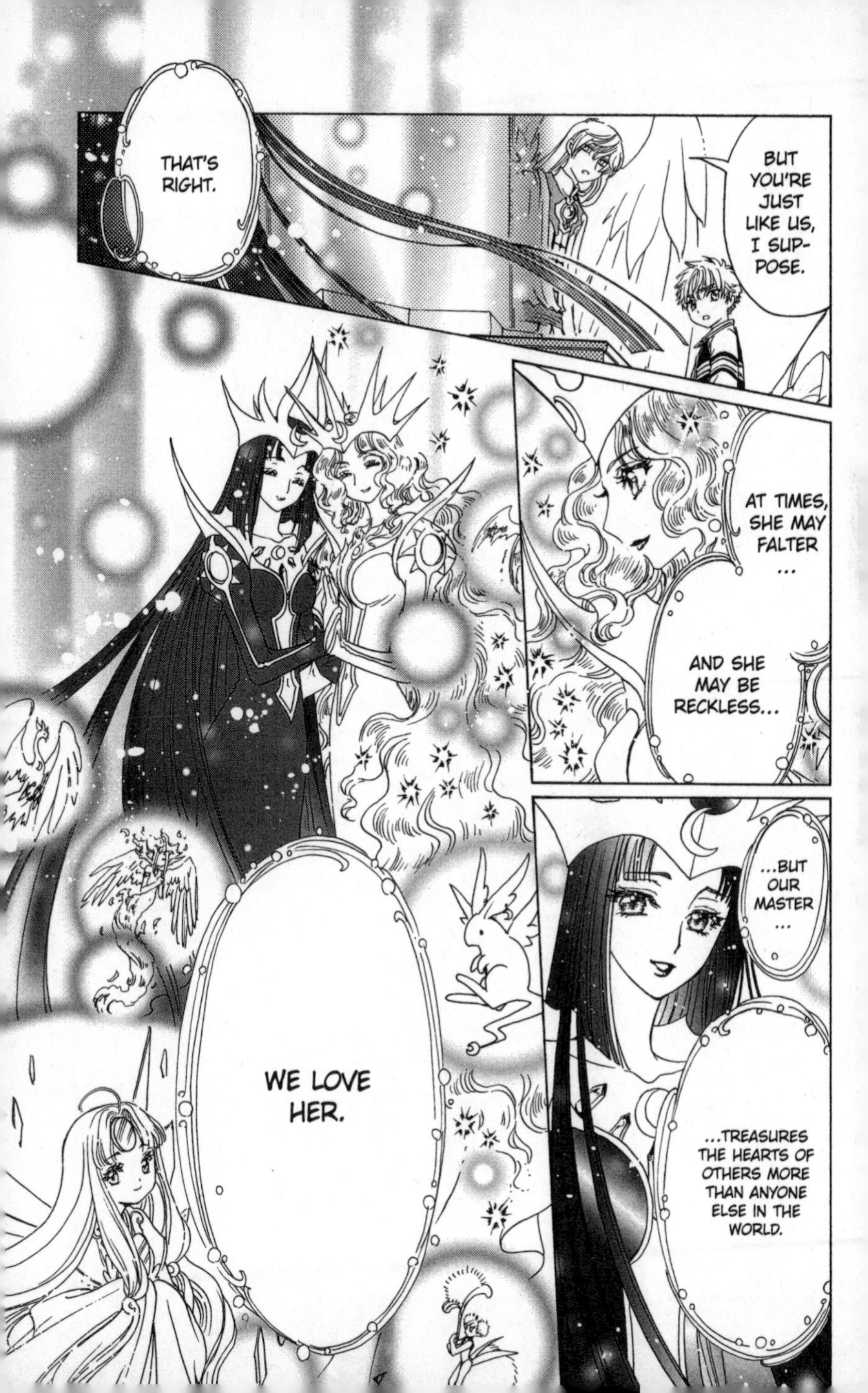
BUT YOU'RE JUST LIKE US, I SUP-POSE.
THAT'S RIGHT.
AT TIMES, SHE MAY FALTER ...
AND SHE MAY BE RECKLESS...
...BUT OUR MASTER ...
...TREASURES THE HEARTS OF OTHERS MORE THAN ANYONE ELSE IN THE WORLD.
WE LOVE HER.

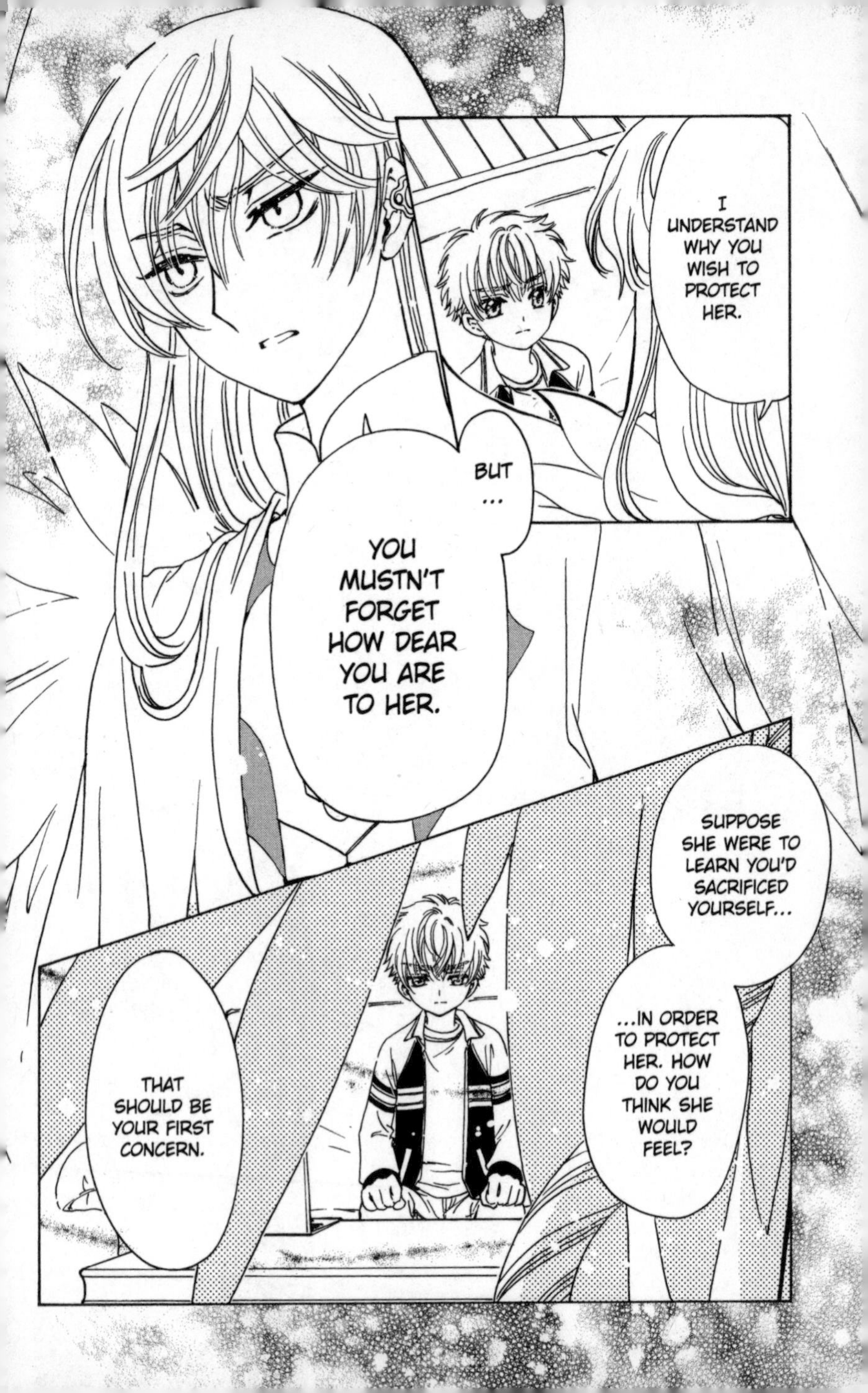
I UNDERSTAND WHY YOU WISH TO PROTECT HER.
BUT ...
YOU MUSTN'T FORGET HOW DEAR YOU ARE TO HER.
SUPPOSE SHE WERE TO LEARN YOU'D SACRIFICED YOURSELF...
...IN ORDER TO PROTECT HER. HOW DO YOU THINK SHE WOULD FEEL?
THAT SHOULD BE YOUR FIRST CONCERN.

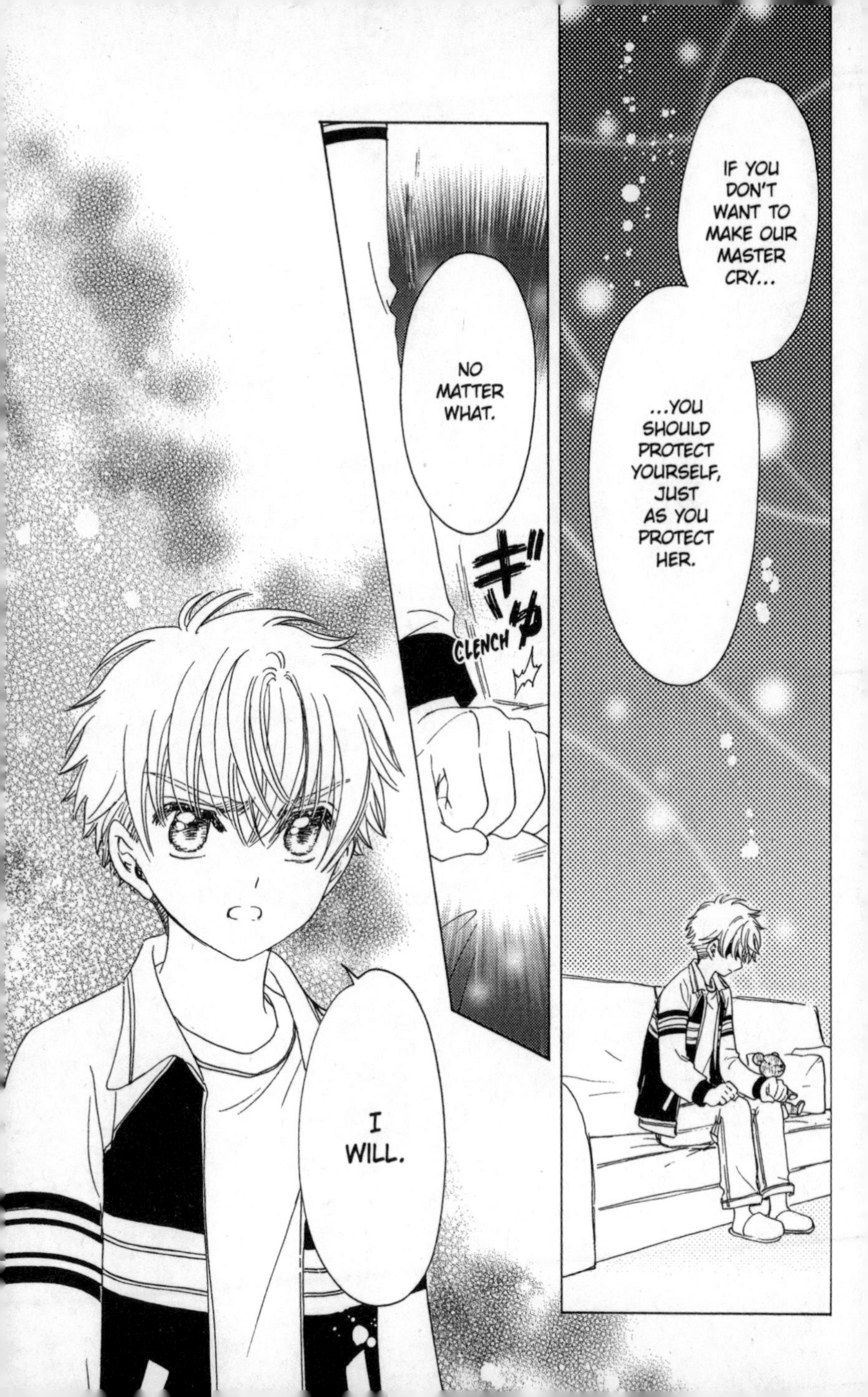
IF YOU DON'T WANT TO MAKE OUR MASTER CRY...
...YOU SHOULD PROTECT YOURSELF, JUST AS YOU PROTECT HER.
NO MATTER WHAT.
ぎゅ
CLENCH
I WILL.

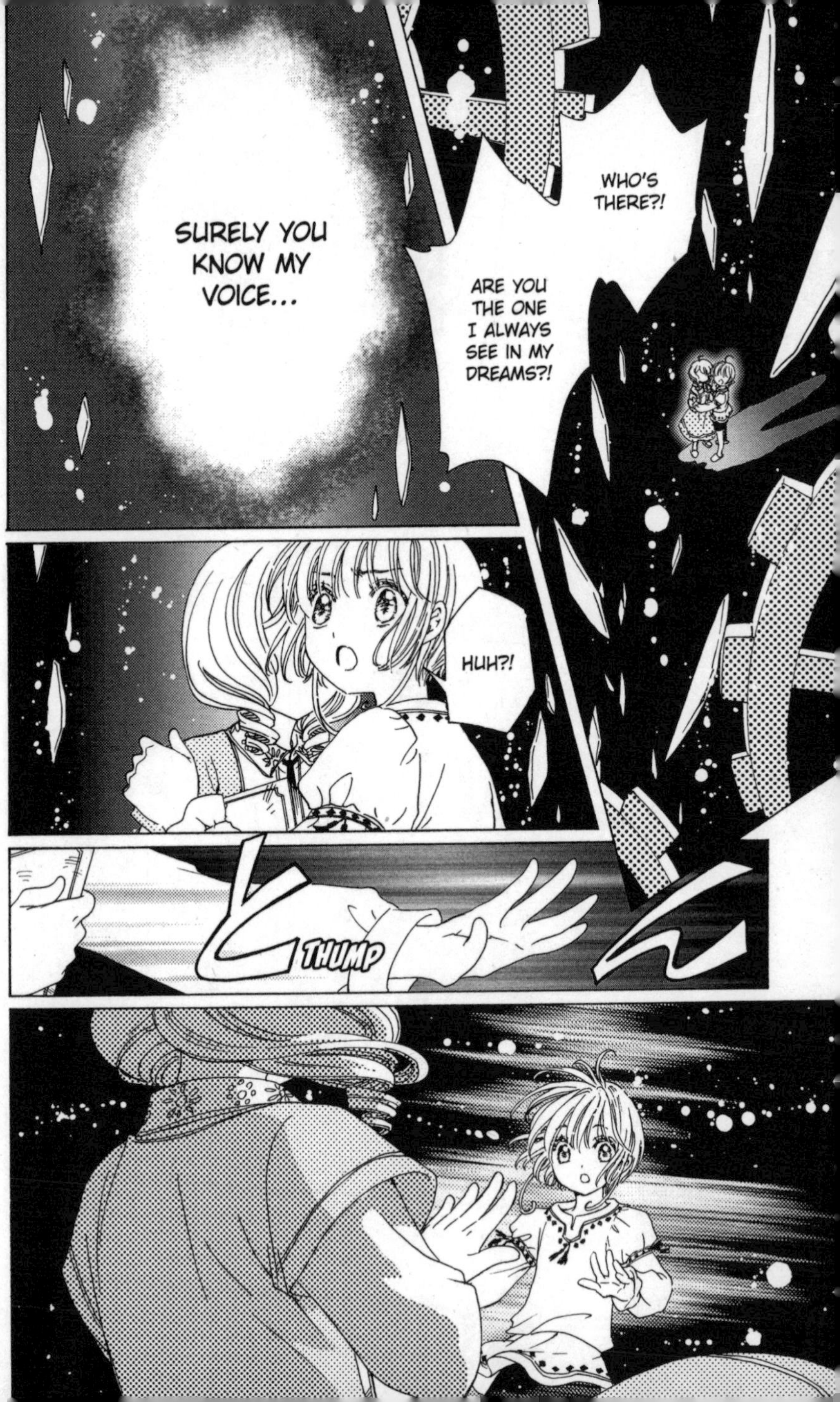
WHO'S THERE?!
ARE YOU THE ONE I ALWAYS SEE IN MY DREAMS?!
SURELY YOU KNOW MY VOICE...
HUH?!
THUMP

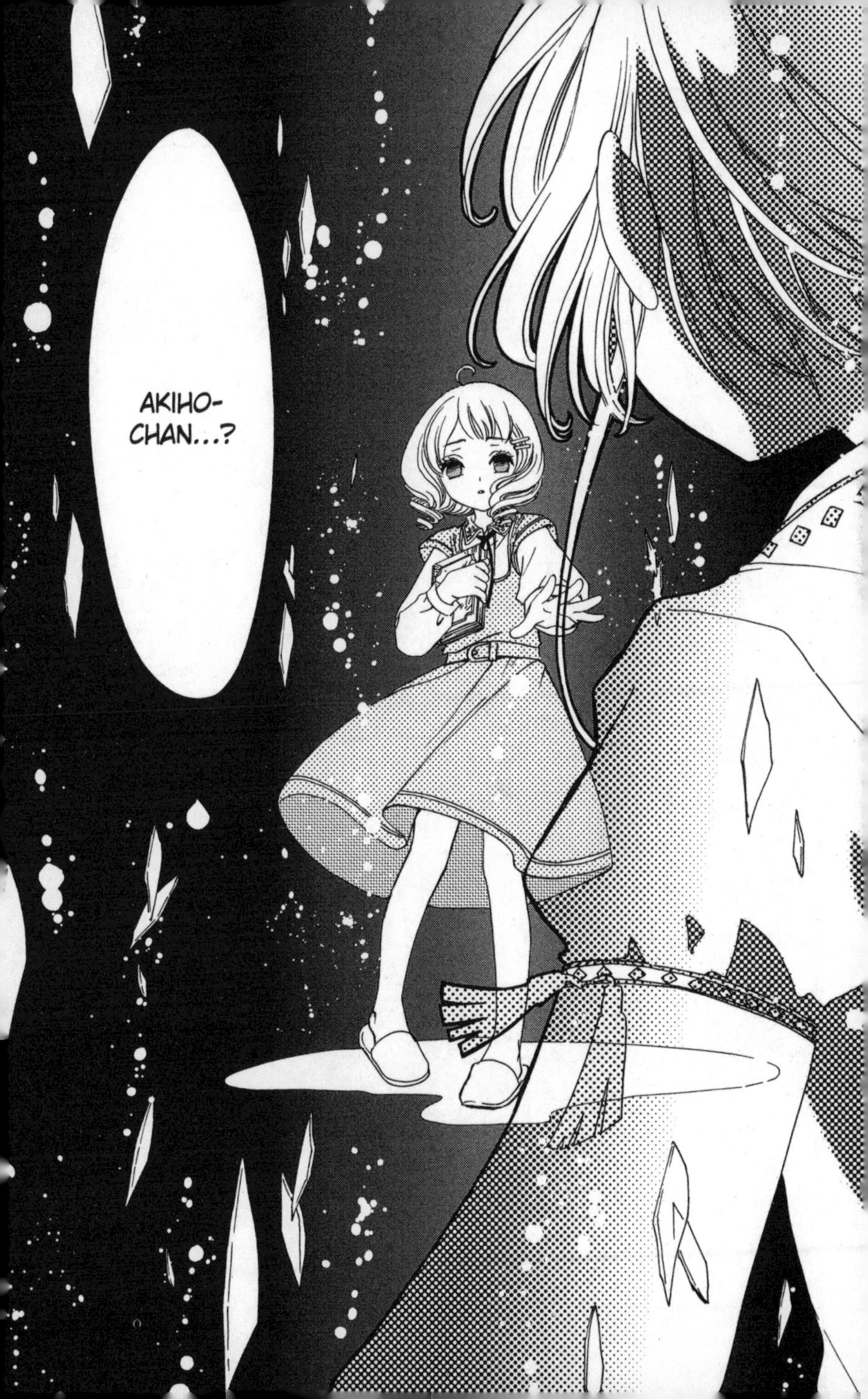
AKIHO-
CHAN...?

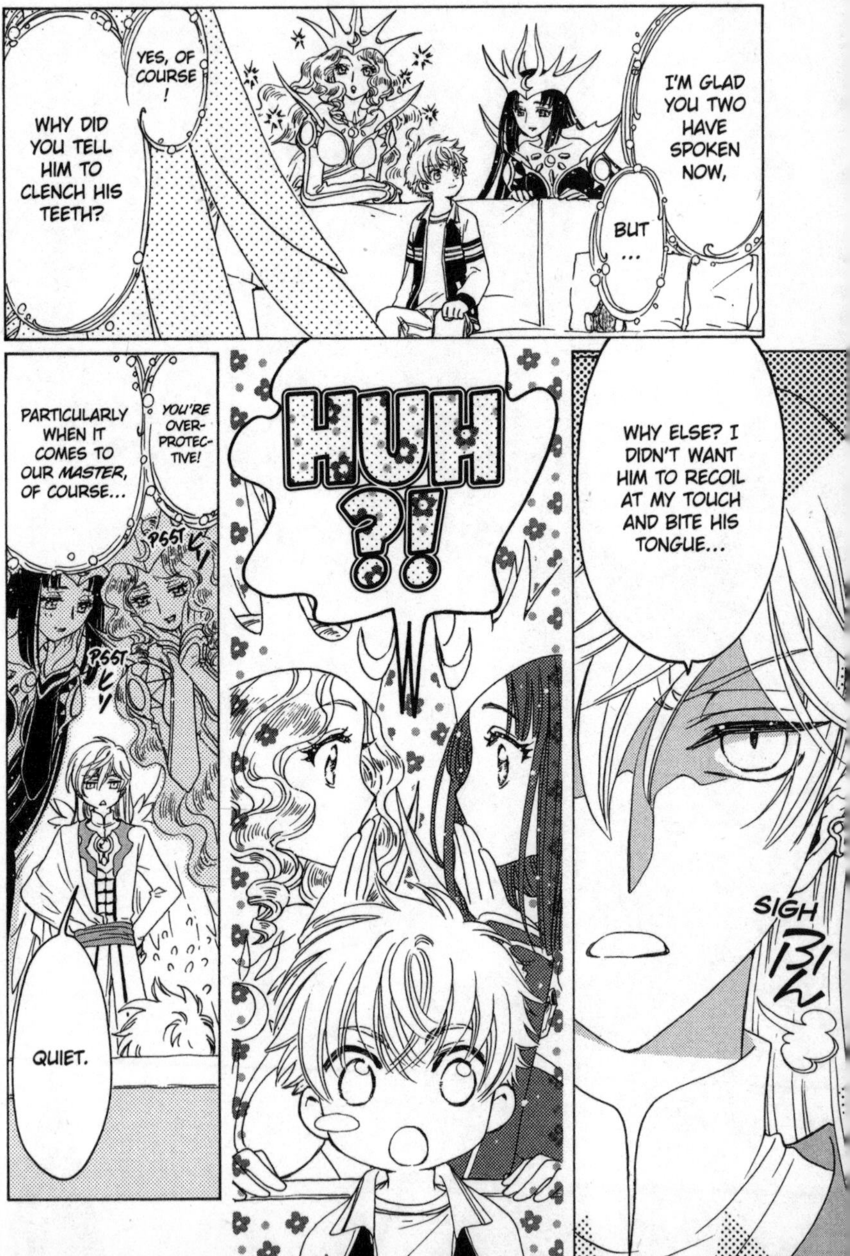
I'M GLAD YOU TWO HAVE SPOKEN NOW,
BUT ...
YES, OF COURSE !
WHY DID YOU TELL HIM TO CLENCH HIS TEETH?
WHY ELSE? I DIDN'T WANT HIM TO RECOIL AT MY TOUCH AND BITE HIS TONGUE...
SIGH
HUH ?!
YOU'RE OVER-PROTECTIVE!
PARTICULARLY WHEN IT COMES TO OUR *MASTER*, OF COURSE...
PSST
PSST
QUIET.

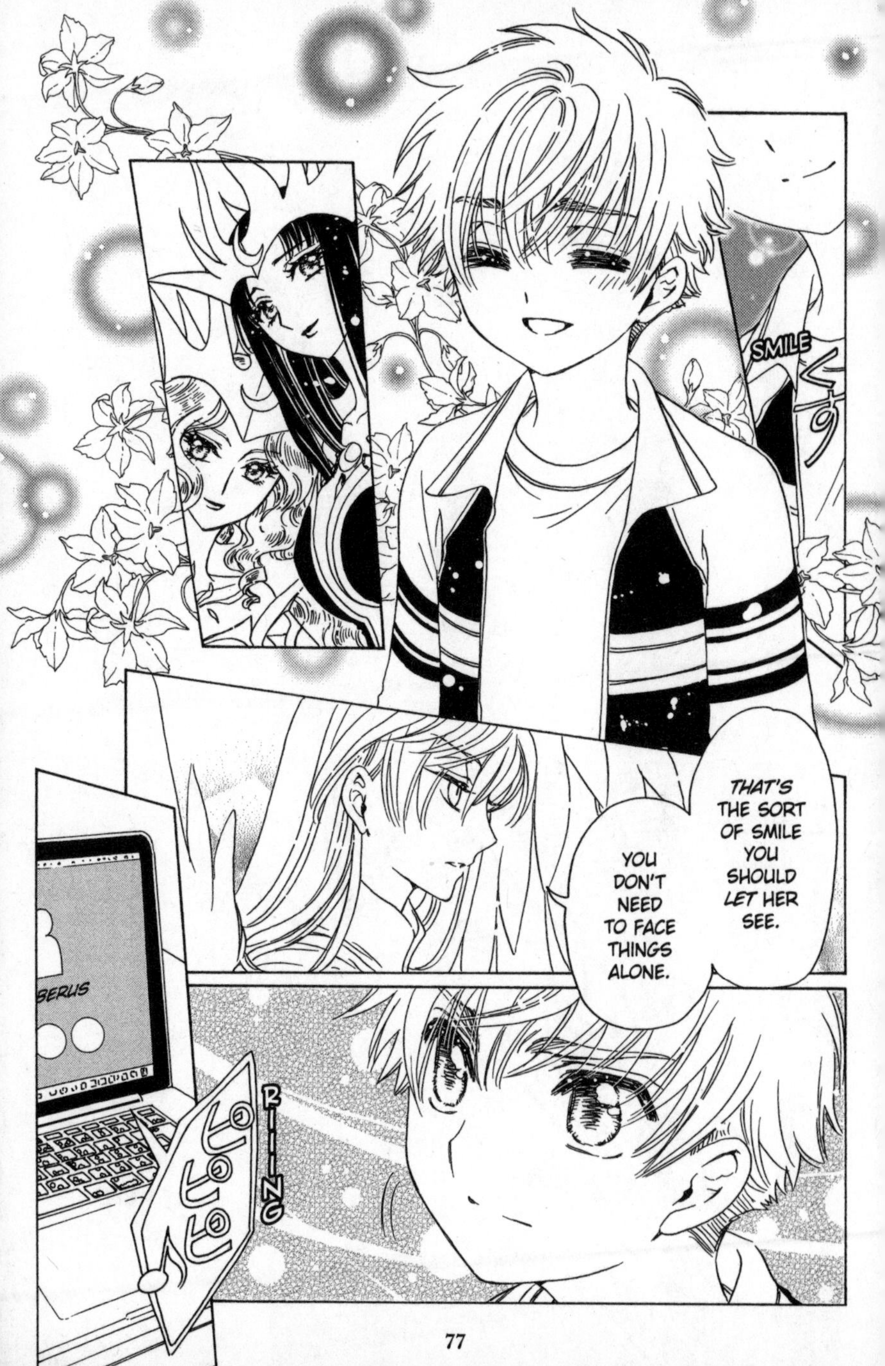
SMILE
くす
THAT'S THE SORT OF SMILE YOU SHOULD LET HER SEE.
YOU DON'T NEED TO FACE THINGS ALONE.
RIIING
ピロピロ♪

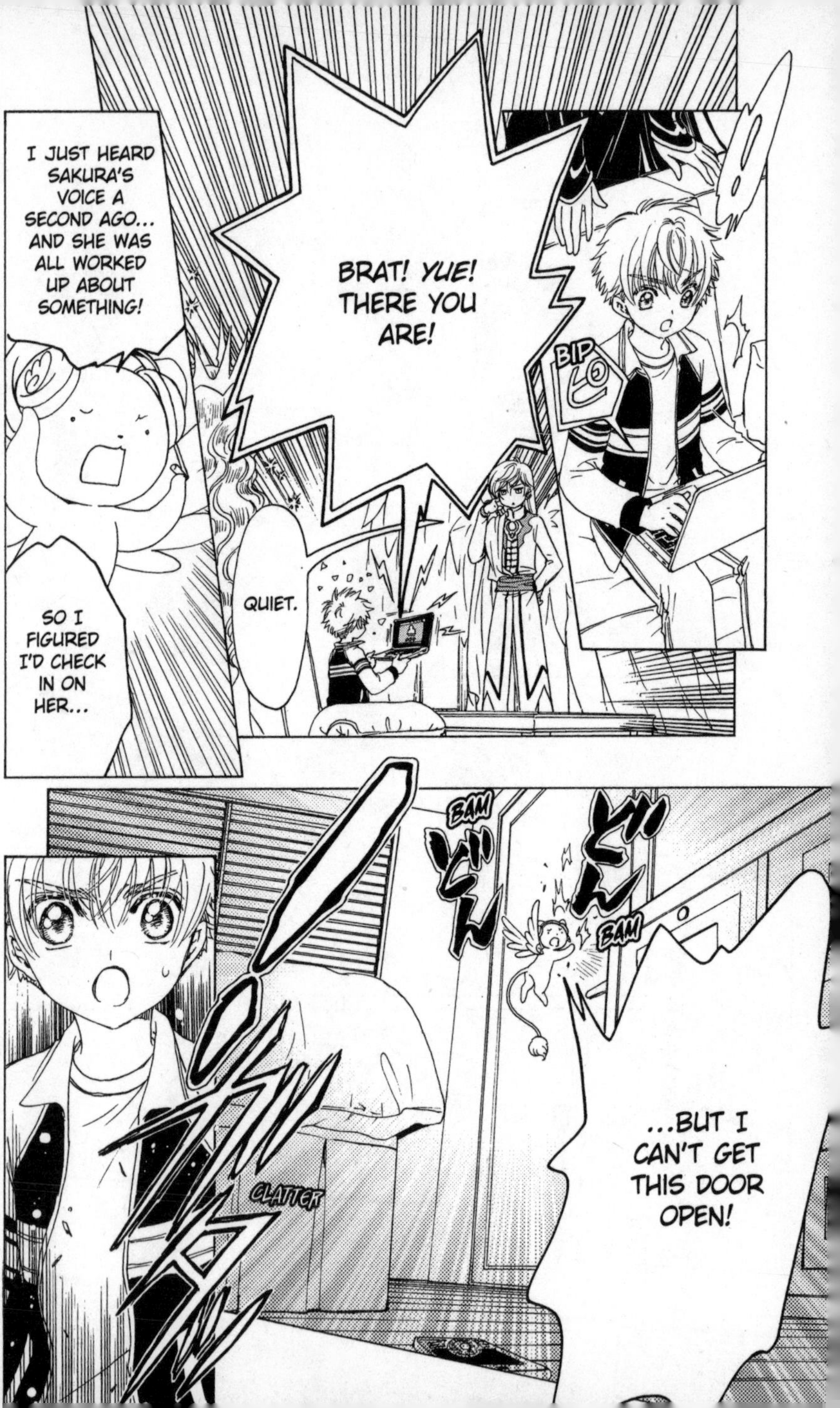
BIP
BRAT! YUE! THERE YOU ARE!
QUIET.
I JUST HEARD SAKURA'S VOICE A SECOND AGO... AND SHE WAS ALL WORKED UP ABOUT SOMETHING!
SO I FIGURED I'D CHECK IN ON HER...
BAM
BAM
...BUT I CAN'T GET THIS DOOR OPEN!
CLATTER

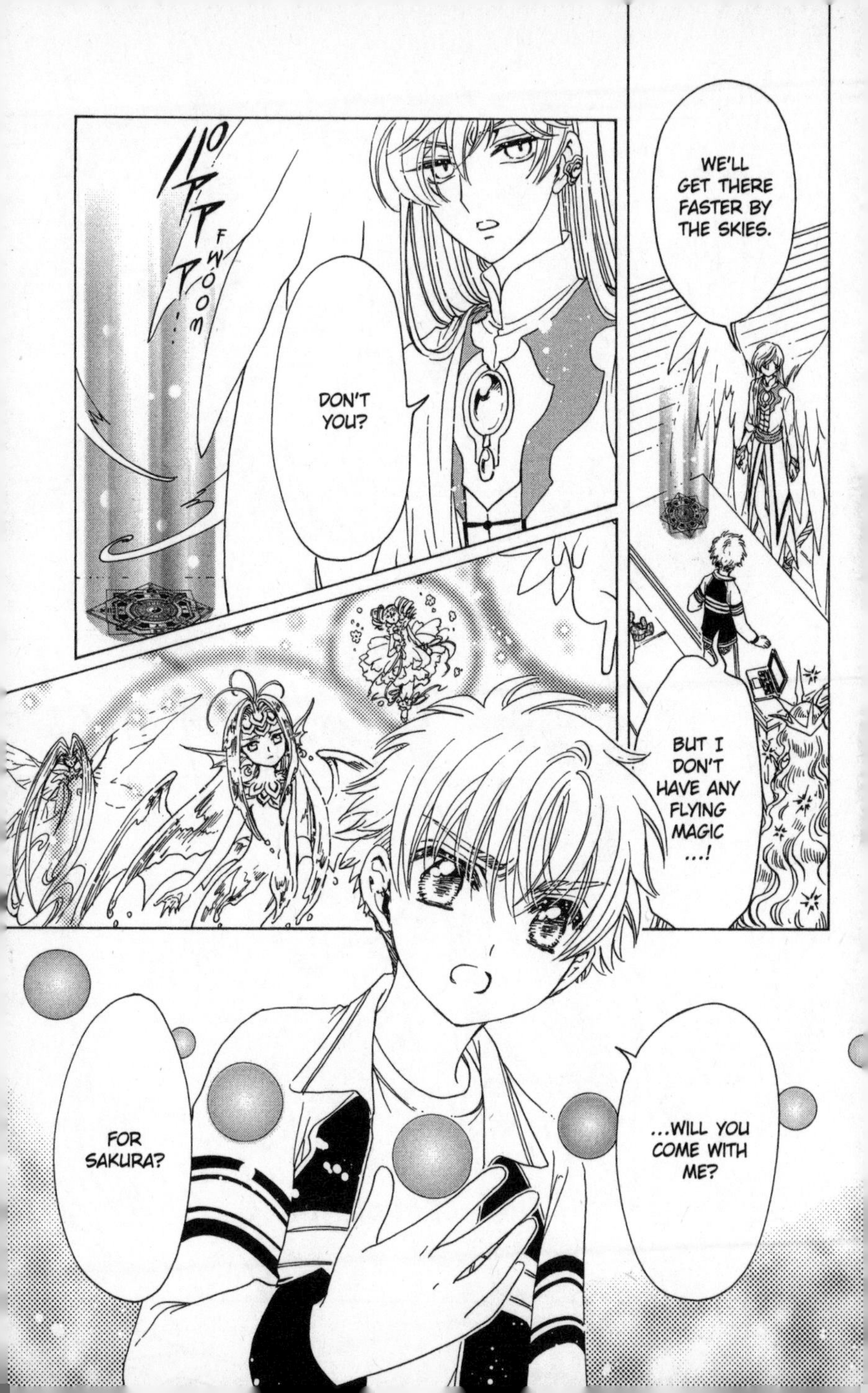
WE'LL GET THERE FASTER BY THE SKIES.
BUT I DON'T HAVE ANY FLYING MAGIC ...!
FWOOM
DON'T YOU?
...WILL YOU COME WITH ME?
FOR SAKURA?

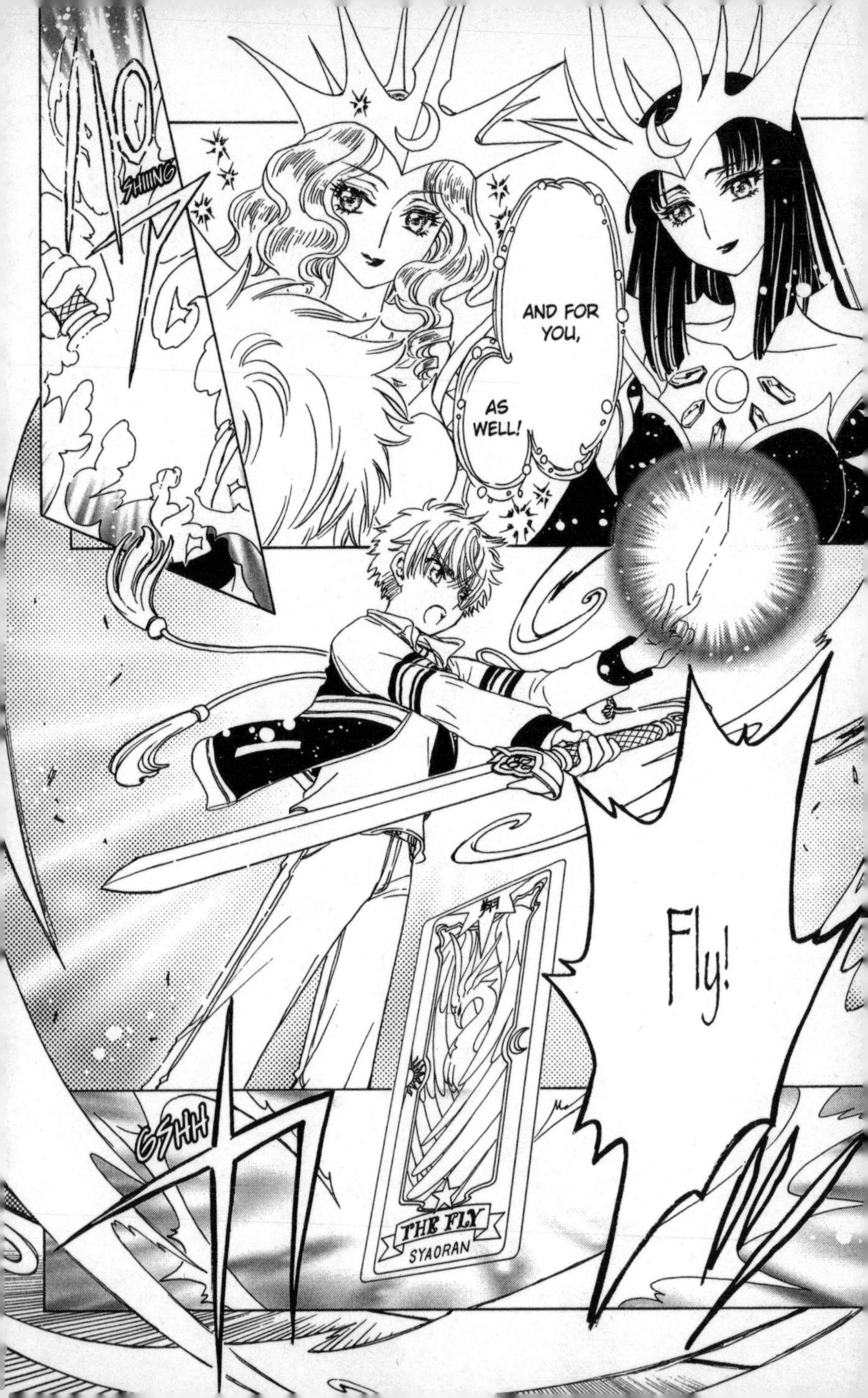
SHIIING
AND FOR YOU,
AS WELL!
Fly!
THE FLY
SYAORAN
GSHH

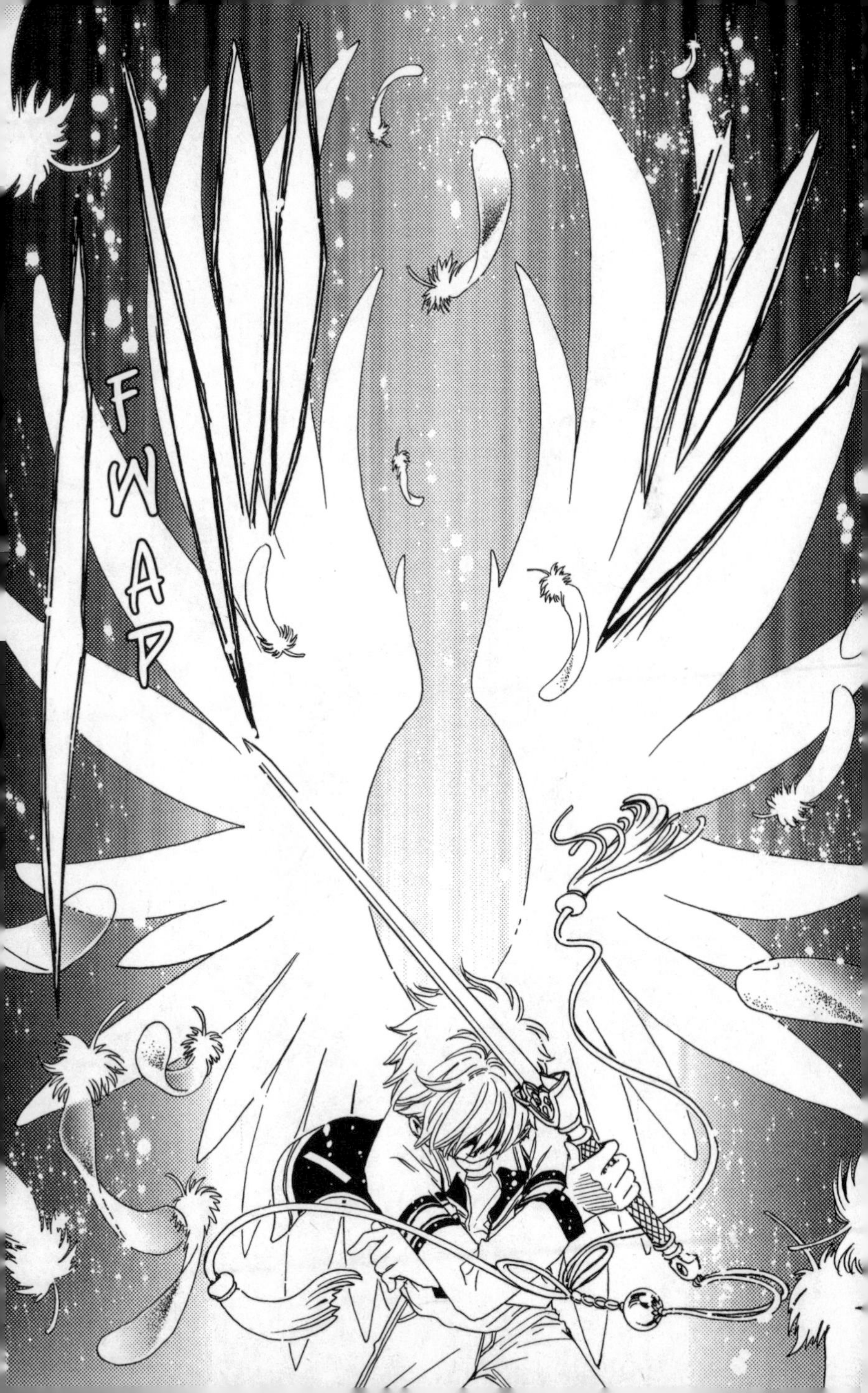
FWAP

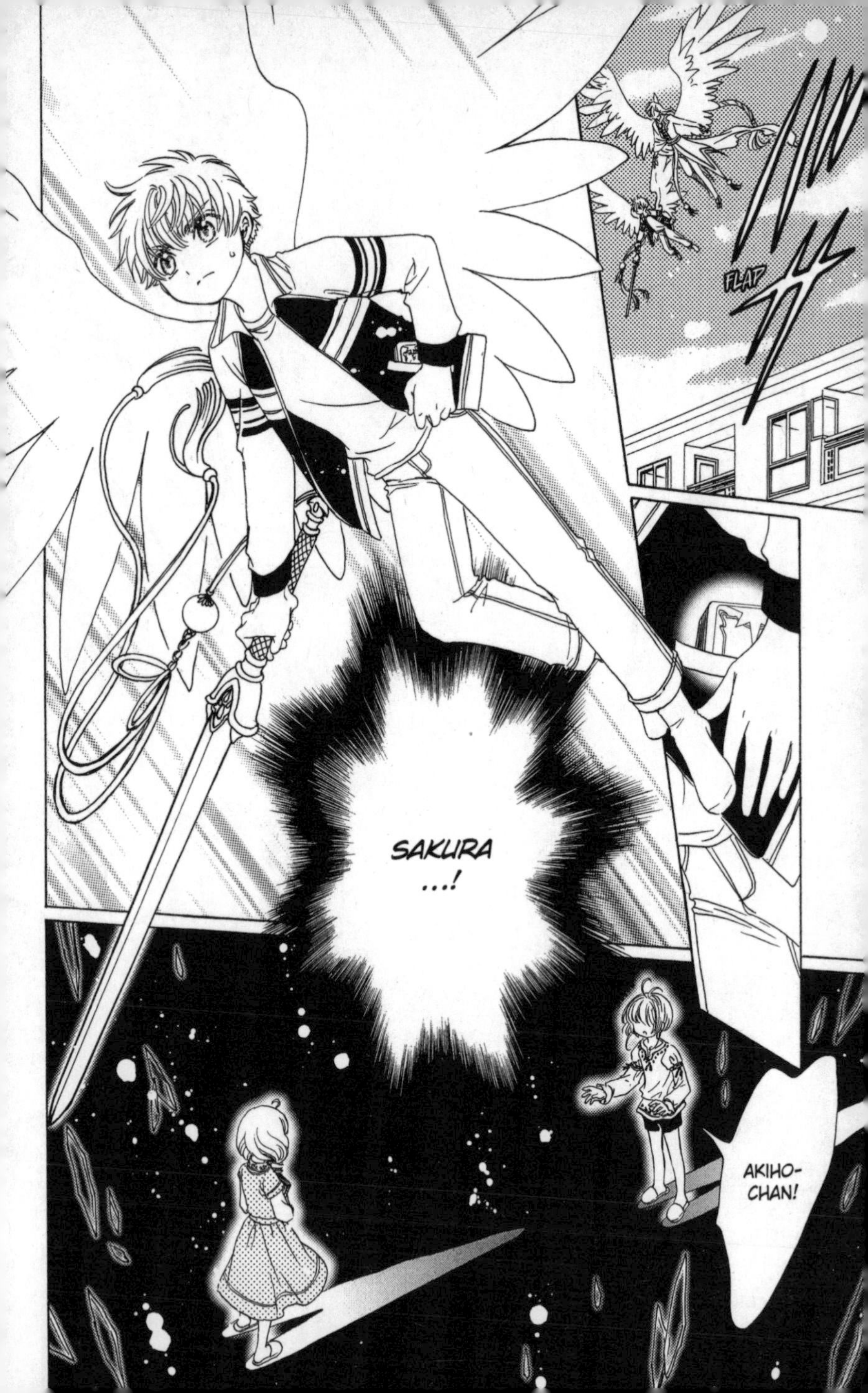
FLAP
SAKURA ...!
AKIHO-CHAN!

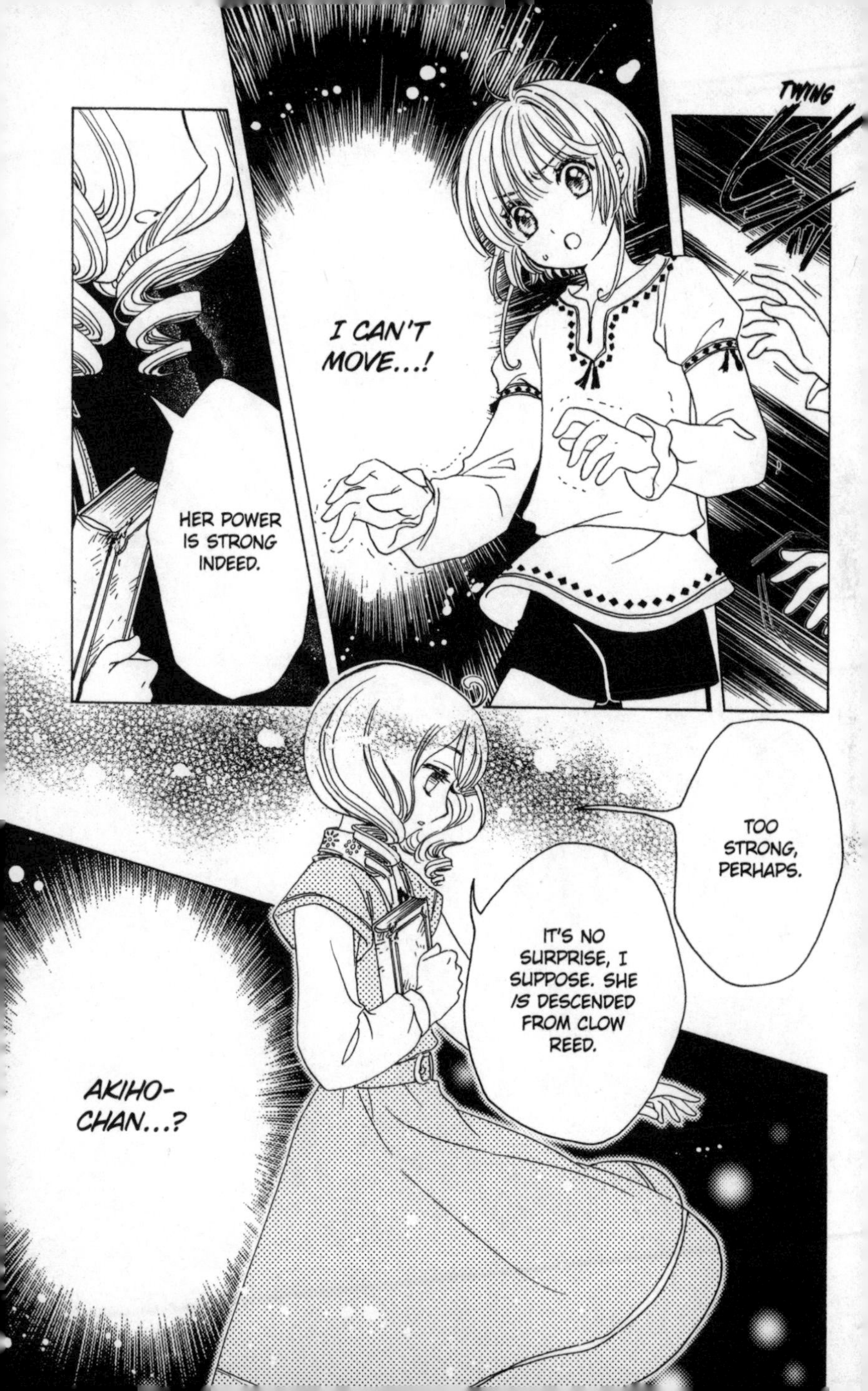
TWING
I CAN'T MOVE...!
HER POWER IS STRONG INDEED.
TOO STRONG, PERHAPS.
IT'S NO SURPRISE, I SUPPOSE. SHE IS DESCENDED FROM CLOW REED.
AKIHO-CHAN...?

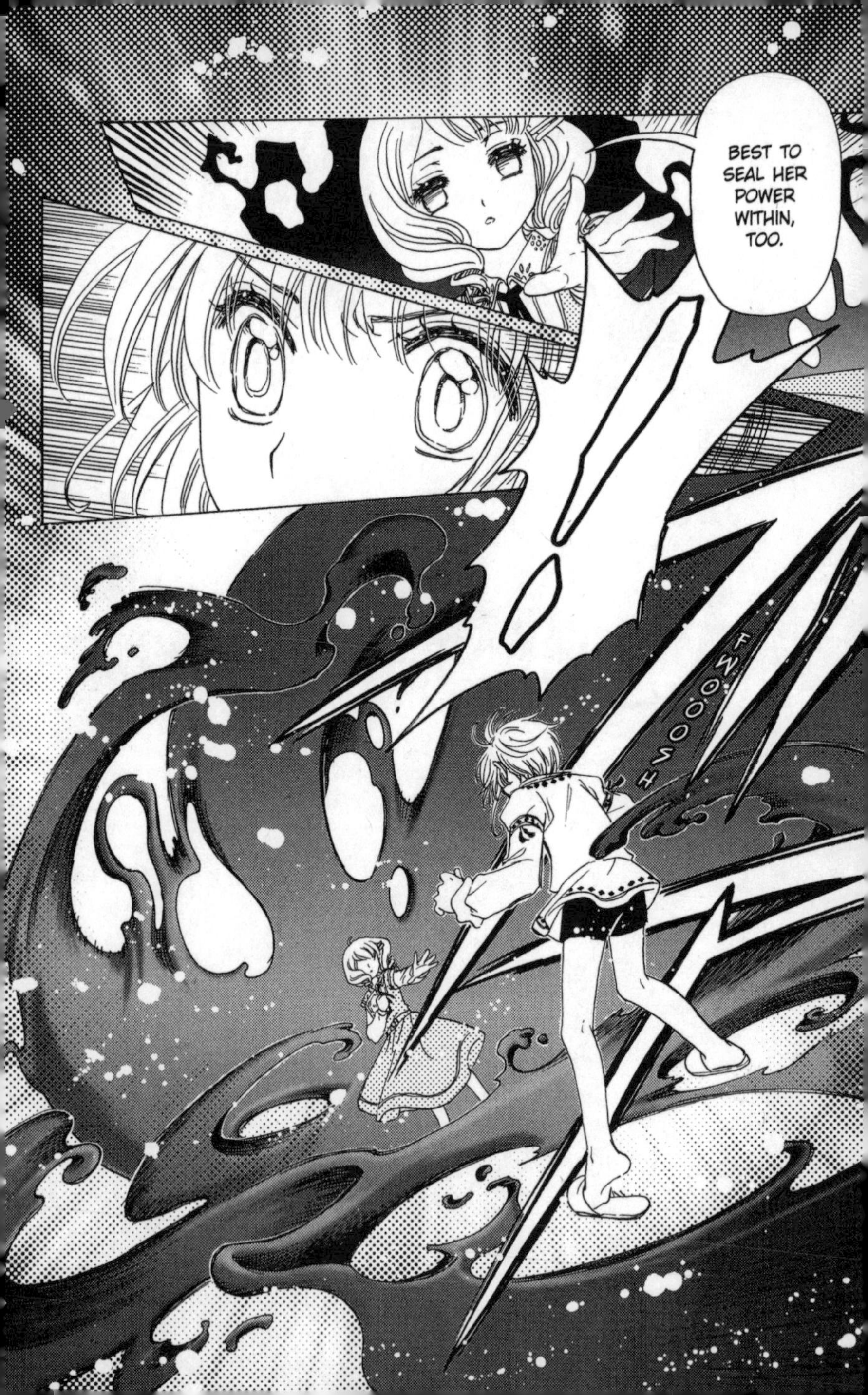
BEST TO SEAL HER POWER WITHIN, TOO.
FWOOOOSH

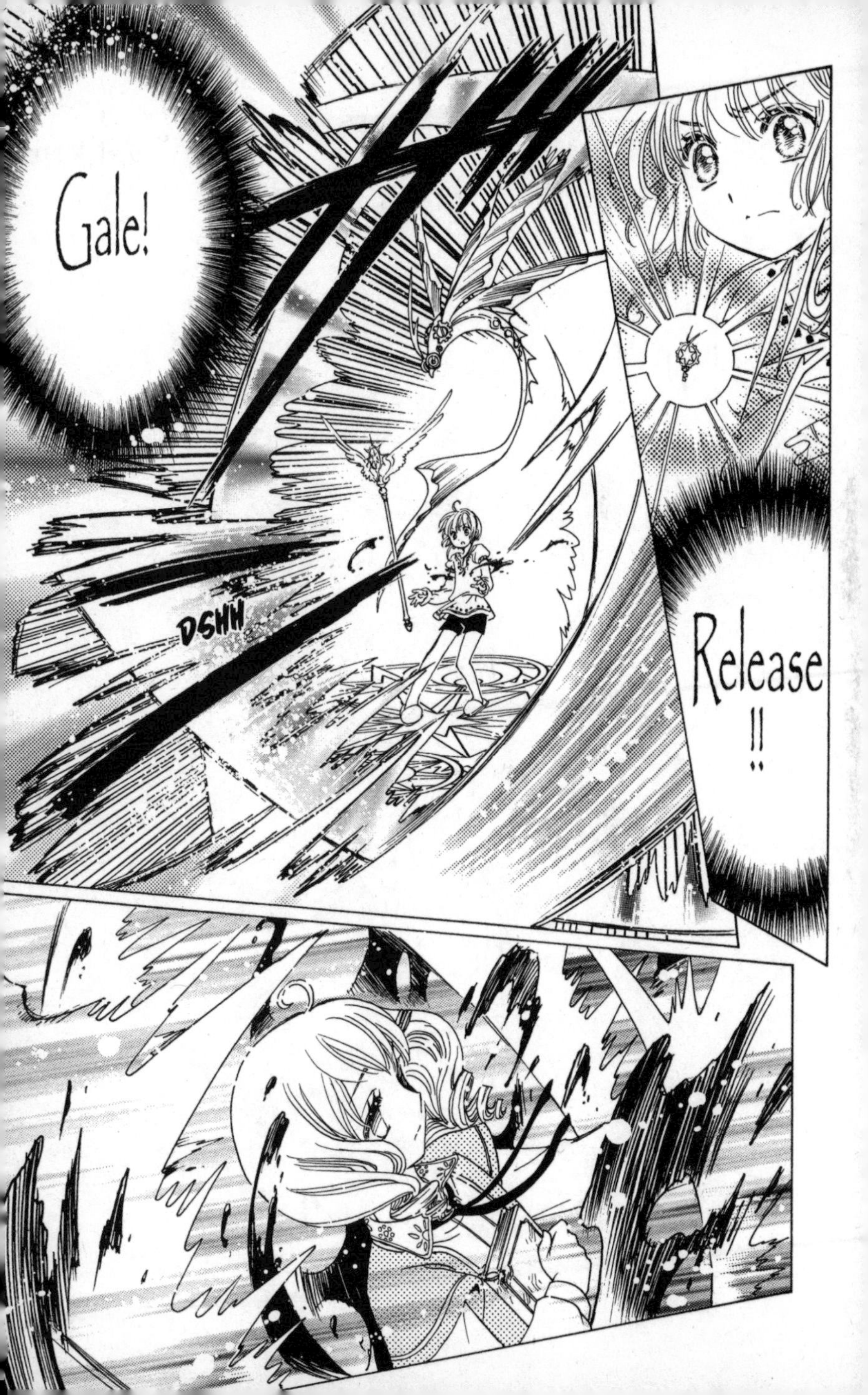
Release !!
Gale!
DSHH

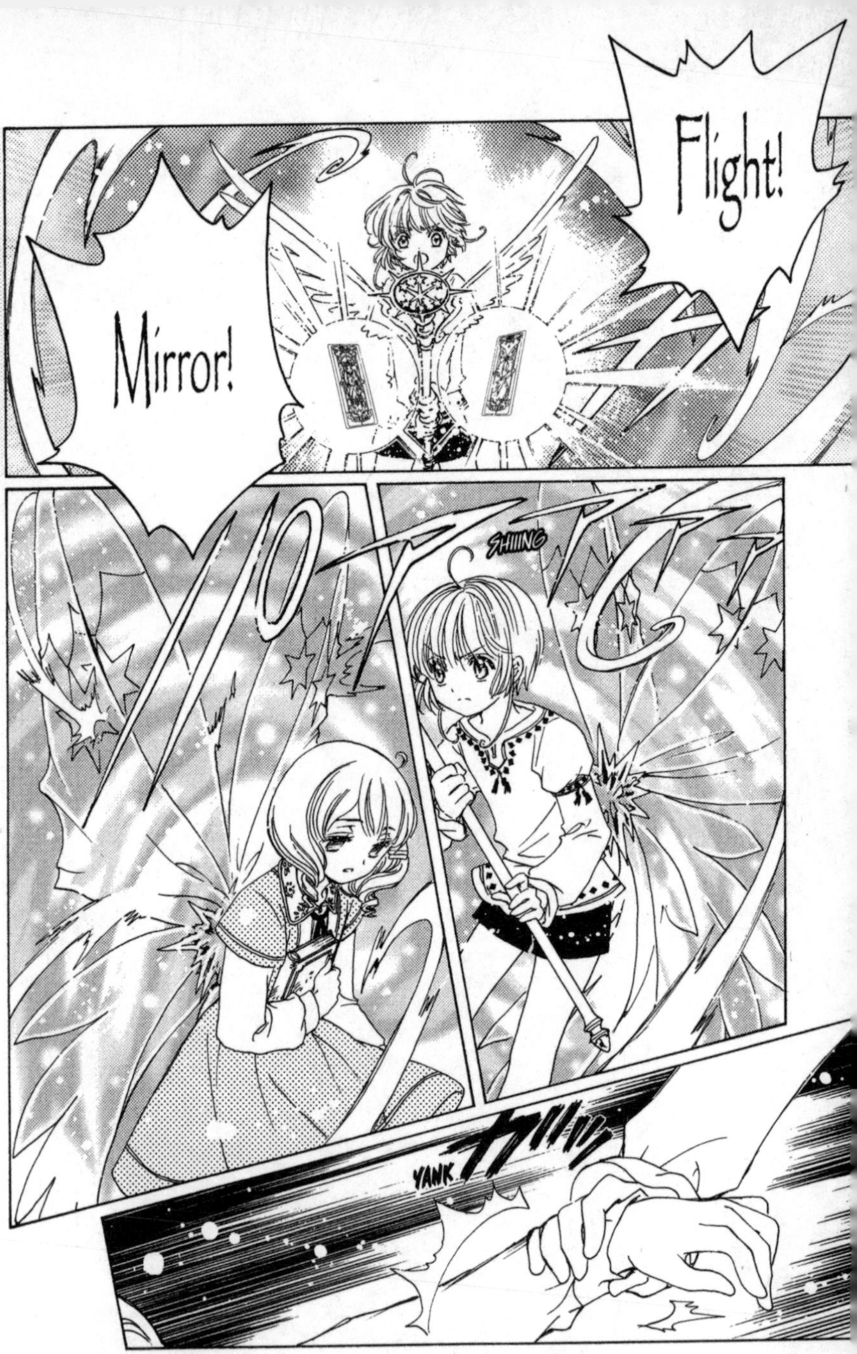
Flight!
Mirror!
SHIIING
YANK

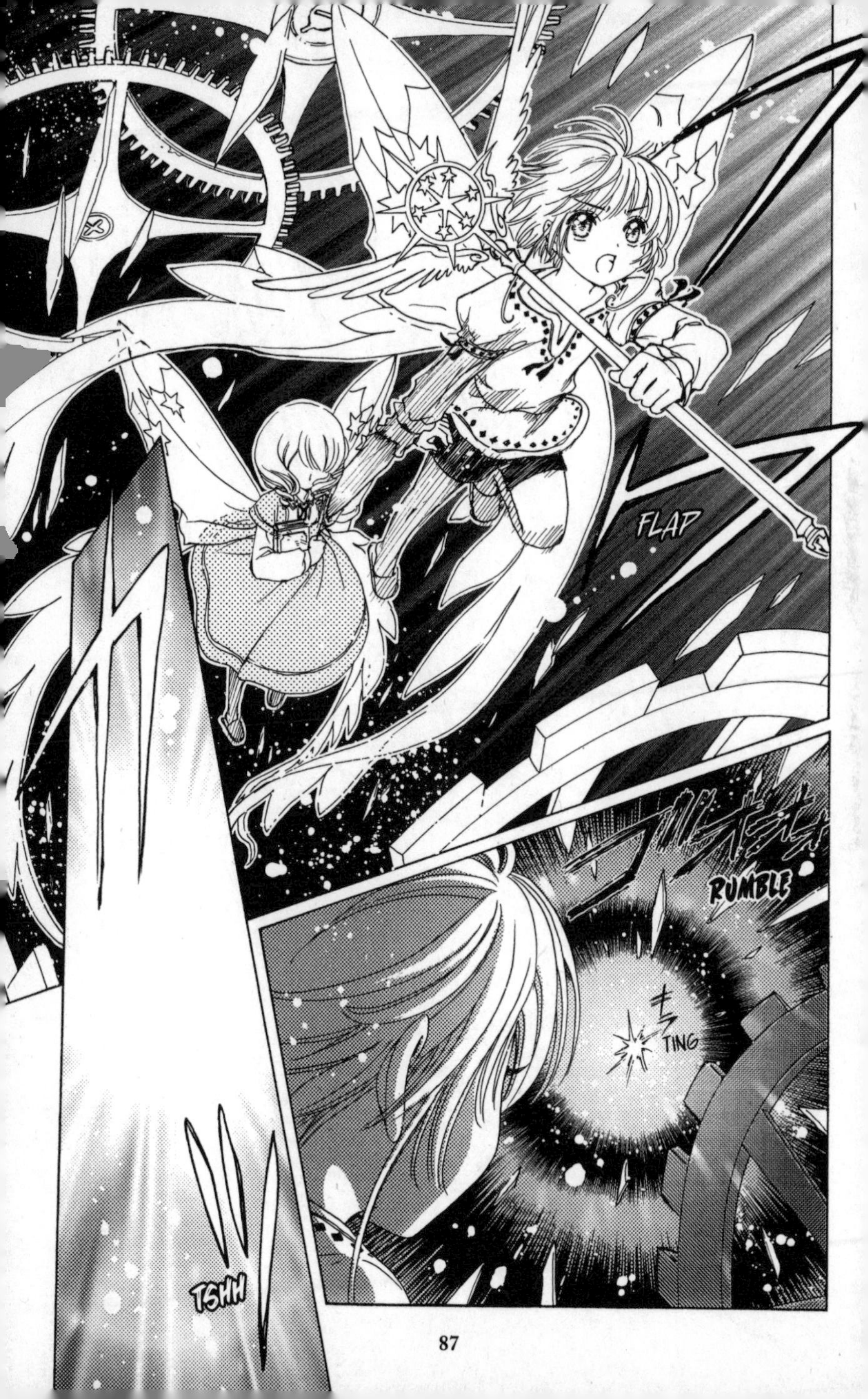
FLAP
RUMBLE
TING
TSHH

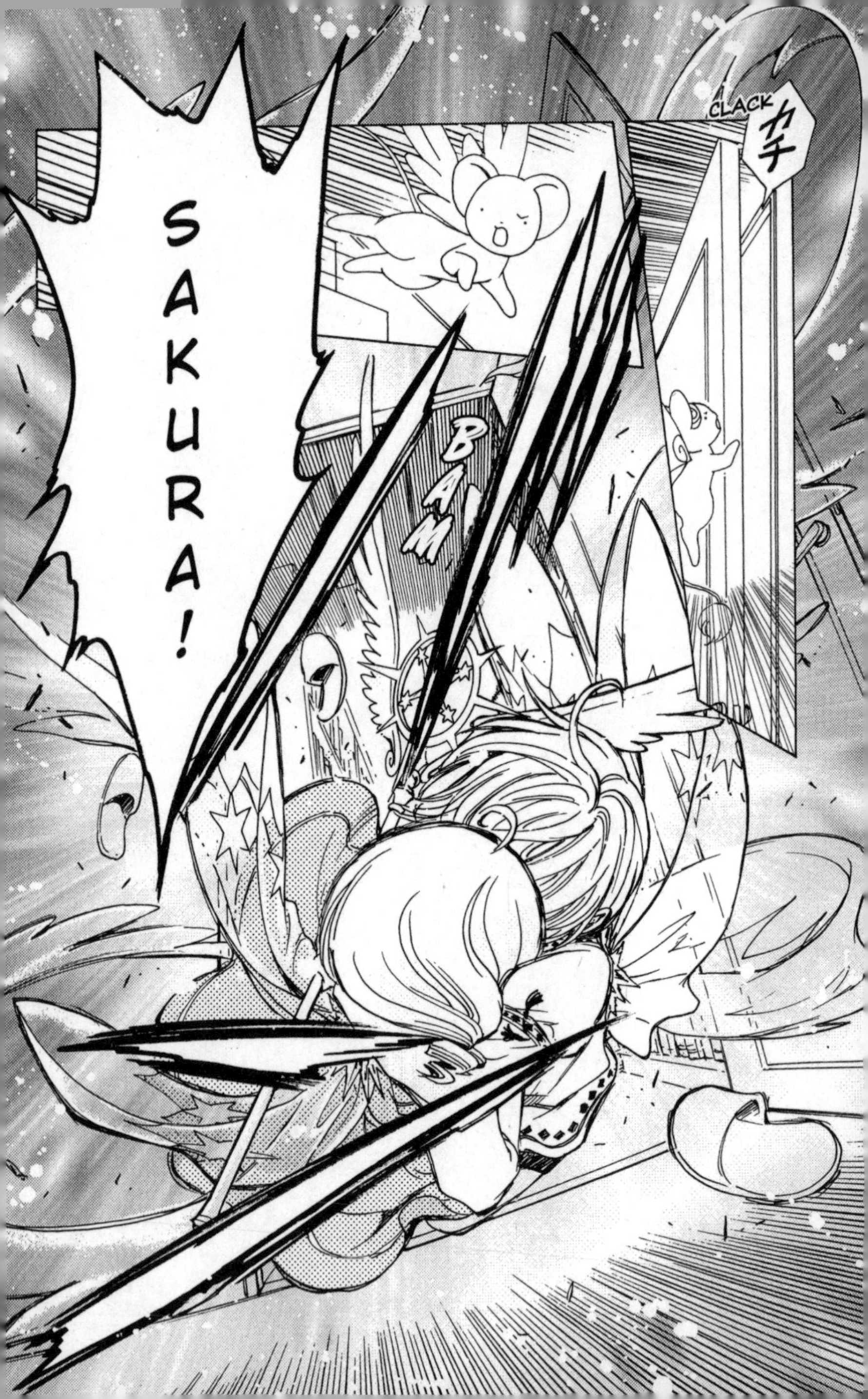
CLACK
カチ
SAKURA!
BAM

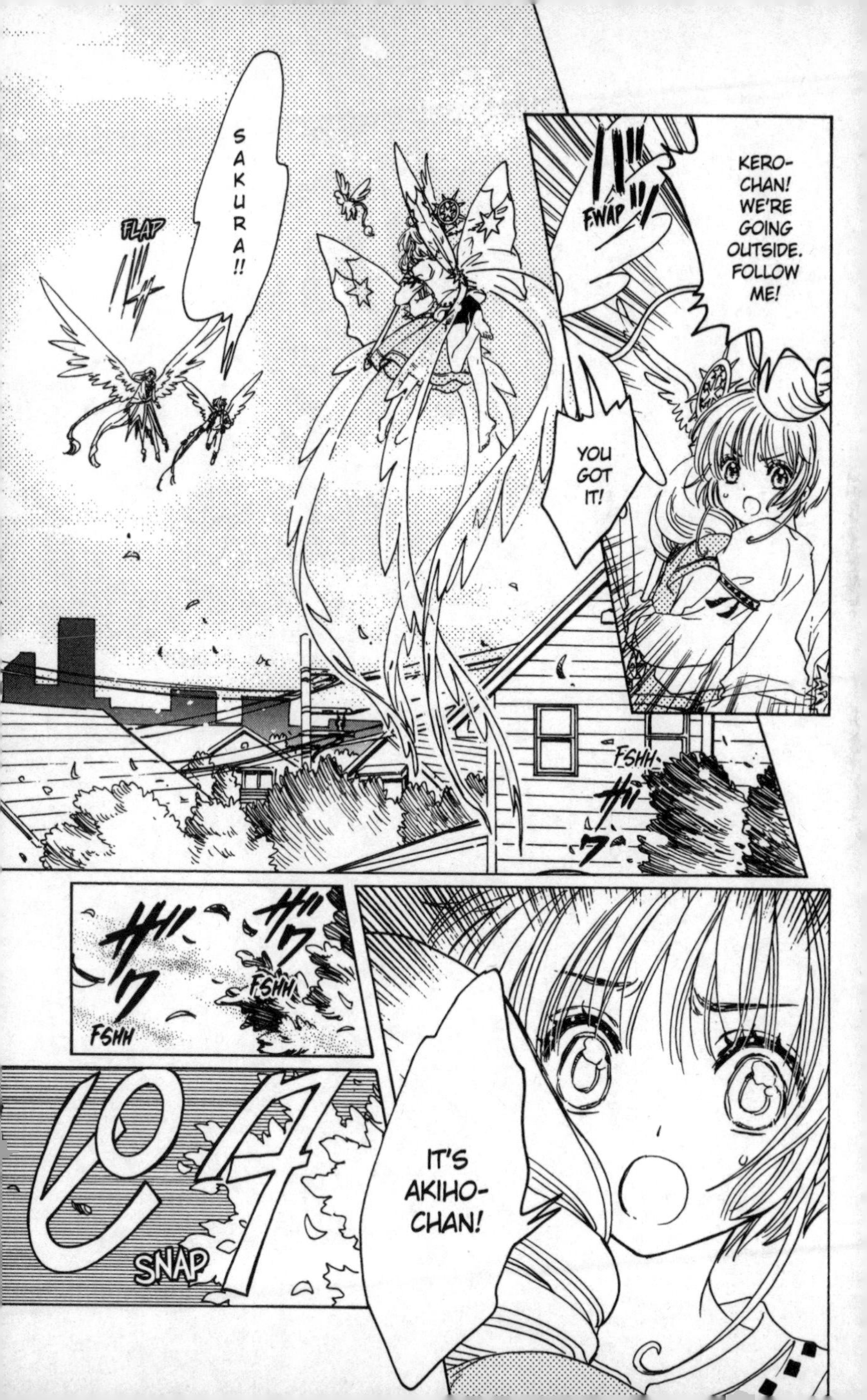
KERO-CHAN! WE'RE GOING OUTSIDE. FOLLOW ME!
FWAP
YOU GOT IT!
SAKURA!!
FLAP
FSHH
IT'S AKIHO-CHAN!
FSHH
FSHH
SNAP

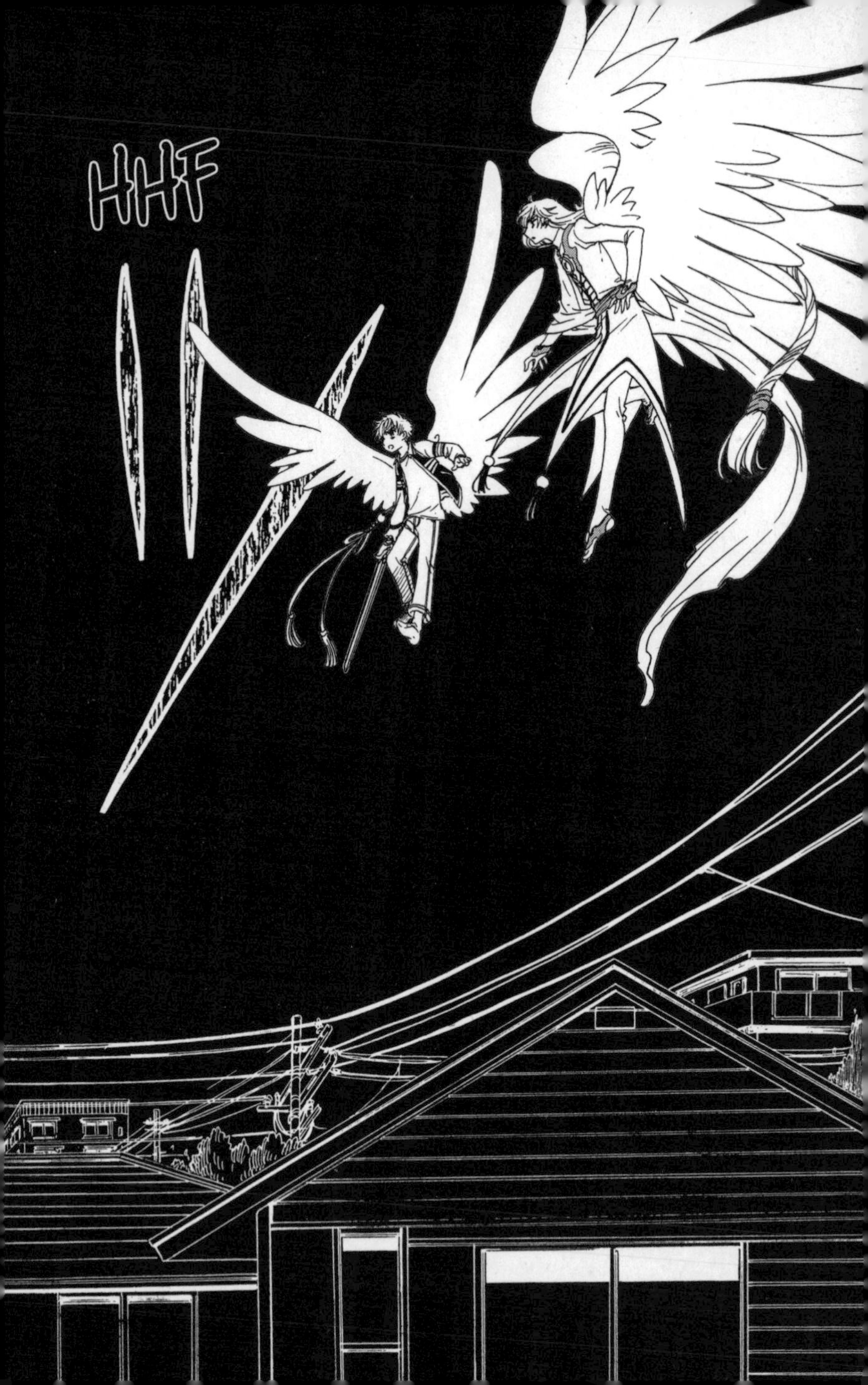
HHF

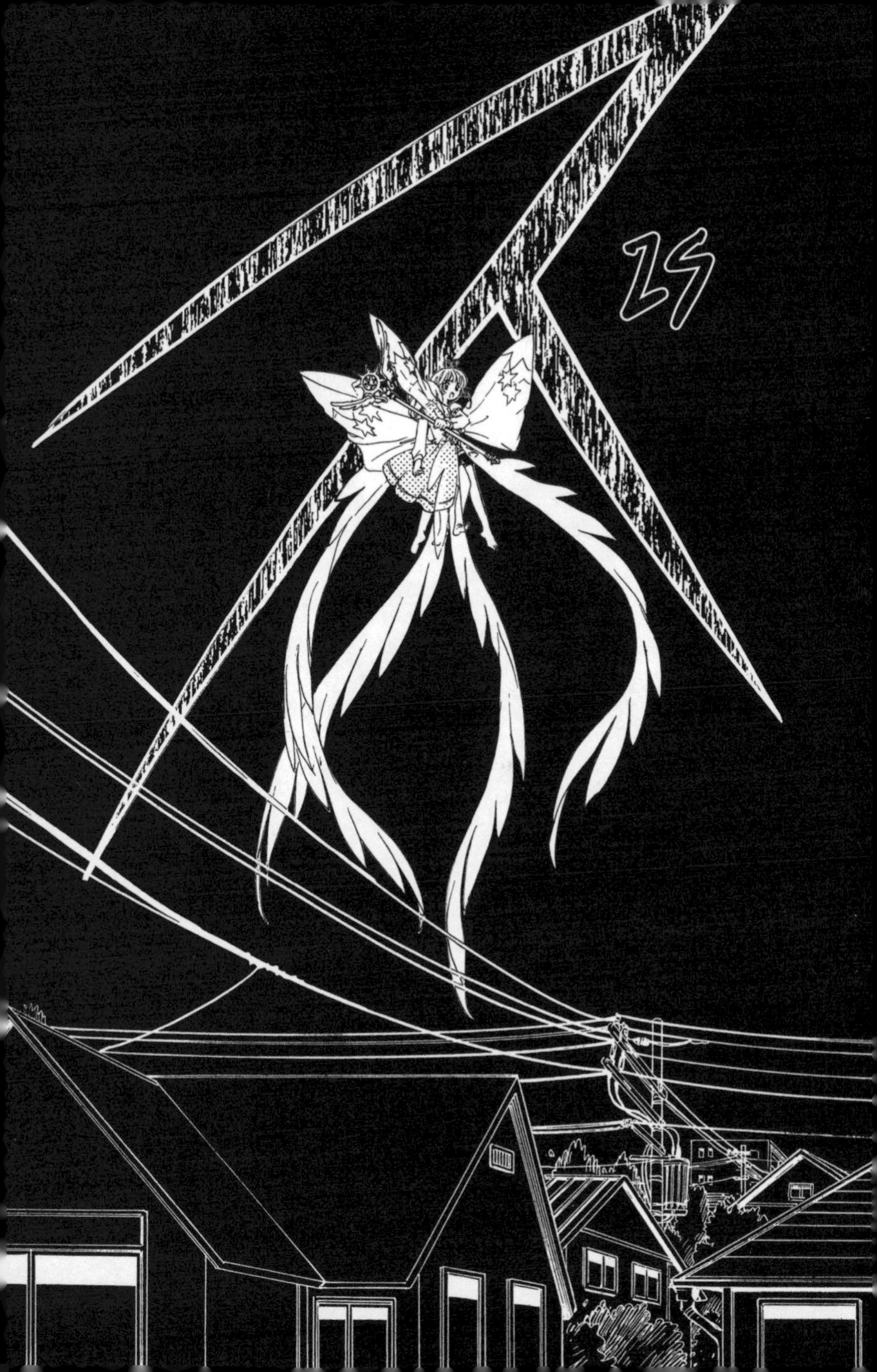
ZS

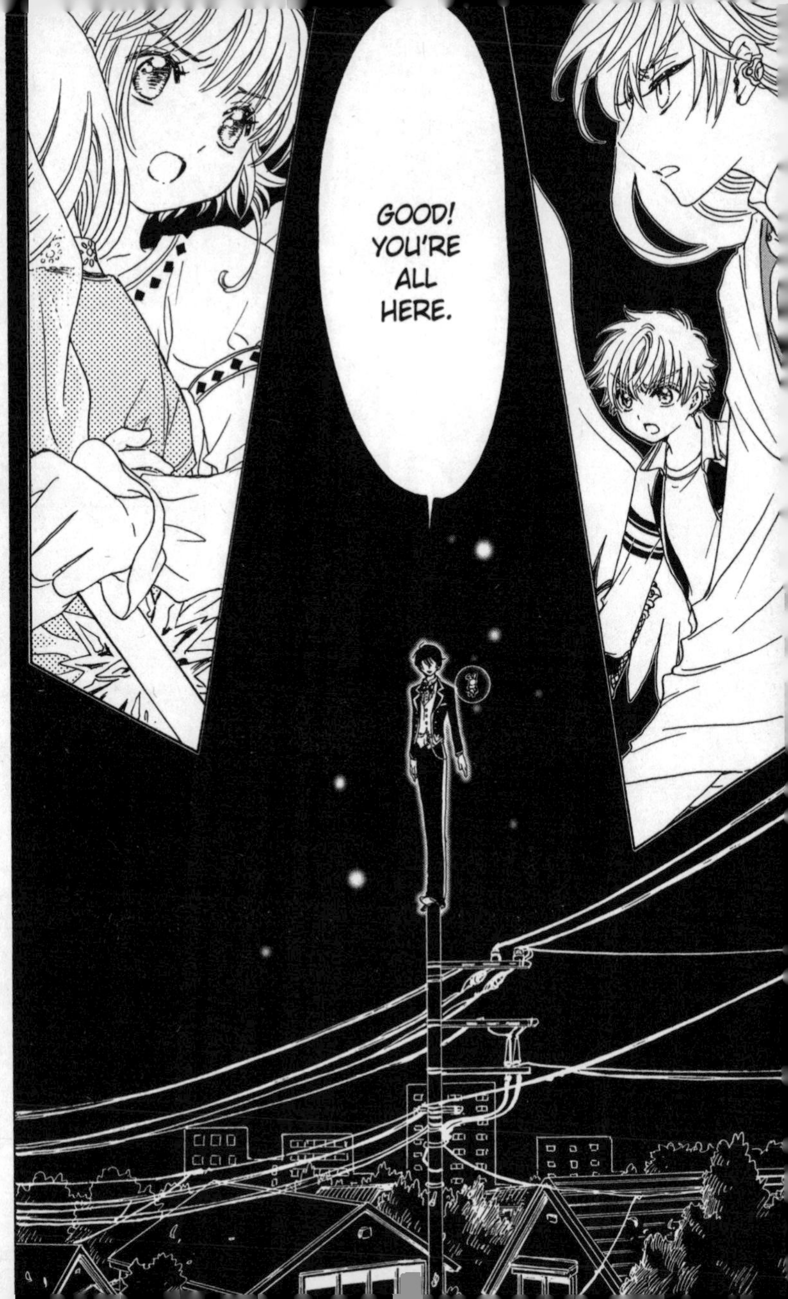
GOOD! YOU'RE ALL HERE.

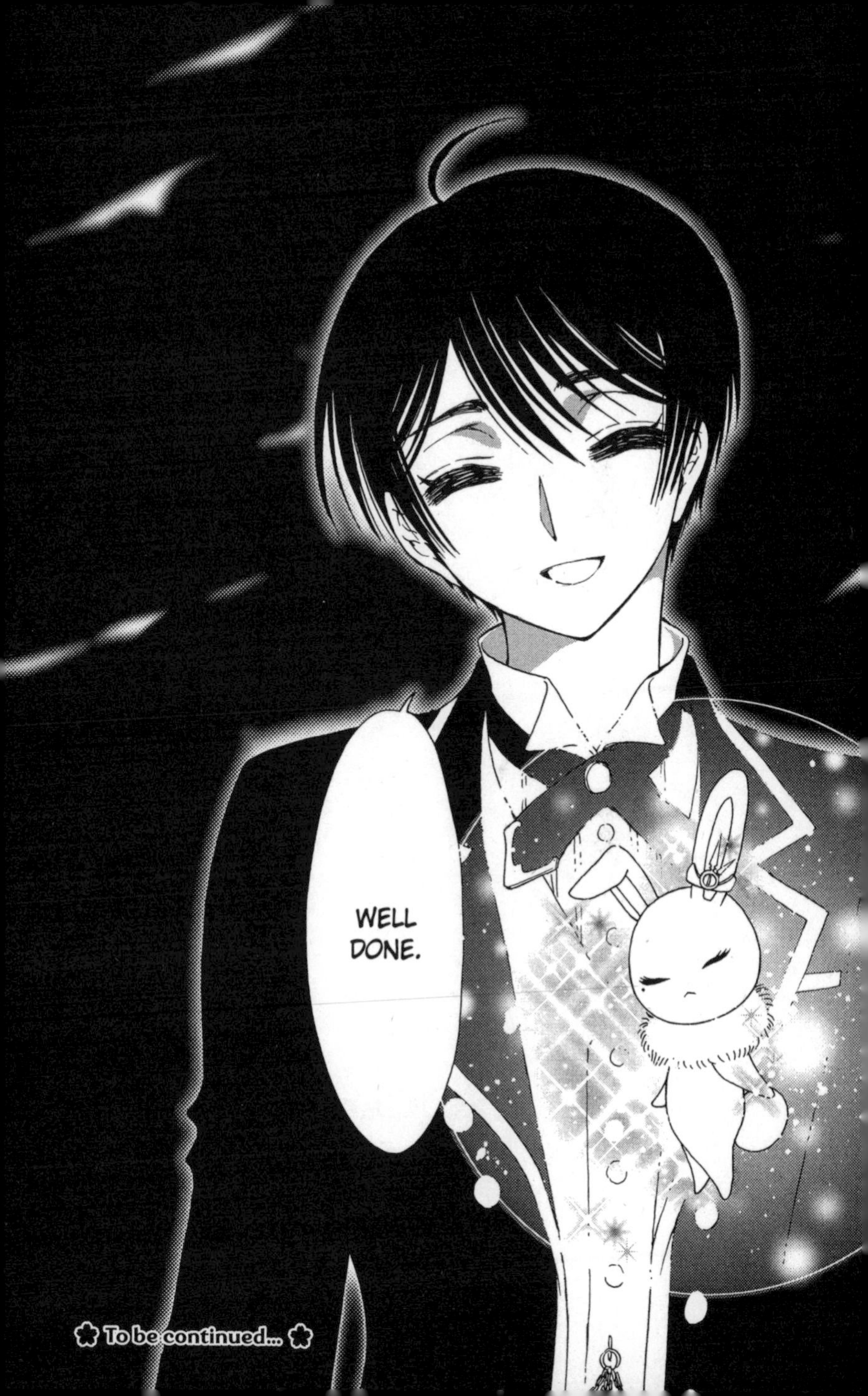
WELL DONE.
To be continued...

Cardcaptor Sakura

CLEAR CARD

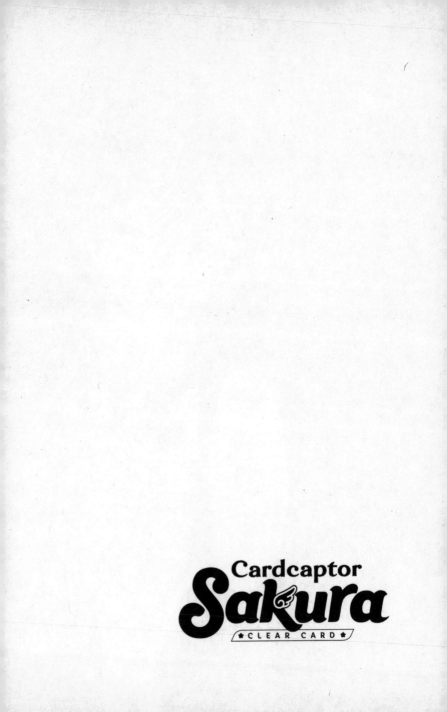

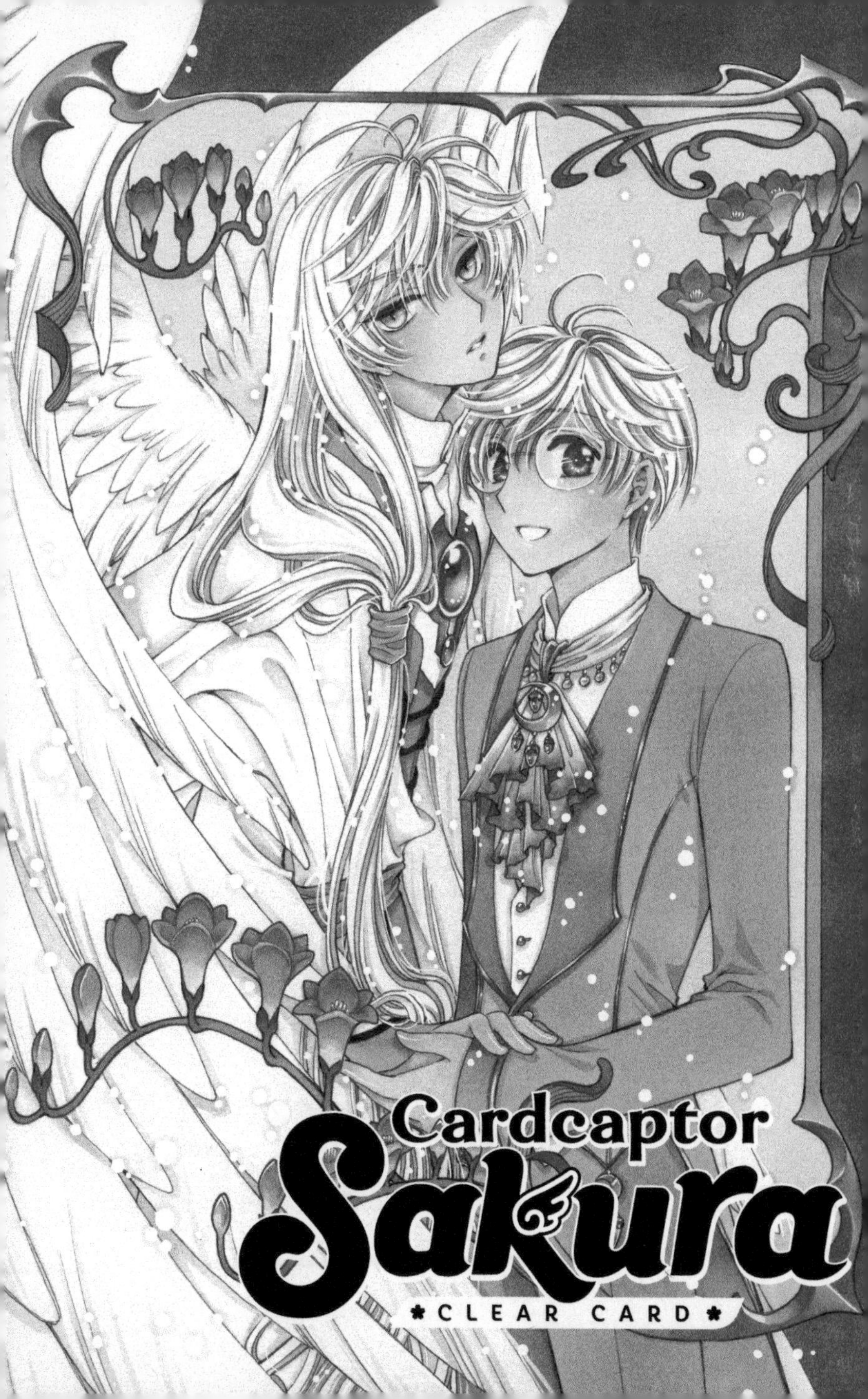
Cardcaptor
Sakura
CLEAR CARD

Cardcaptor Sakura
CLEAR CARD

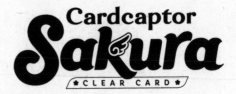

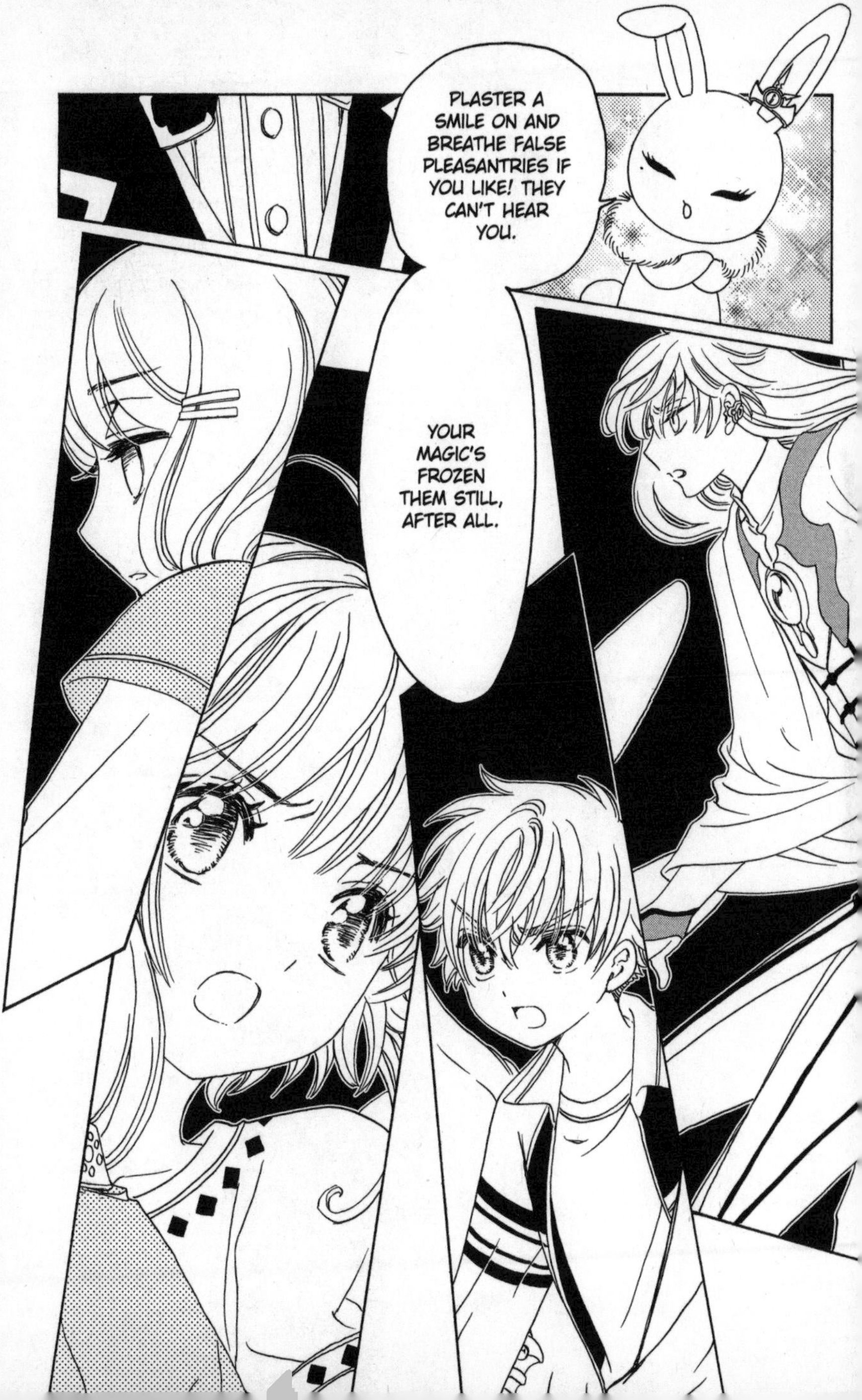
PLASTER A SMILE ON AND BREATHE FALSE PLEASANTRIES IF YOU LIKE! THEY CAN'T HEAR YOU.
YOUR MAGIC'S FROZEN THEM STILL, AFTER ALL.

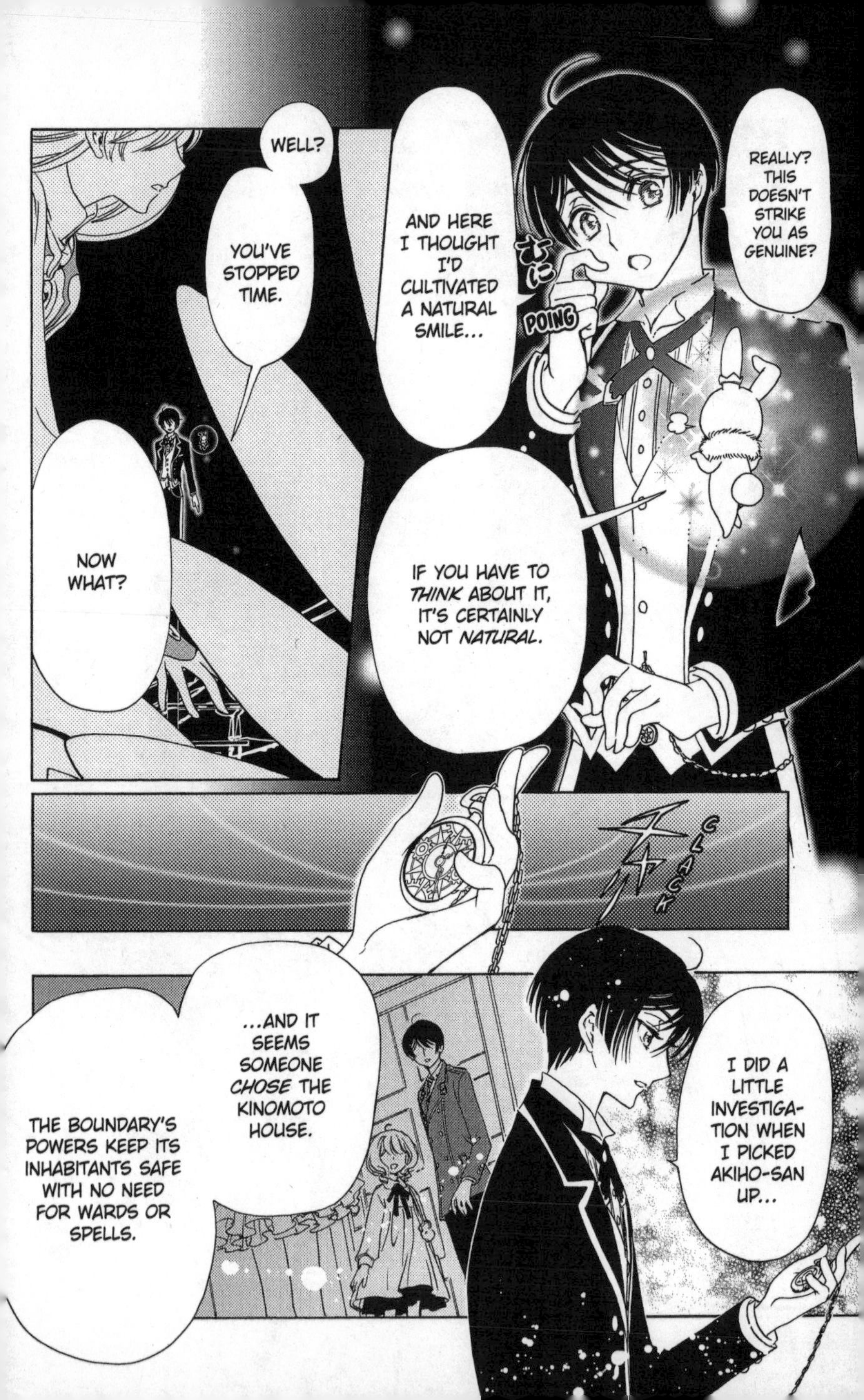
REALLY? THIS DOESN'T STRIKE YOU AS GENUINE?
むに
POING
AND HERE I THOUGHT I'D CULTIVATED A NATURAL SMILE...
IF YOU HAVE TO *THINK* ABOUT IT, IT'S CERTAINLY NOT *NATURAL*.
WELL?
YOU'VE STOPPED TIME.
NOW WHAT?
CLACK
I DID A LITTLE INVESTIGATION WHEN I PICKED AKIHO-SAN UP...
...AND IT SEEMS SOMEONE *CHOSE* THE KINOMOTO HOUSE.
THE BOUNDARY'S POWERS KEEP ITS INHABITANTS SAFE WITH NO NEED FOR WARDS OR SPELLS.

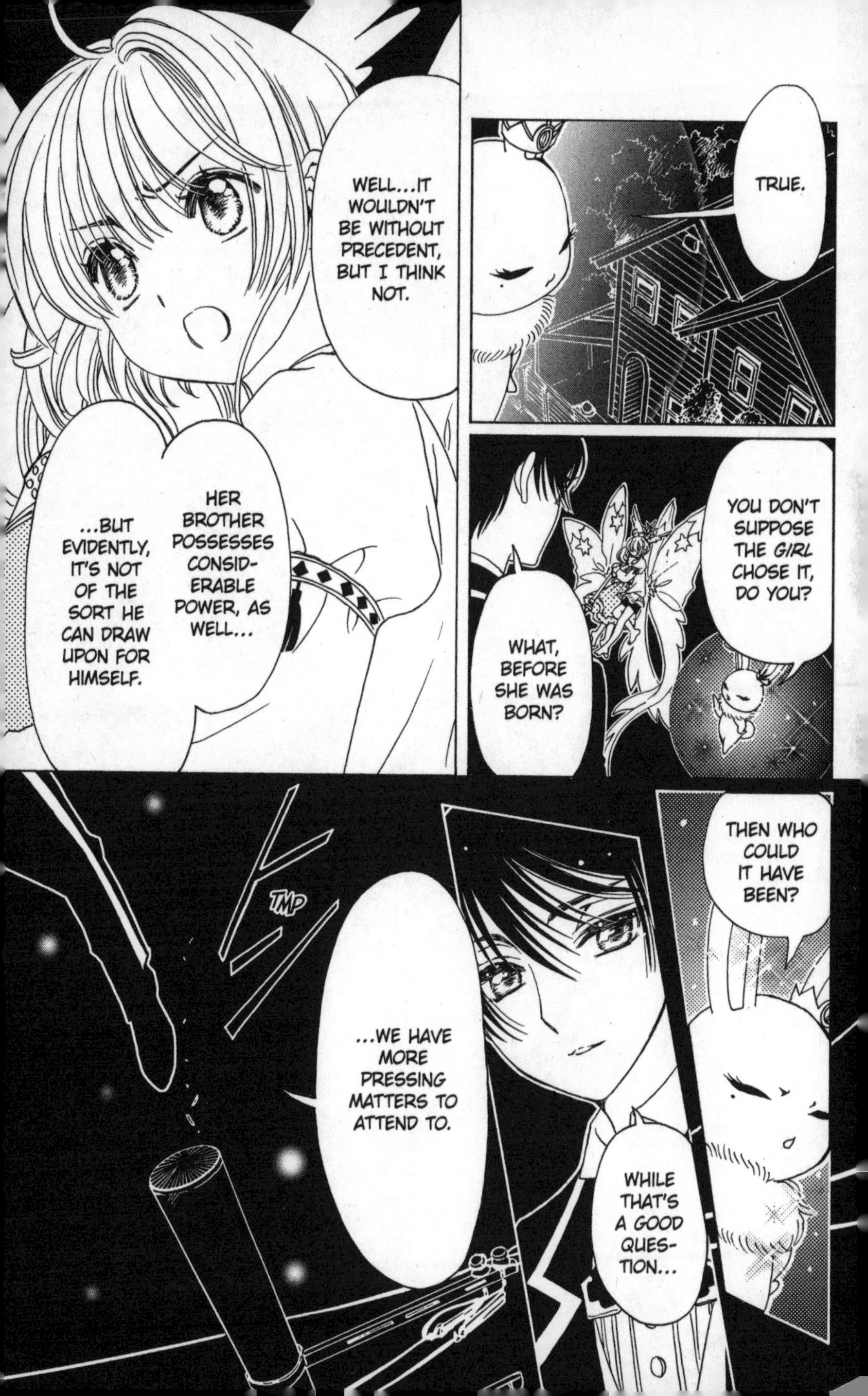
TRUE.
YOU DON'T SUPPOSE THE *GIRL* CHOSE IT, DO YOU?
WHAT, BEFORE SHE WAS BORN?
WELL...IT WOULDN'T BE WITHOUT PRECEDENT, BUT I THINK NOT.
HER BROTHER POSSESSES CONSID-ERABLE POWER, AS WELL...
...BUT EVIDENTLY, IT'S NOT OF THE SORT HE CAN DRAW UPON FOR HIMSELF.
THEN WHO COULD IT HAVE BEEN?
WHILE THAT'S A GOOD QUES-TION...
TMP
...WE HAVE MORE PRESSING MATTERS TO ATTEND TO.

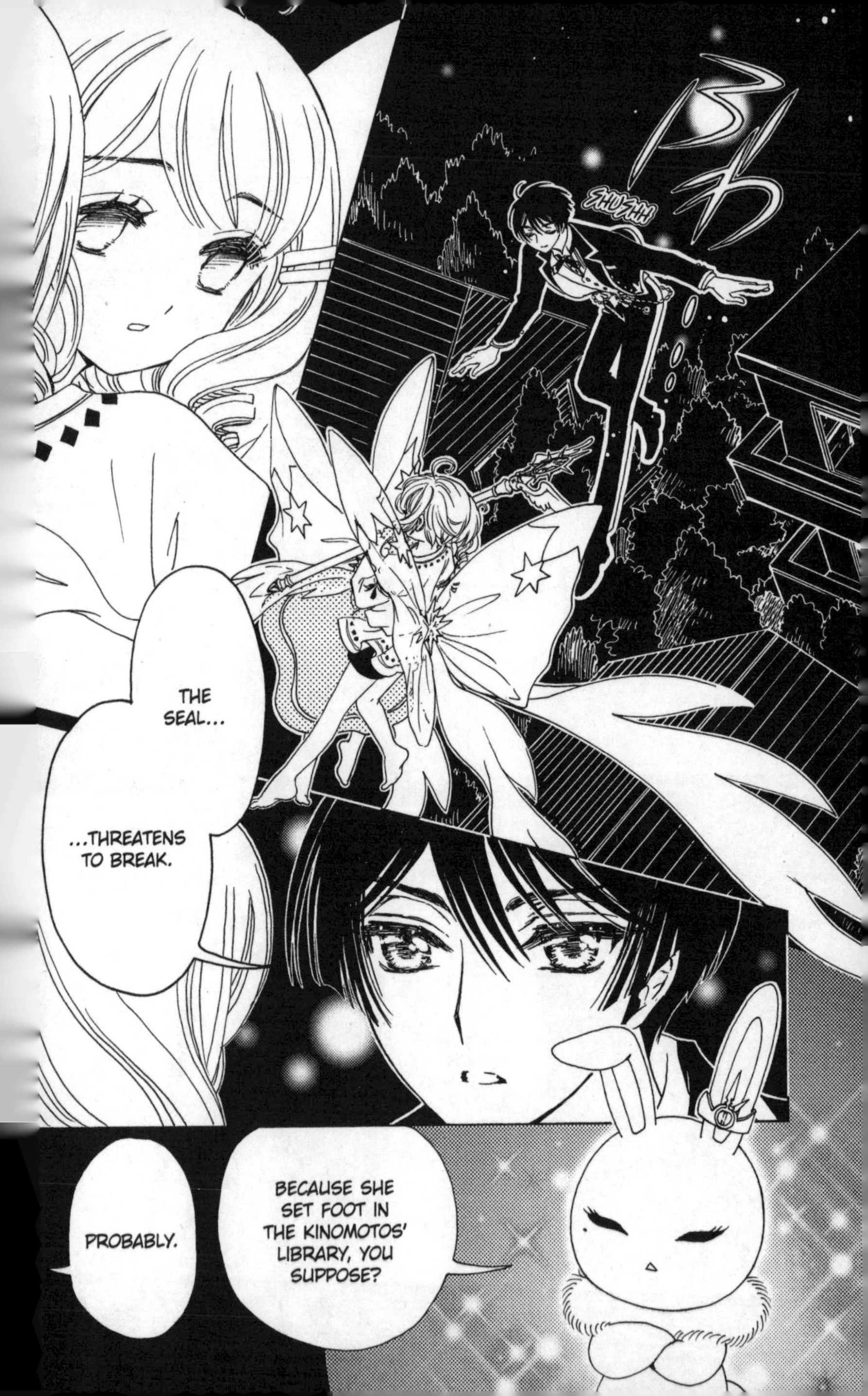
SHUSHH
THE SEAL...
...THREATENS TO BREAK.
BECAUSE SHE SET FOOT IN THE KINOMOTOS' LIBRARY, YOU SUPPOSE?
PROBABLY.

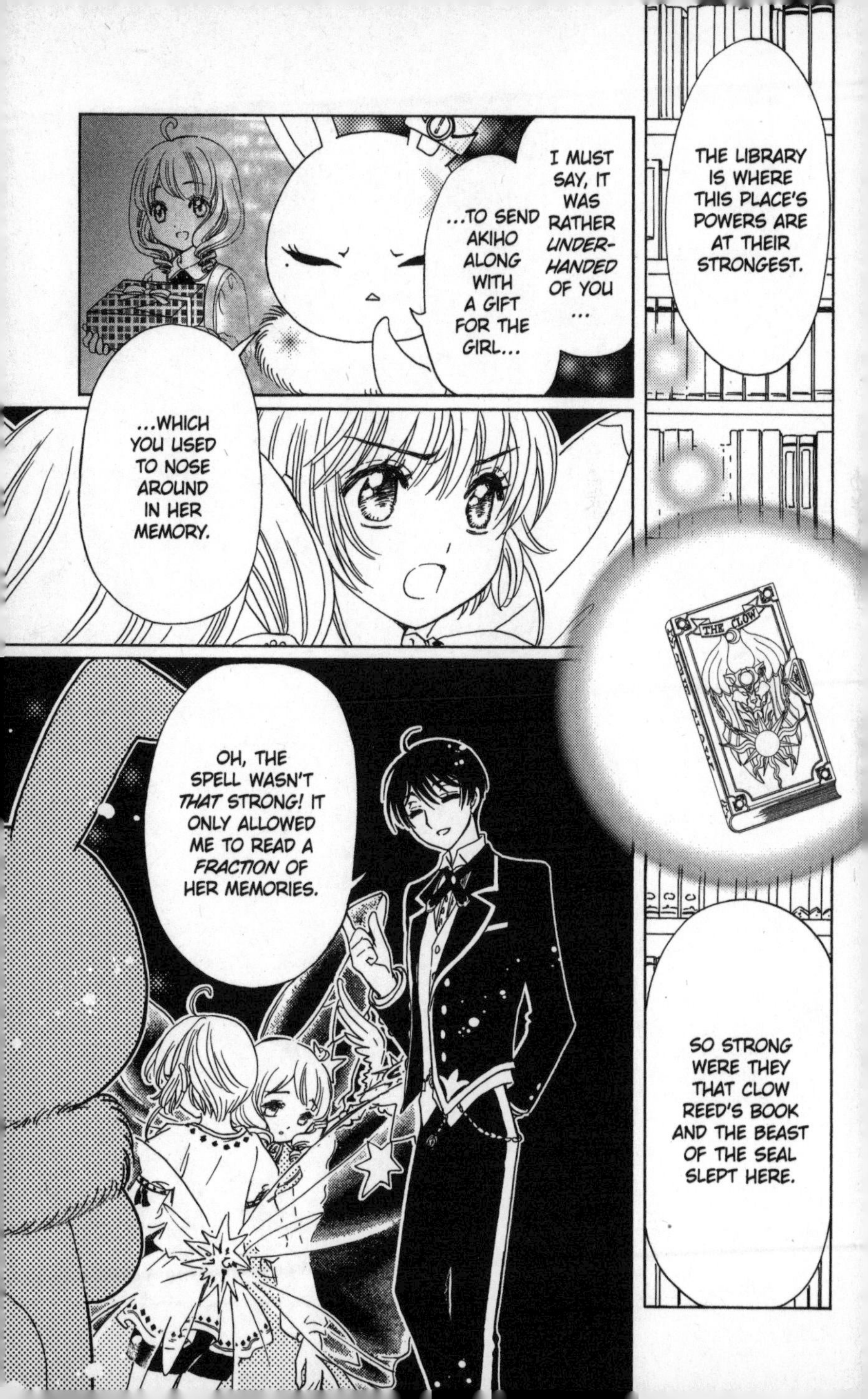
THE LIBRARY IS WHERE THIS PLACE'S POWERS ARE AT THEIR STRONGEST.
SO STRONG WERE THEY THAT CLOW REED'S BOOK AND THE BEAST OF THE SEAL SLEPT HERE.
THE CLOW
I MUST SAY, IT WAS RATHER *UNDER-HANDED* OF YOU ...
...TO SEND AKIHO ALONG WITH A GIFT FOR THE GIRL...
...WHICH YOU USED TO NOSE AROUND IN HER MEMORY.
OH, THE SPELL WASN'T *THAT* STRONG! IT ONLY ALLOWED ME TO READ A *FRACTION* OF HER MEMORIES.

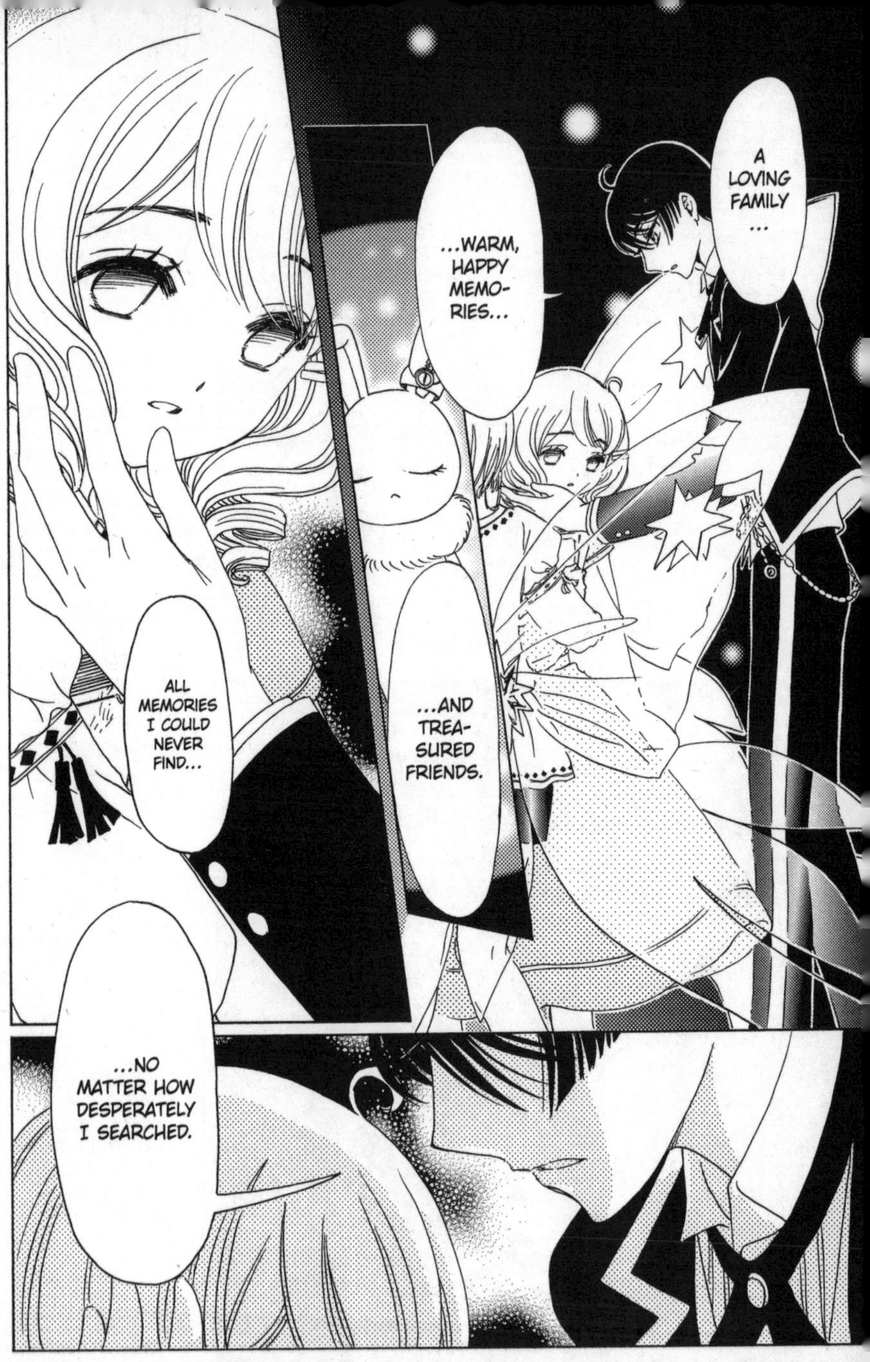
A LOVING FAMILY ...
...WARM, HAPPY MEMO-RIES...
...AND TREA-SURED FRIENDS.
ALL MEMORIES I COULD NEVER FIND...
...NO MATTER HOW DESPERATELY I SEARCHED.

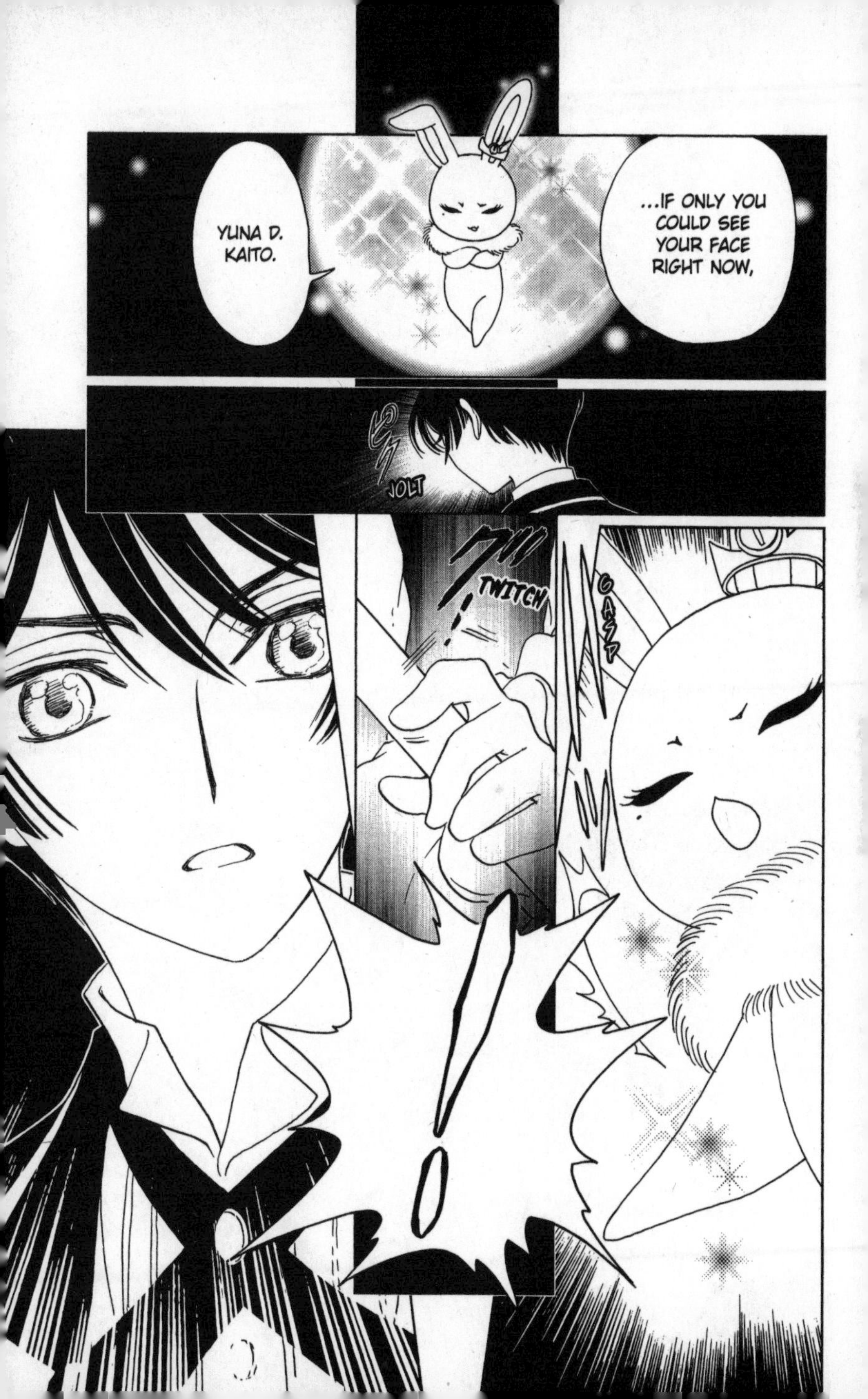
...IF ONLY YOU COULD SEE YOUR FACE RIGHT NOW,
YUNA D. KAITO.
JOLT
GASP
TWITCH

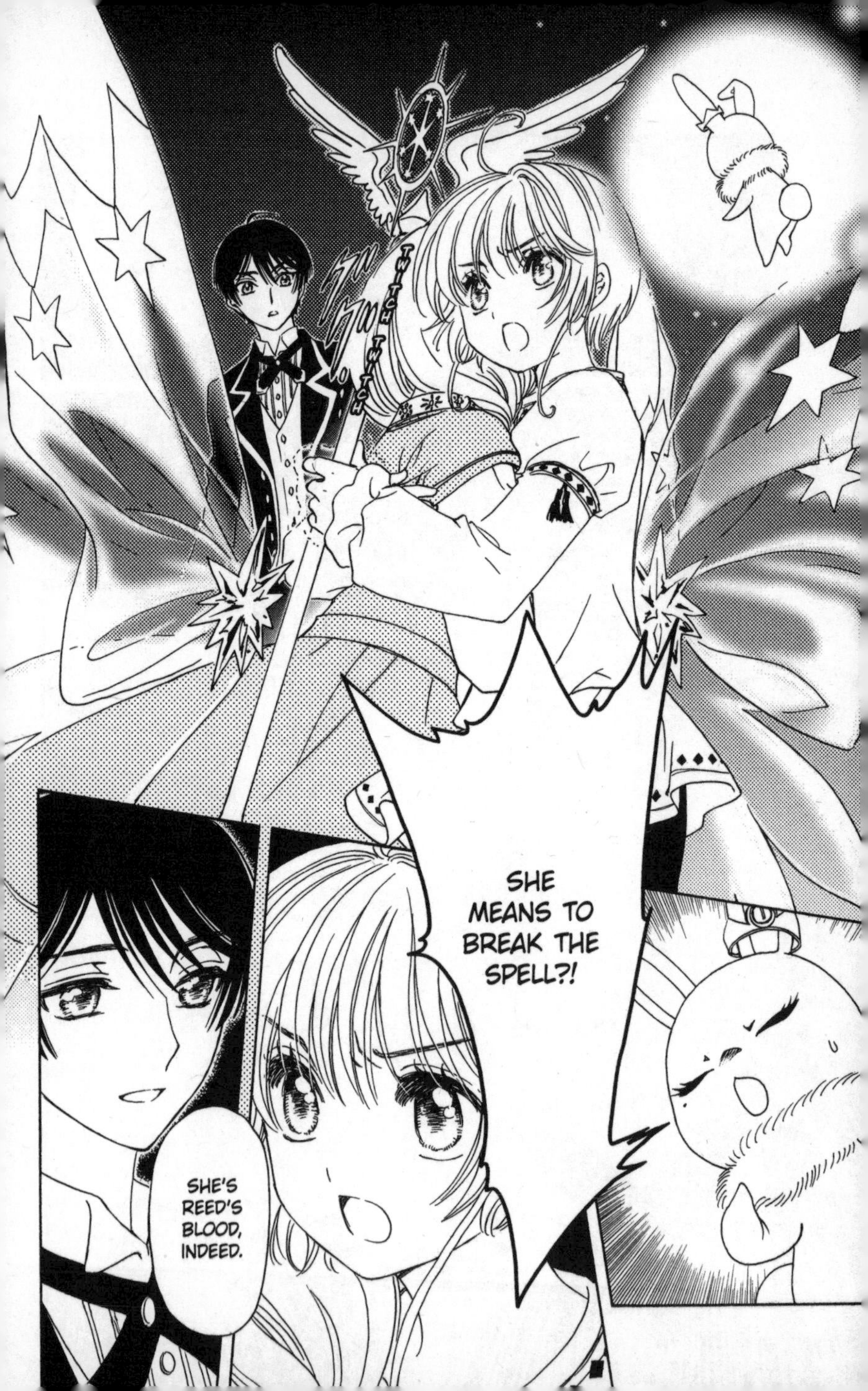
TWITCH TWITCH
SHE MEANS TO BREAK THE SPELL?!
SHE'S REED'S BLOOD, INDEED.

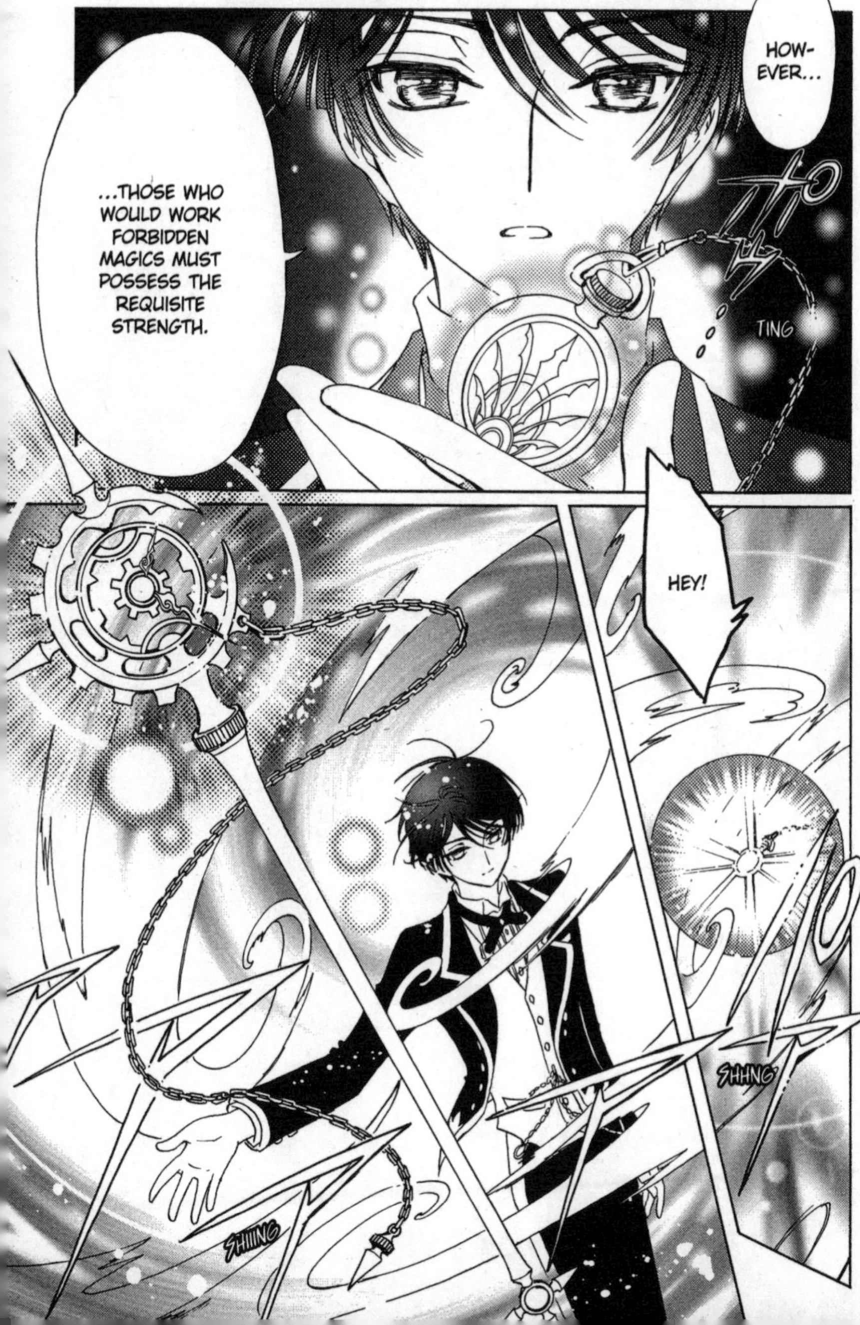
HOW-EVER...
...THOSE WHO WOULD WORK FORBIDDEN MAGICS MUST POSSESS THE REQUISITE STRENGTH.
TING
HEY!
SHHNG
SHIIING

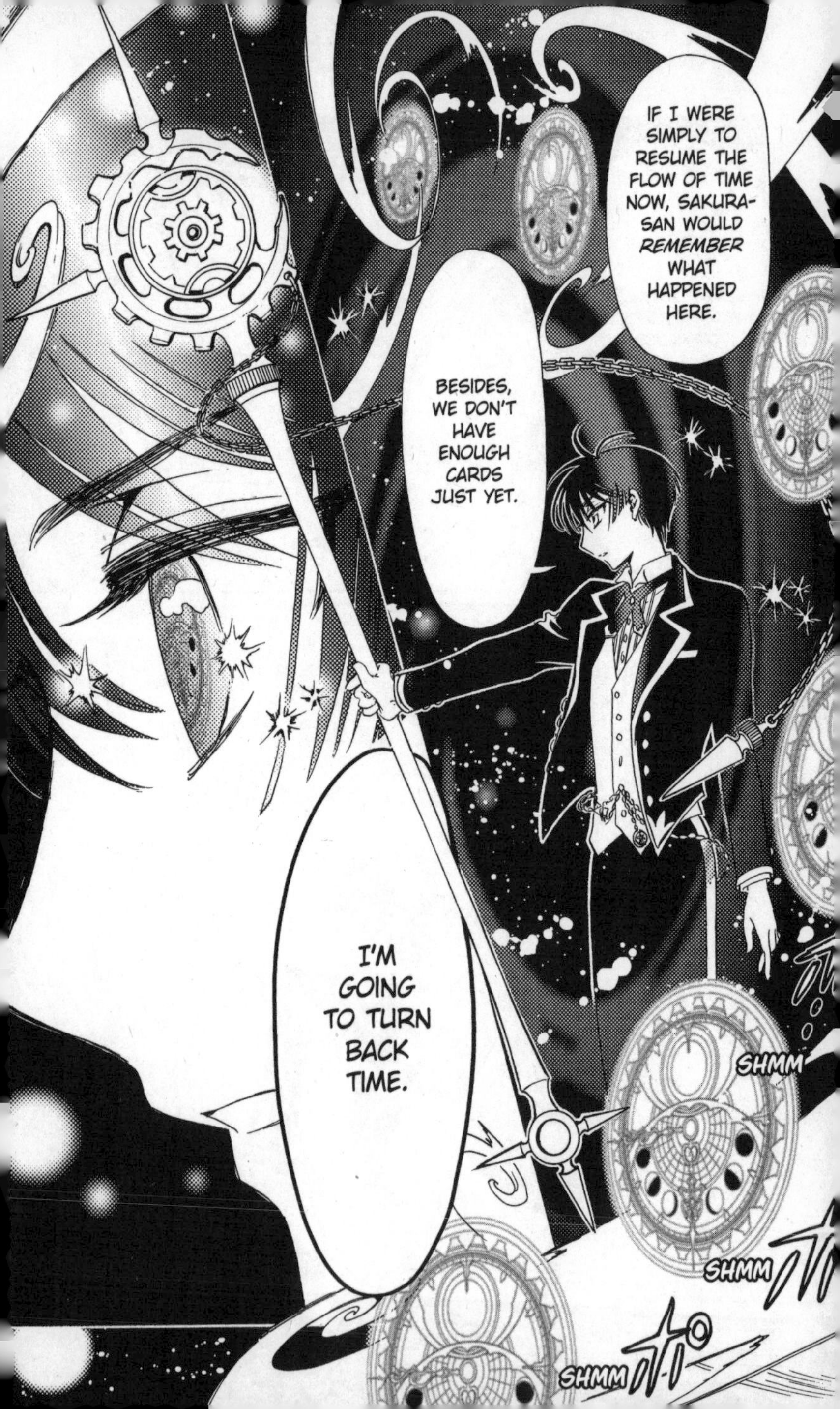
IF I WERE SIMPLY TO RESUME THE FLOW OF TIME NOW, SAKURA-SAN WOULD *REMEMBER* WHAT HAPPENED HERE.
BESIDES, WE DON'T HAVE ENOUGH CARDS JUST YET.
I'M GOING TO TURN BACK TIME.
SHMM
SHMM
SHMM

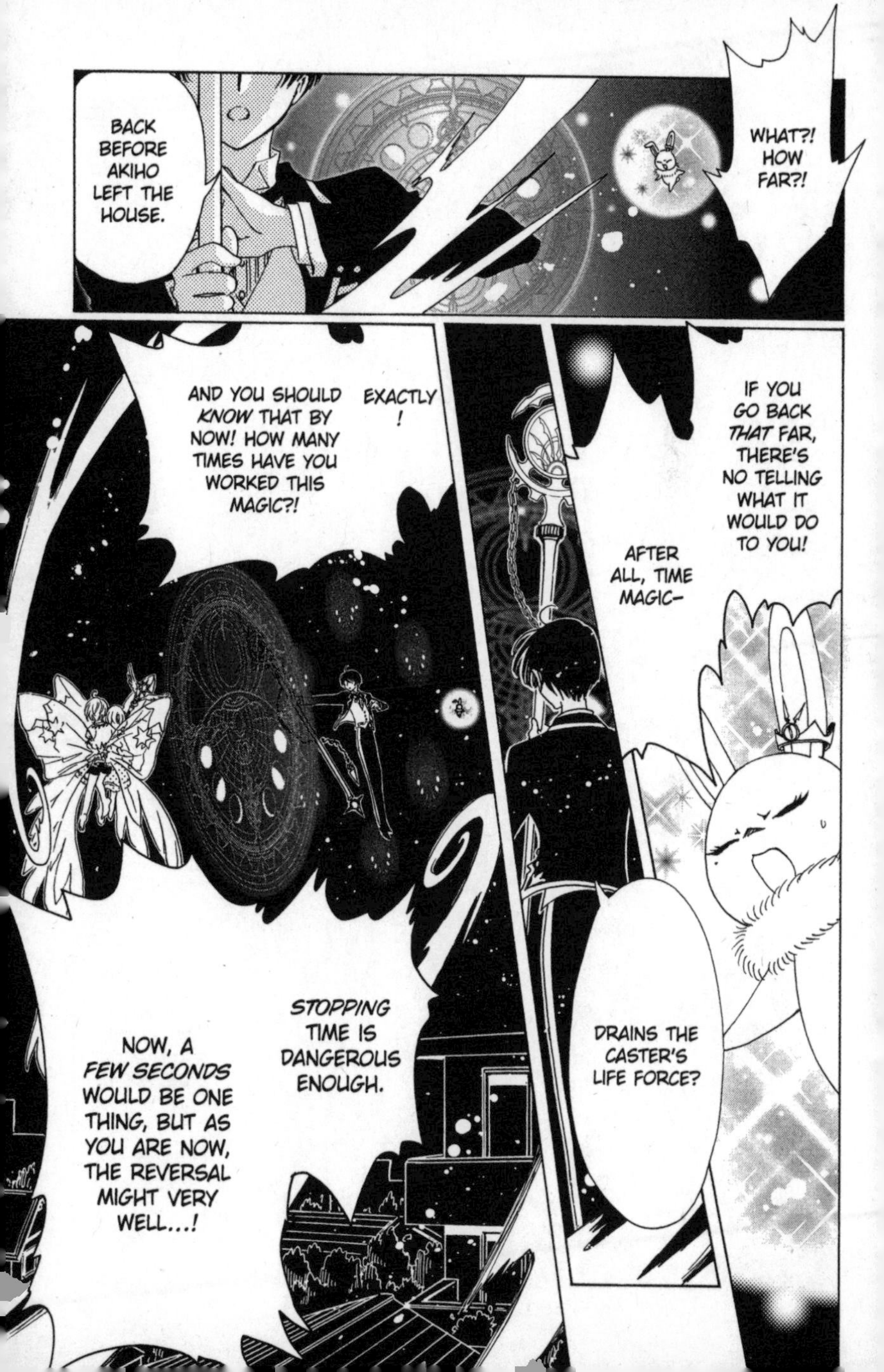
WHAT?! HOW FAR?!
BACK BEFORE AKIHO LEFT THE HOUSE.
IF YOU GO BACK *THAT* FAR, THERE'S NO TELLING WHAT IT WOULD DO TO YOU!
AFTER ALL, TIME MAGIC—
DRAINS THE CASTER'S LIFE FORCE?
EXACTLY!
AND YOU SHOULD *KNOW* THAT BY NOW! HOW MANY TIMES HAVE YOU WORKED THIS MAGIC?!
STOPPING TIME IS DANGEROUS ENOUGH.
NOW, A *FEW SECONDS* WOULD BE ONE THING, BUT AS YOU ARE NOW, THE REVERSAL MIGHT VERY WELL...!

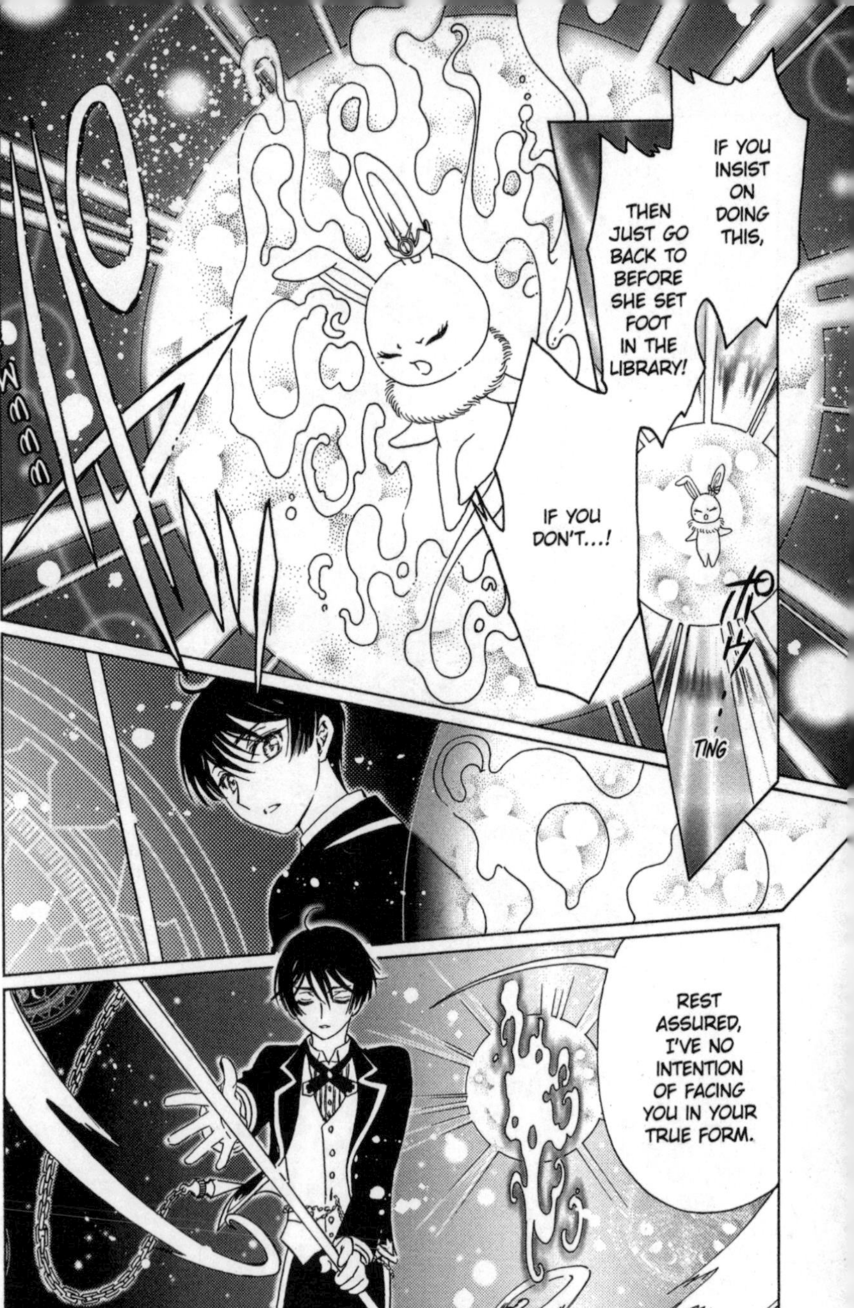
IF YOU INSIST ON DOING THIS,
THEN JUST GO BACK TO BEFORE SHE SET FOOT IN THE LIBRARY!
FWEEEE
IF YOU DON'T...!
TING
REST ASSURED, I'VE NO INTENTION OF FACING YOU IN YOUR TRUE FORM.

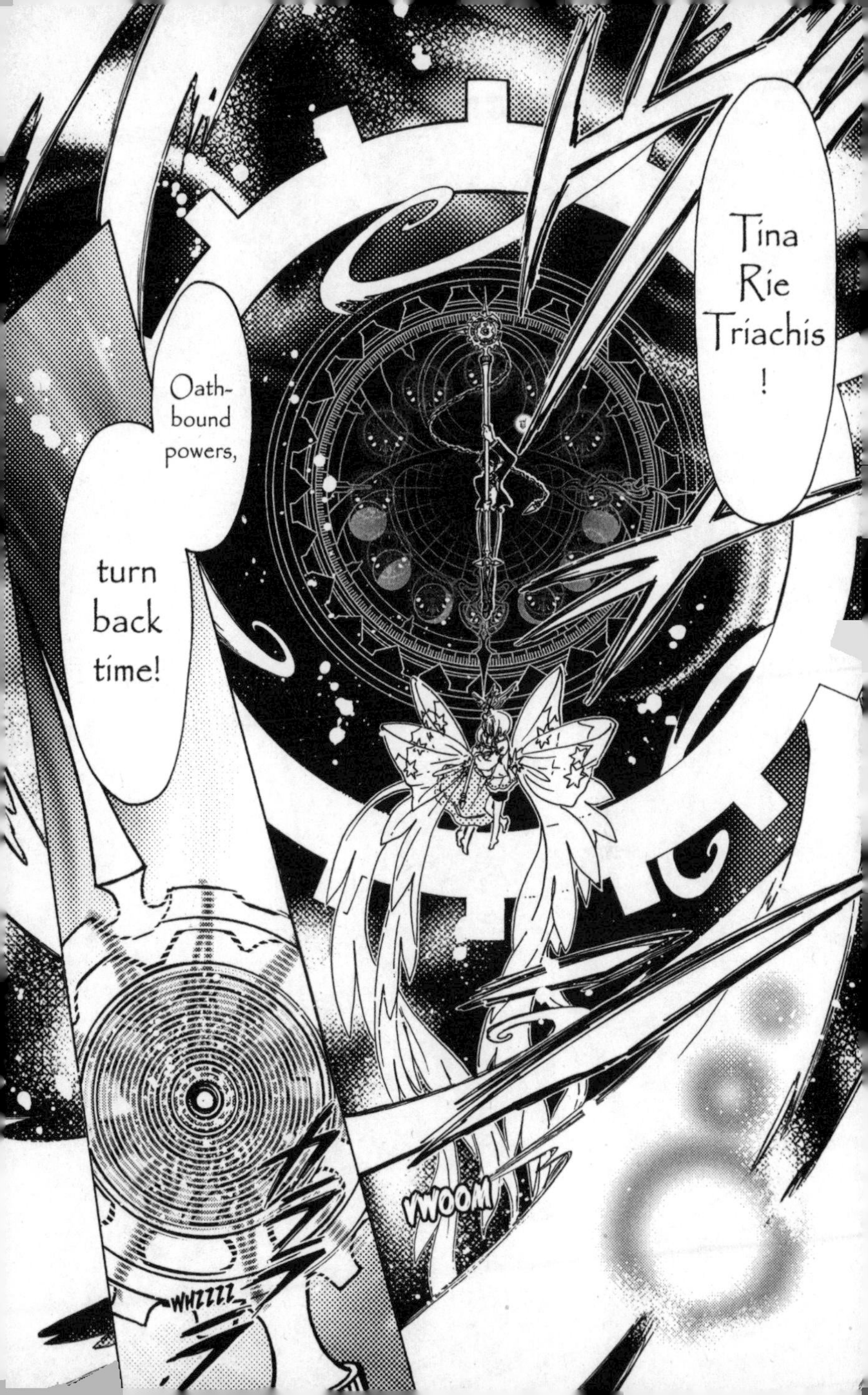
Tina Rie Triachis!
Oath-bound powers,
turn back time!
VWOOM
WHZZZZ

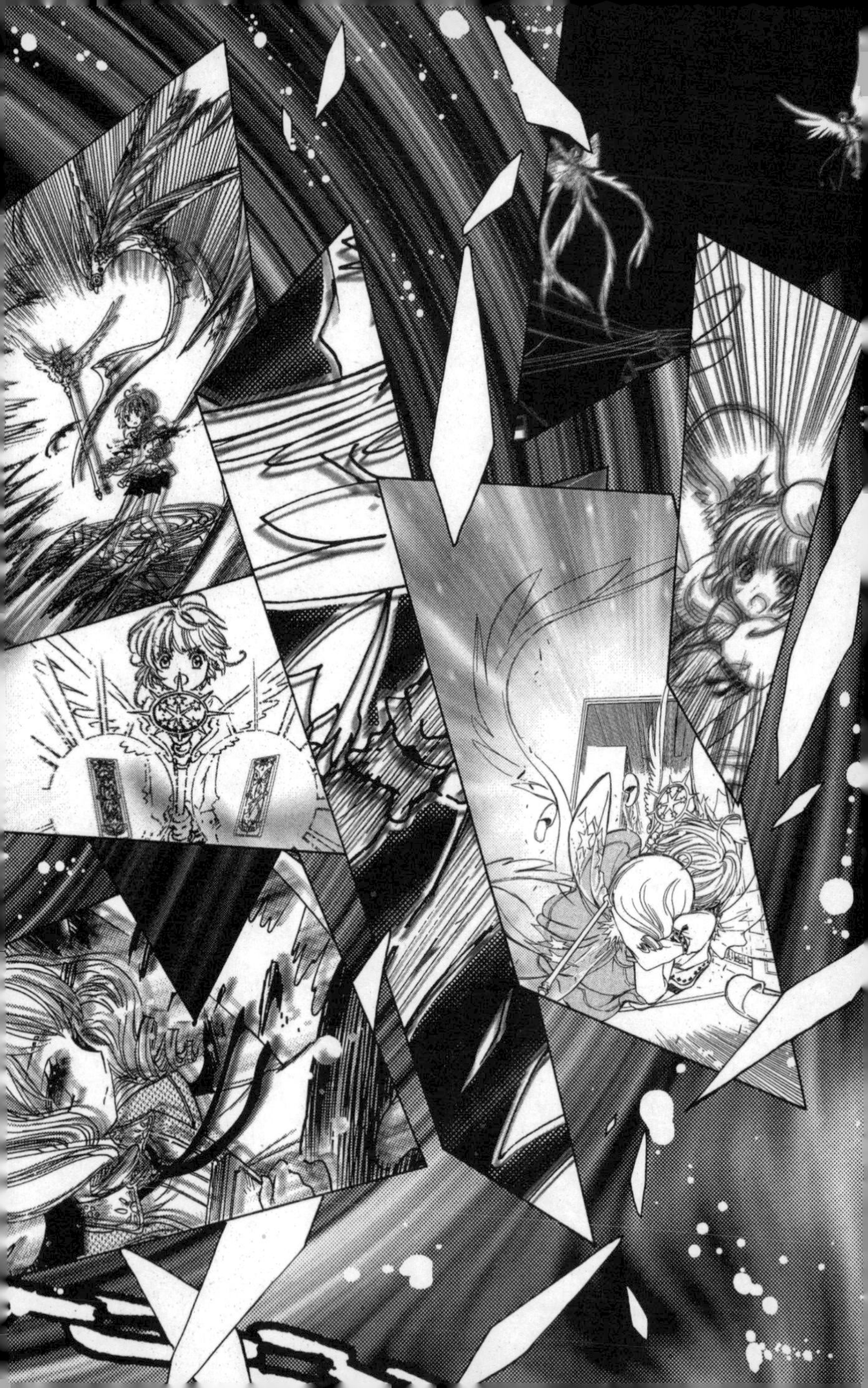

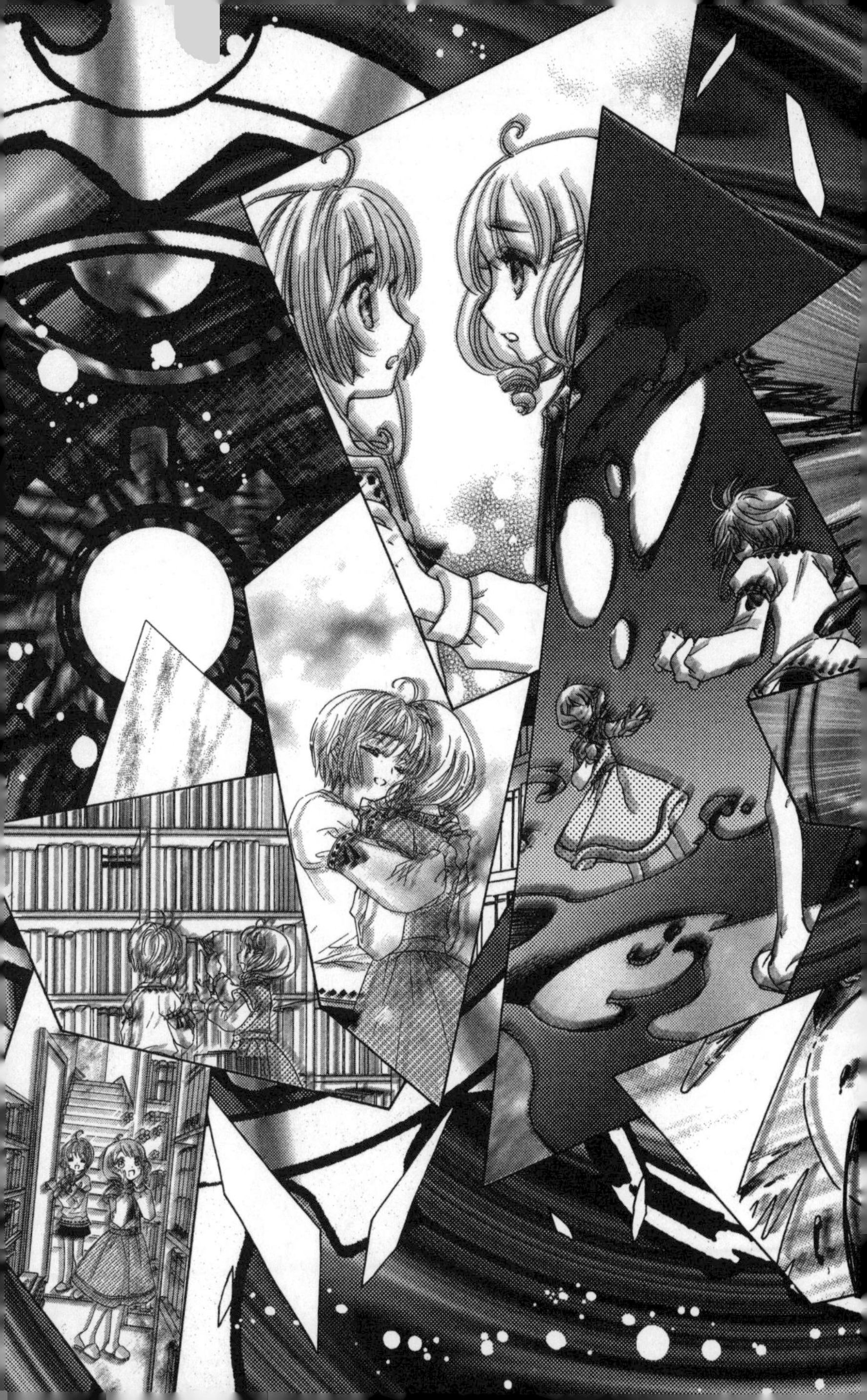

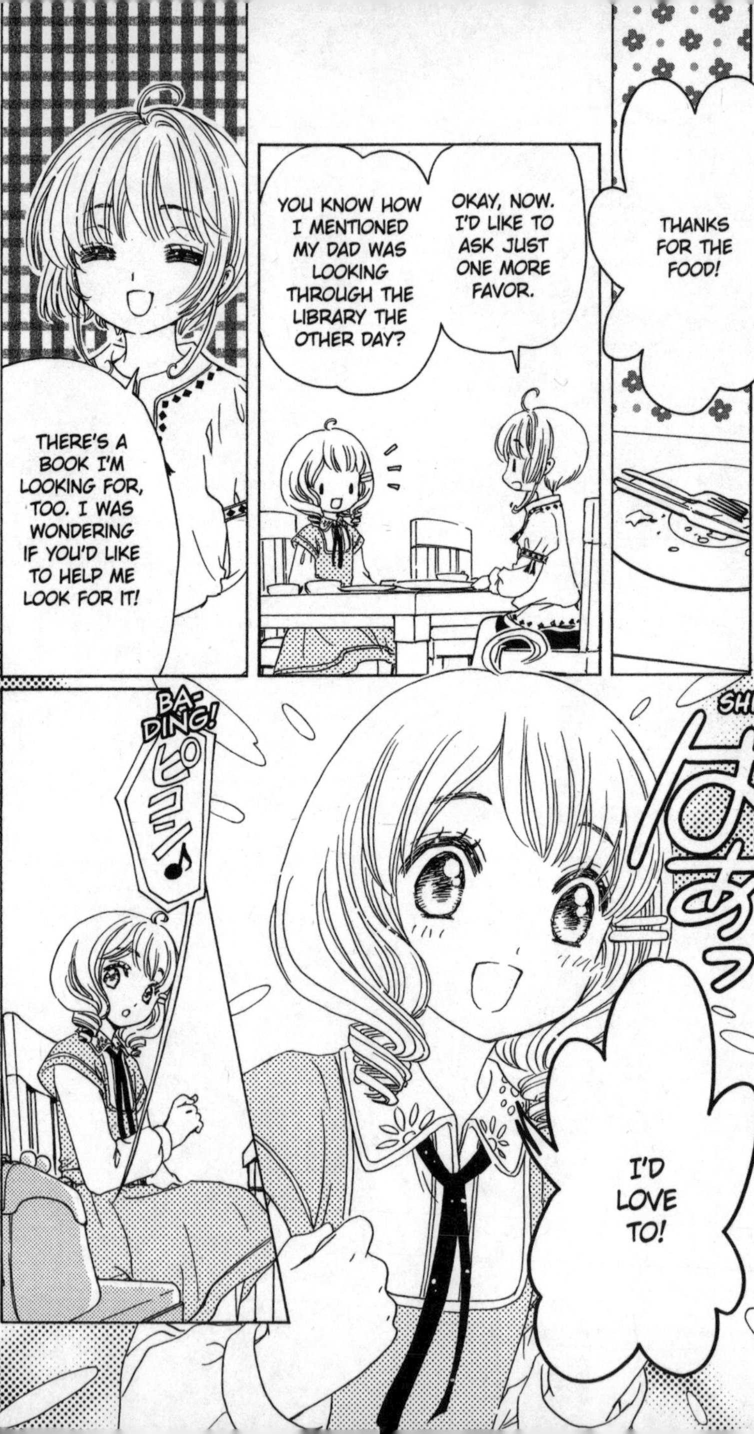
THANKS FOR THE FOOD!
OKAY, NOW. I'D LIKE TO ASK JUST ONE MORE FAVOR.
YOU KNOW HOW I MENTIONED MY DAD WAS LOOKING THROUGH THE LIBRARY THE OTHER DAY?
THERE'S A BOOK I'M LOOKING FOR, TOO. I WAS WONDERING IF YOU'D LIKE TO HELP ME LOOK FOR IT!
SHINE
ぱあっ
BA-DING!
ピコン♪
I'D LOVE TO!

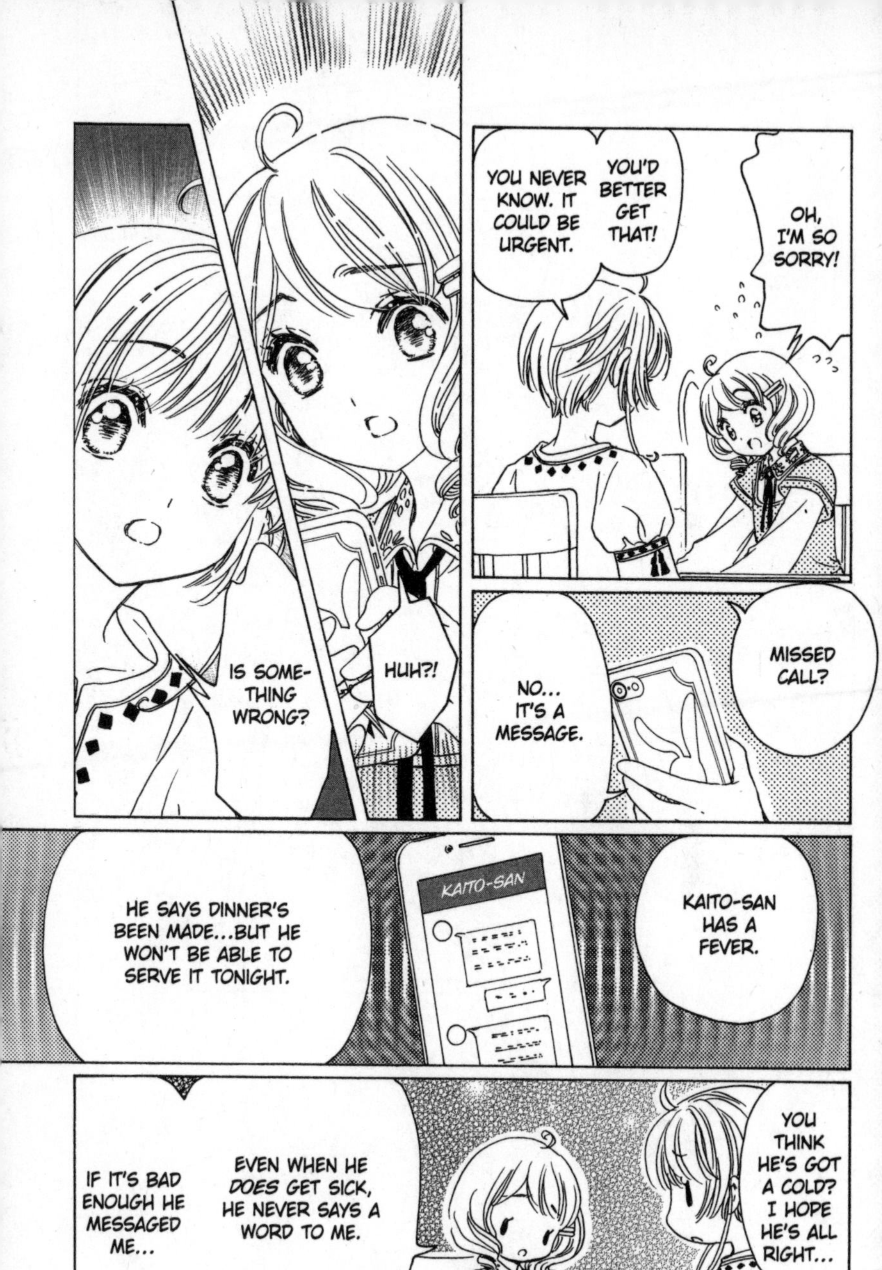
OH, I'M SO SORRY!
YOU'D BETTER GET THAT!
YOU NEVER KNOW. IT COULD BE URGENT.
MISSED CALL?
NO... IT'S A MESSAGE.
HUH?!
IS SOME-THING WRONG?
KAITO-SAN HAS A FEVER.
KAITO-SAN
HE SAYS DINNER'S BEEN MADE...BUT HE WON'T BE ABLE TO SERVE IT TONIGHT.
YOU THINK HE'S GOT A COLD? I HOPE HE'S ALL RIGHT...
EVEN WHEN HE *DOES* GET SICK, HE NEVER SAYS A WORD TO ME.
IF IT'S BAD ENOUGH HE MESSAGED ME...

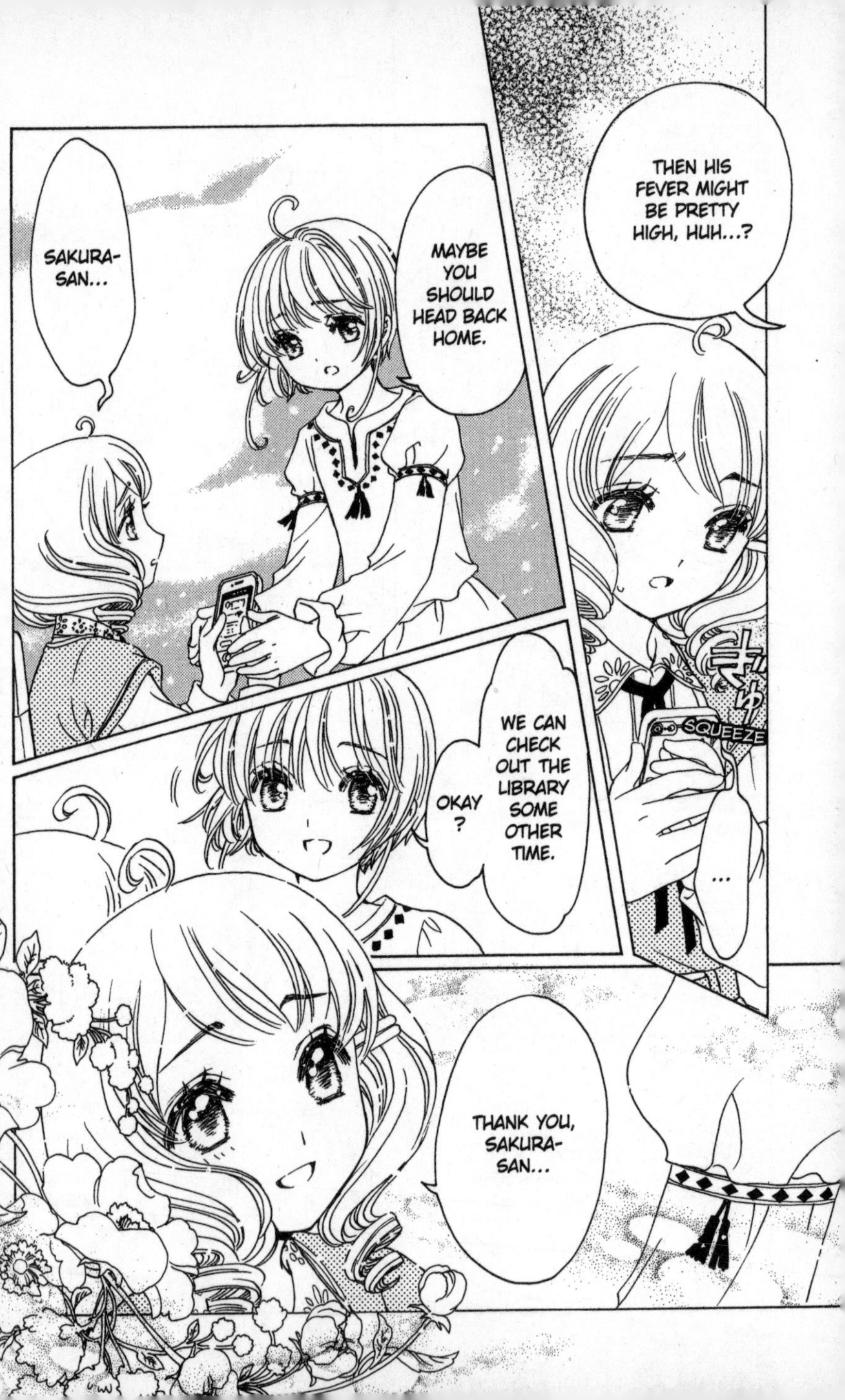
THEN HIS FEVER MIGHT BE PRETTY HIGH, HUH...?
SQUEEZE
...
MAYBE YOU SHOULD HEAD BACK HOME.
SAKURA-SAN...
WE CAN CHECK OUT THE LIBRARY SOME OTHER TIME.
OKAY?
THANK YOU, SAKURA-SAN...

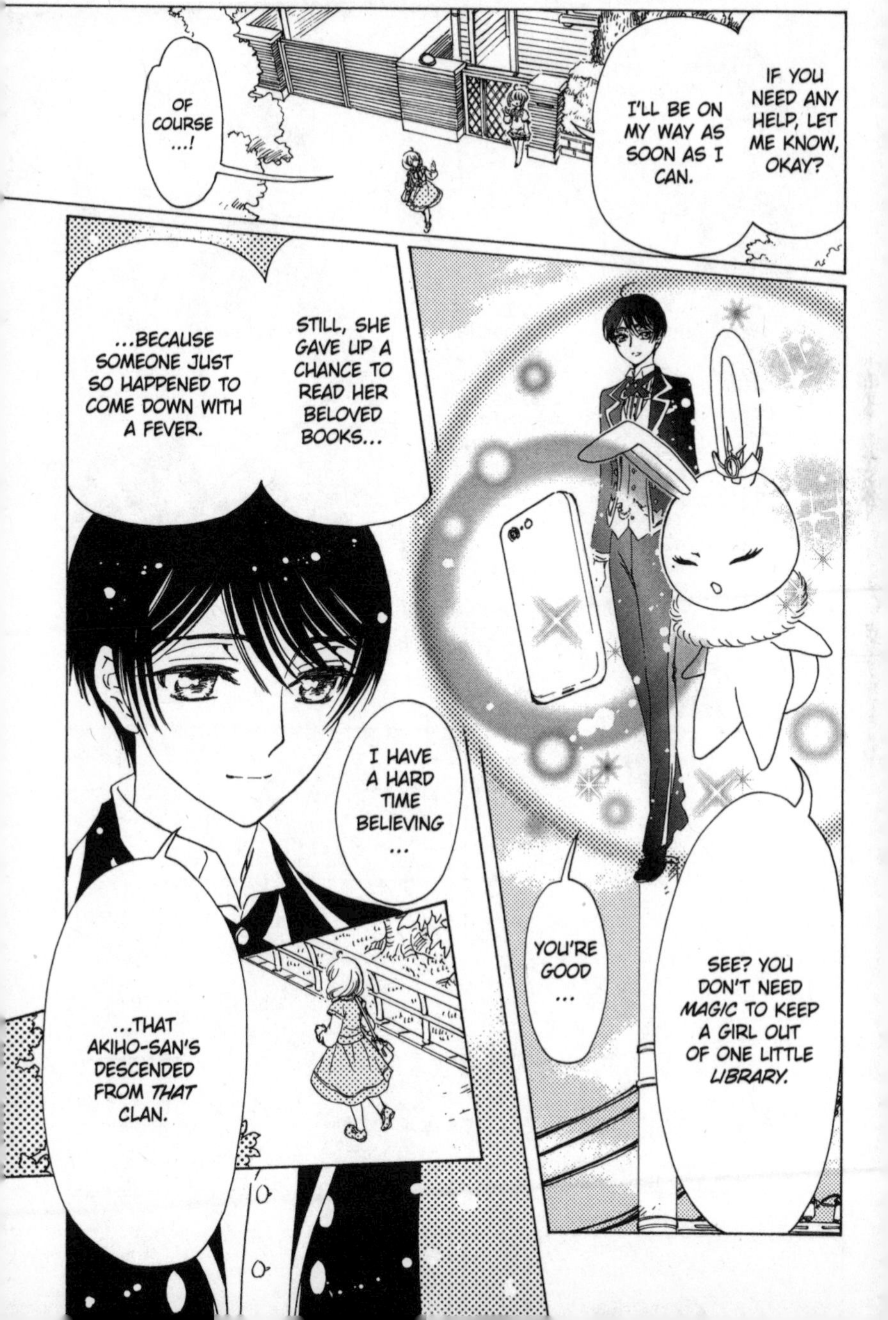
IF YOU NEED ANY HELP, LET ME KNOW, OKAY?
I'LL BE ON MY WAY AS SOON AS I CAN.
OF COURSE ...!
SEE? YOU DON'T NEED *MAGIC* TO KEEP A GIRL OUT OF ONE LITTLE *LIBRARY*.
YOU'RE GOOD ...
STILL, SHE GAVE UP A CHANCE TO READ HER BELOVED BOOKS...
...BECAUSE SOMEONE JUST SO HAPPENED TO COME DOWN WITH A FEVER.
I HAVE A HARD TIME BELIEVING ...
...THAT AKIHO-SAN'S DESCENDED FROM *THAT* CLAN.

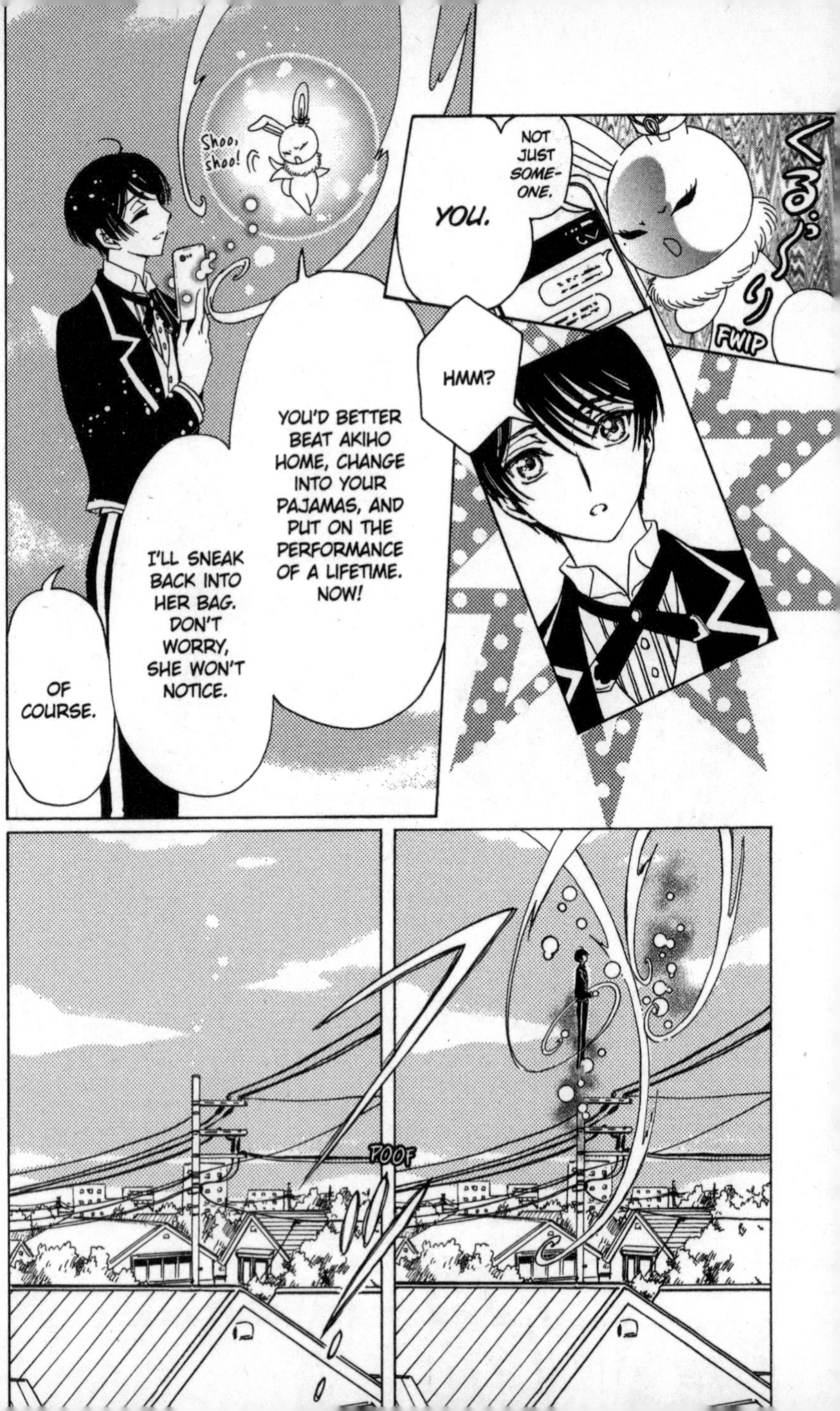
NOT JUST SOME-ONE.
YOU.
FWIP
HMM?
Shoo, shoo!
YOU'D BETTER BEAT AKIHO HOME, CHANGE INTO YOUR PAJAMAS, AND PUT ON THE PERFORMANCE OF A LIFETIME. NOW!
I'LL SNEAK BACK INTO HER BAG. DON'T WORRY, SHE WON'T NOTICE.
OF COURSE.
POOF

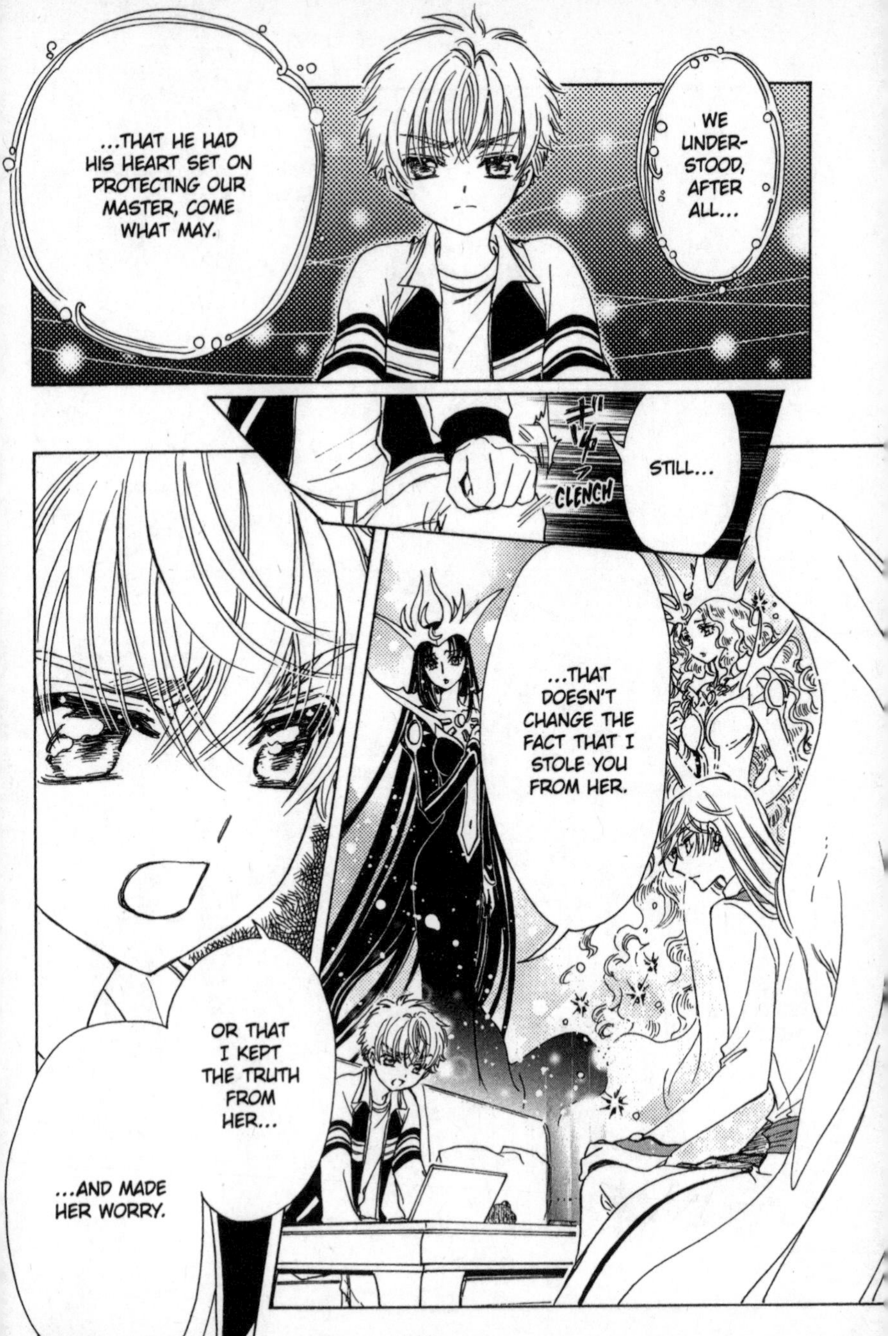
WE UNDER-STOOD, AFTER ALL...
...THAT HE HAD HIS HEART SET ON PROTECTING OUR MASTER, COME WHAT MAY.
CLENCH
STILL...
...THAT DOESN'T CHANGE THE FACT THAT I STOLE YOU FROM HER.
OR THAT I KEPT THE TRUTH FROM HER...
...AND MADE HER WORRY.

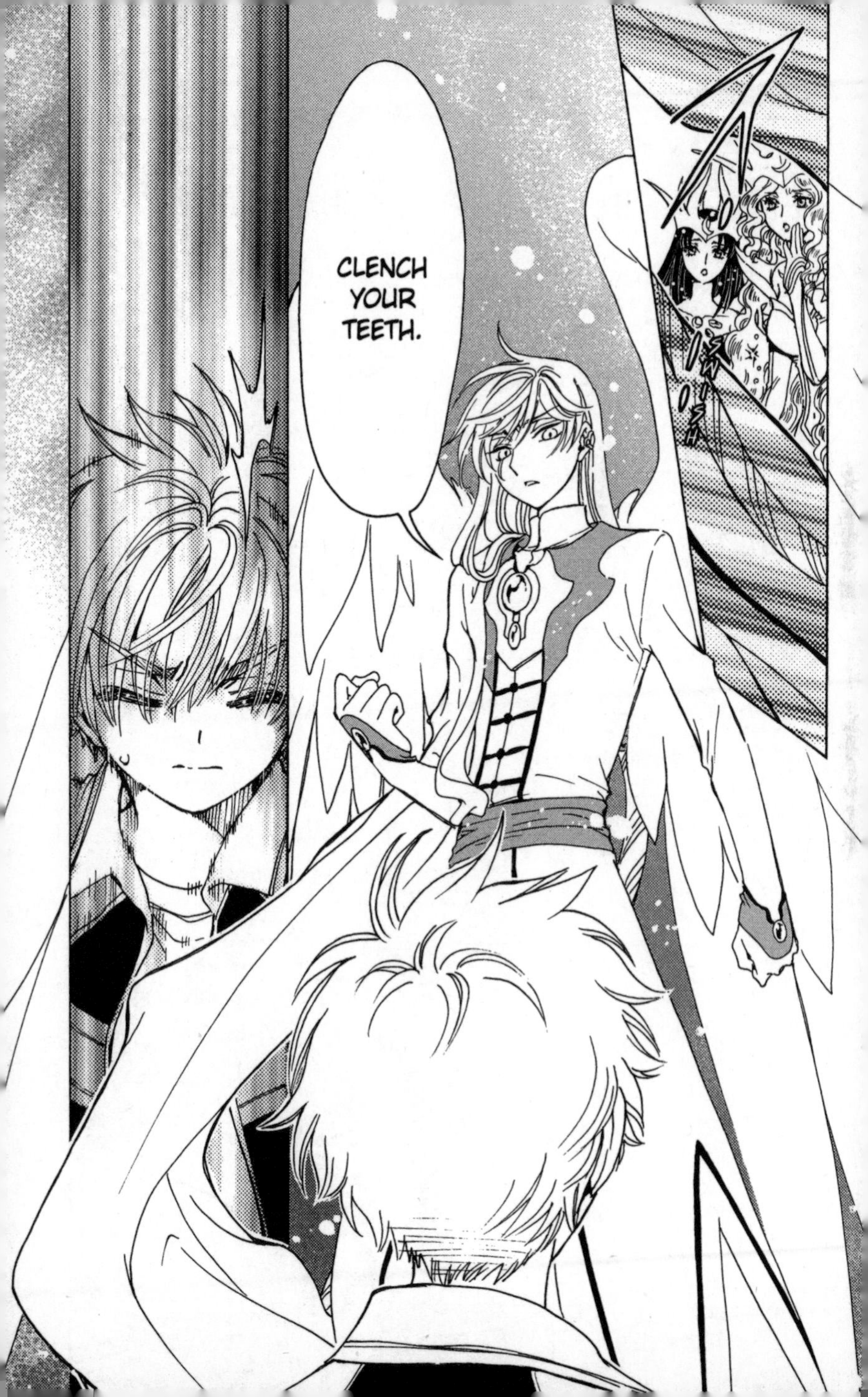
SWISH
CLENCH YOUR TEETH.

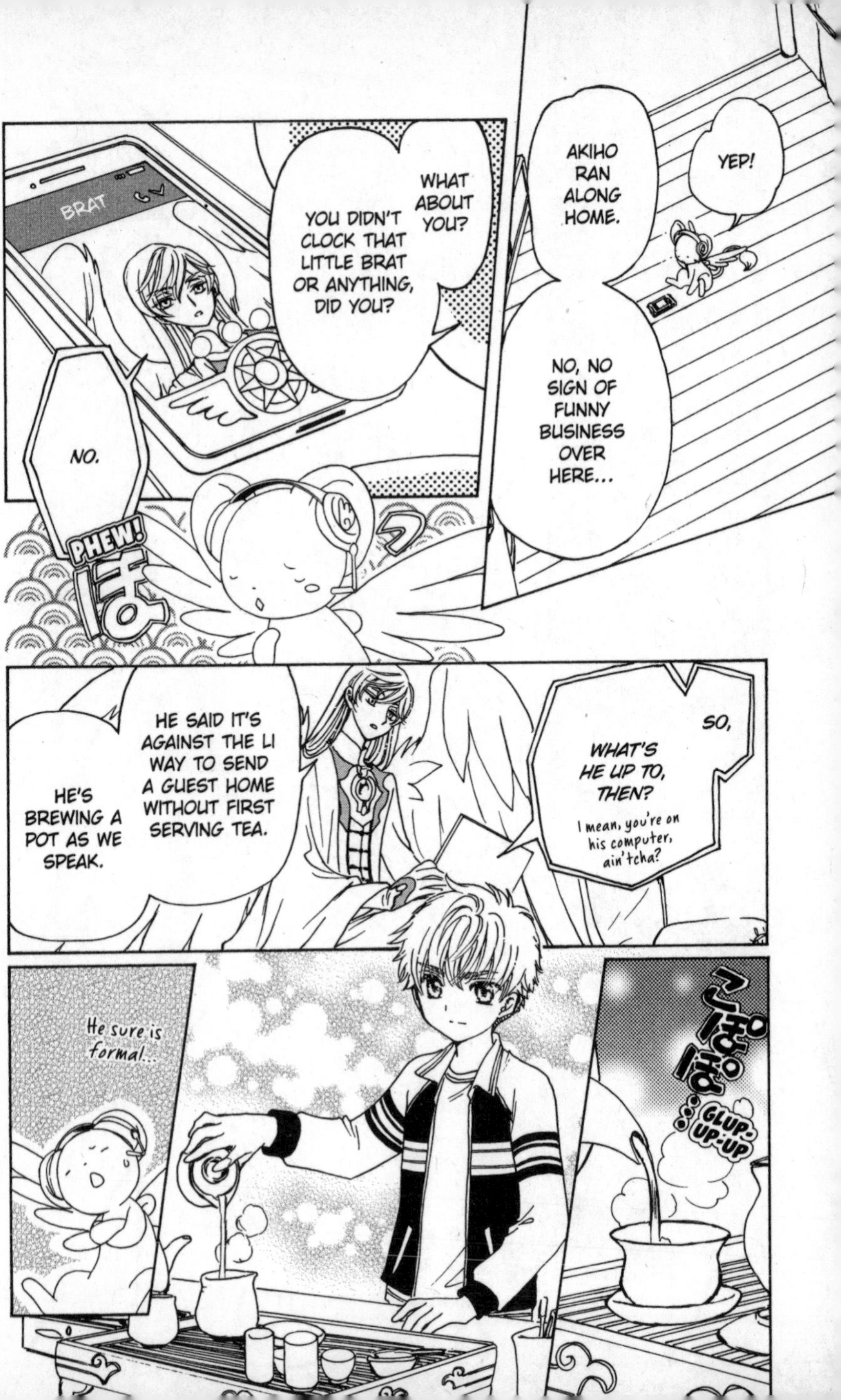

YEP!
AKIHO RAN ALONG HOME.
NO, NO SIGN OF FUNNY BUSINESS OVER HERE...
WHAT ABOUT YOU?
YOU DIDN'T CLOCK THAT LITTLE BRAT OR ANYTHING, DID YOU?
BRAT
NO.
PHEW!
ほ
SO,
WHAT'S HE UP TO, THEN?
I mean, you're on his computer, ain'tcha?
HE SAID IT'S AGAINST THE LI WAY TO SEND A GUEST HOME WITHOUT FIRST SERVING TEA.
HE'S BREWING A POT AS WE SPEAK.
こぽぽ…
GLUP-UP-UP
He sure is formal...

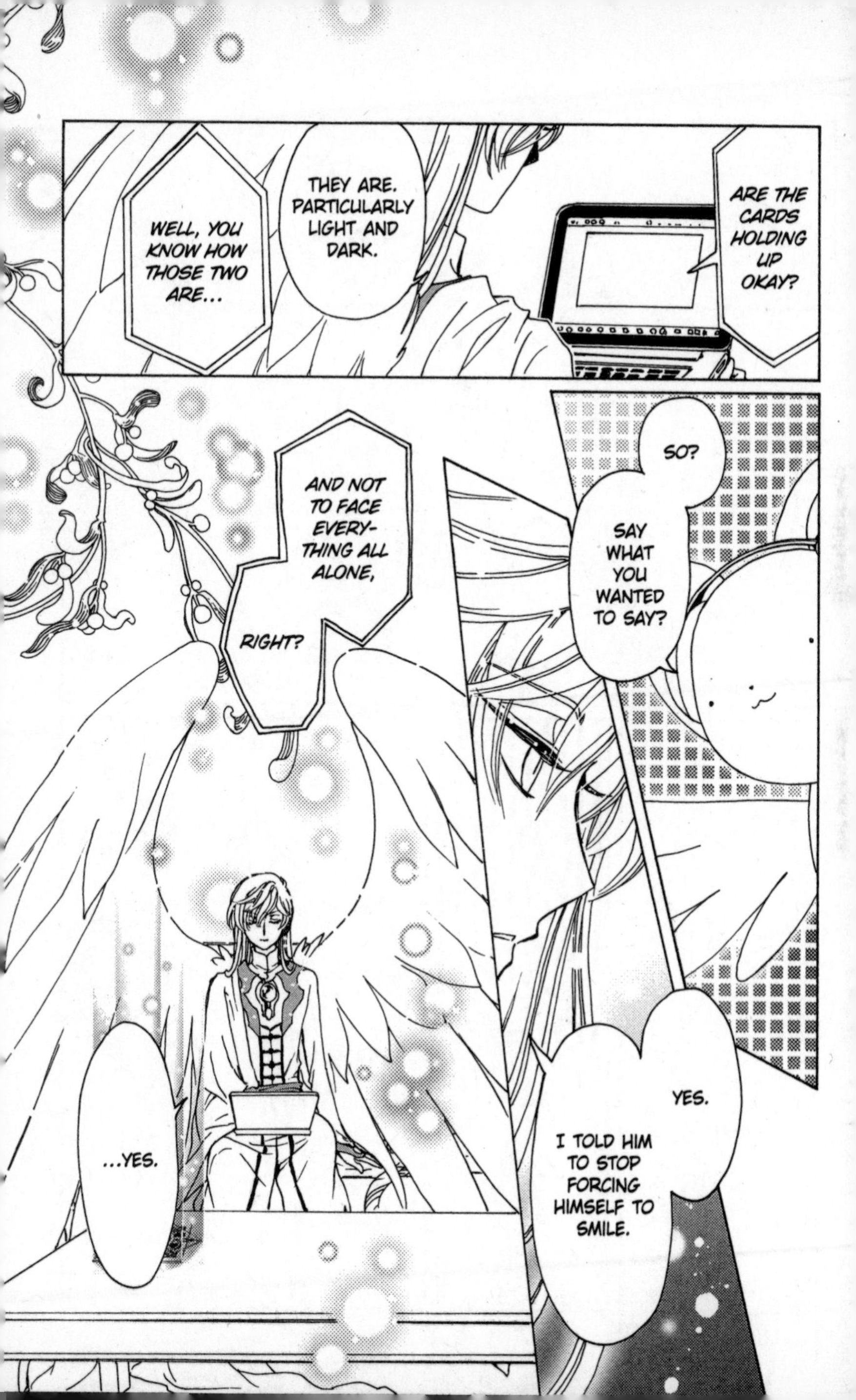
ARE THE CARDS HOLDING UP OKAY?
THEY ARE. PARTICULARLY LIGHT AND DARK.
WELL, YOU KNOW HOW THOSE TWO ARE…
SO?
SAY WHAT YOU WANTED TO SAY?
YES.
I TOLD HIM TO STOP FORCING HIMSELF TO SMILE.
AND NOT TO FACE EVERY-THING ALL ALONE,
RIGHT?
…YES.

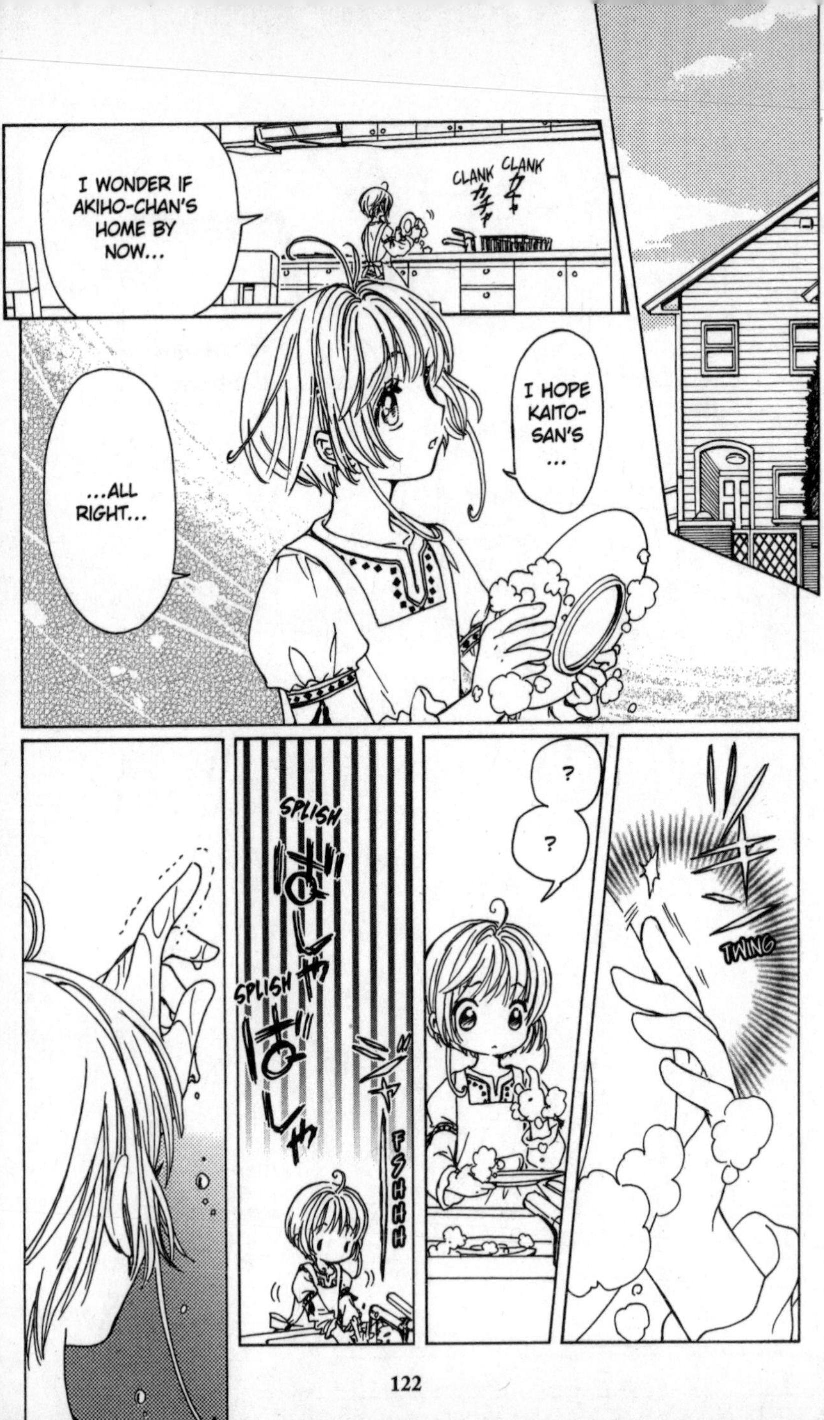
CLANK CLANK
I WONDER IF AKIHO-CHAN'S HOME BY NOW...
I HOPE KAITO-SAN'S ...
...ALL RIGHT...
TWING
?
?
SPLISH
SPLISH
FSHHHH

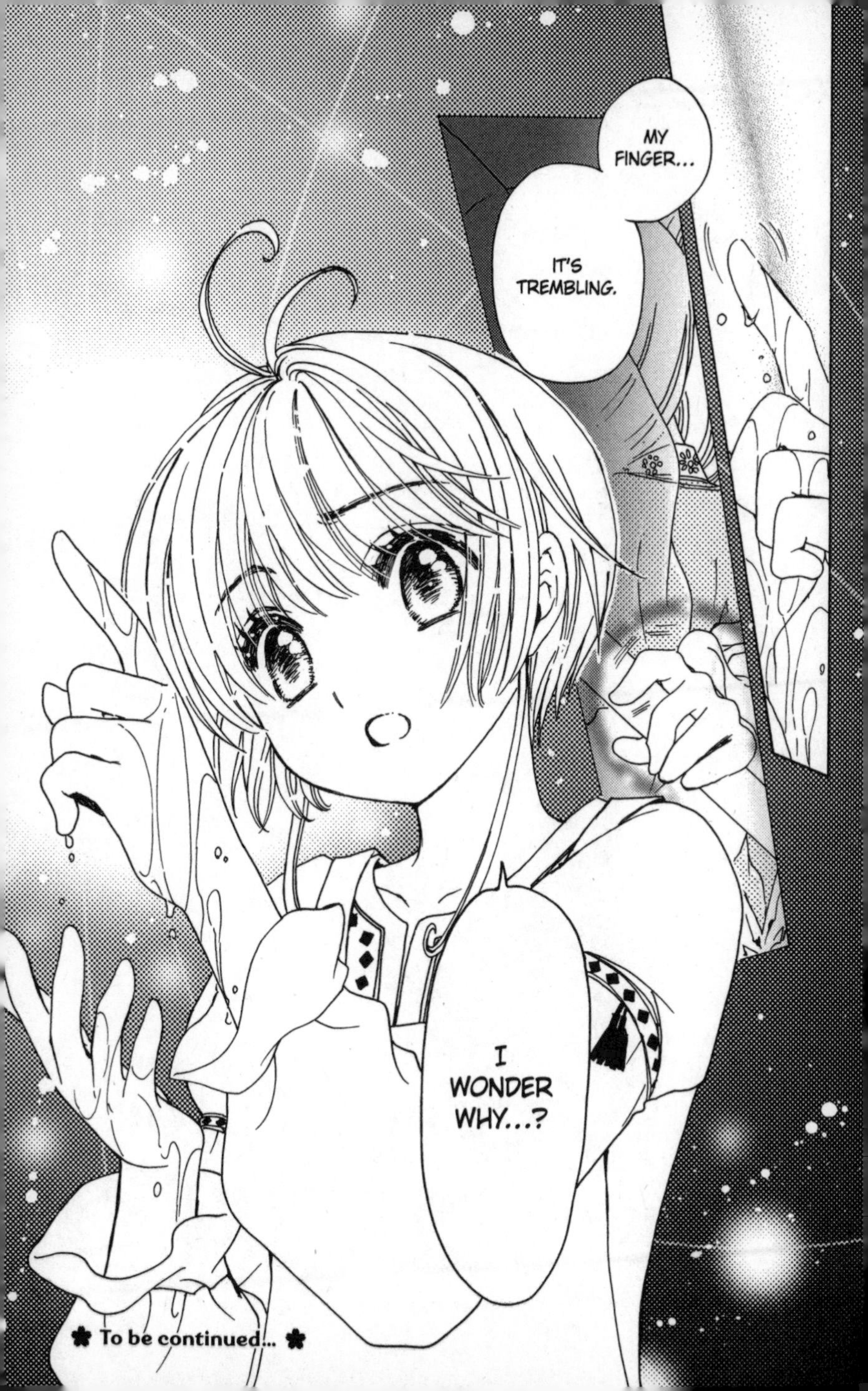
MY FINGER...
IT'S TREMBLING.
I WONDER WHY...?
To be continued...

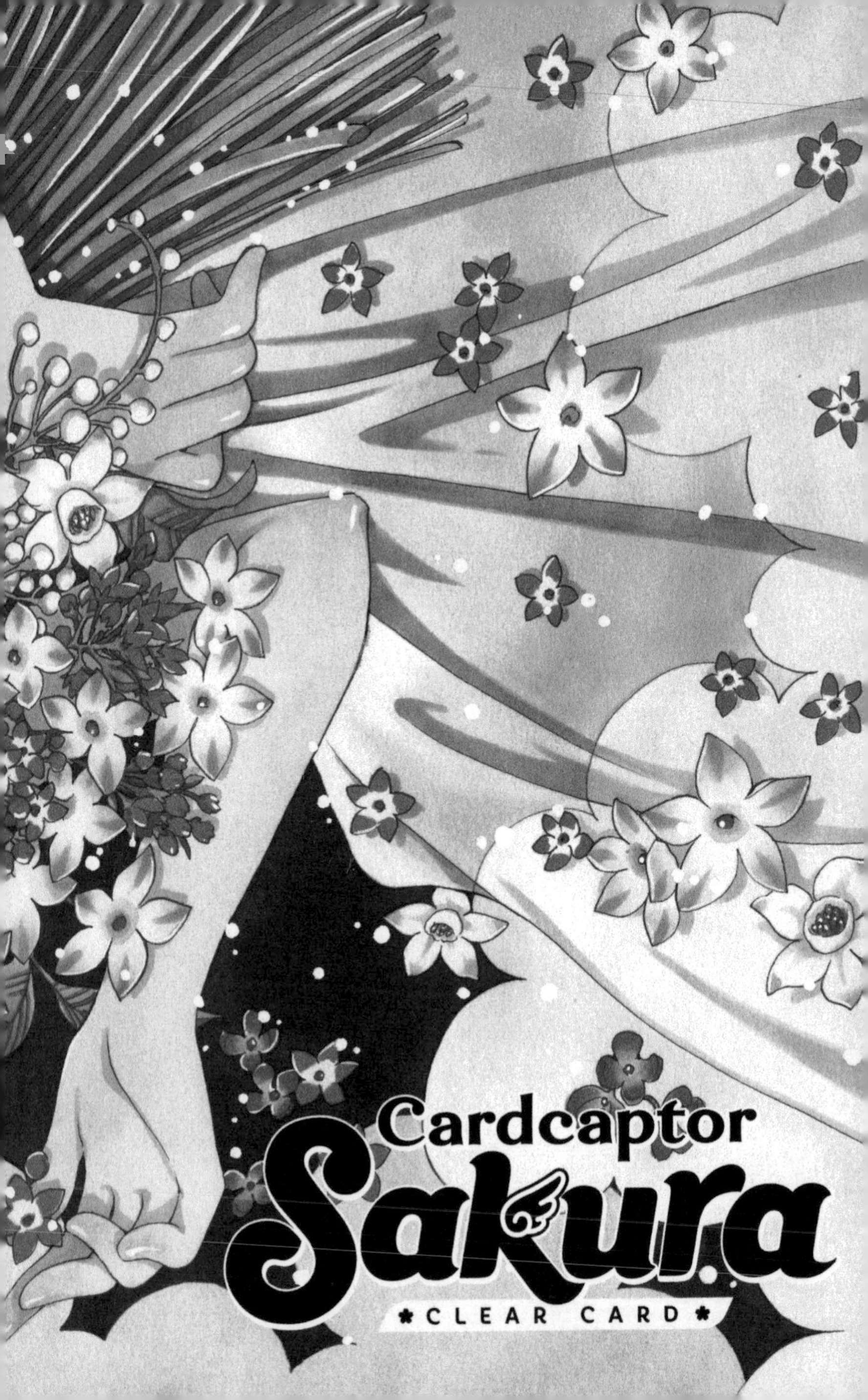
Cardcaptor
Sakura
CLEAR CARD

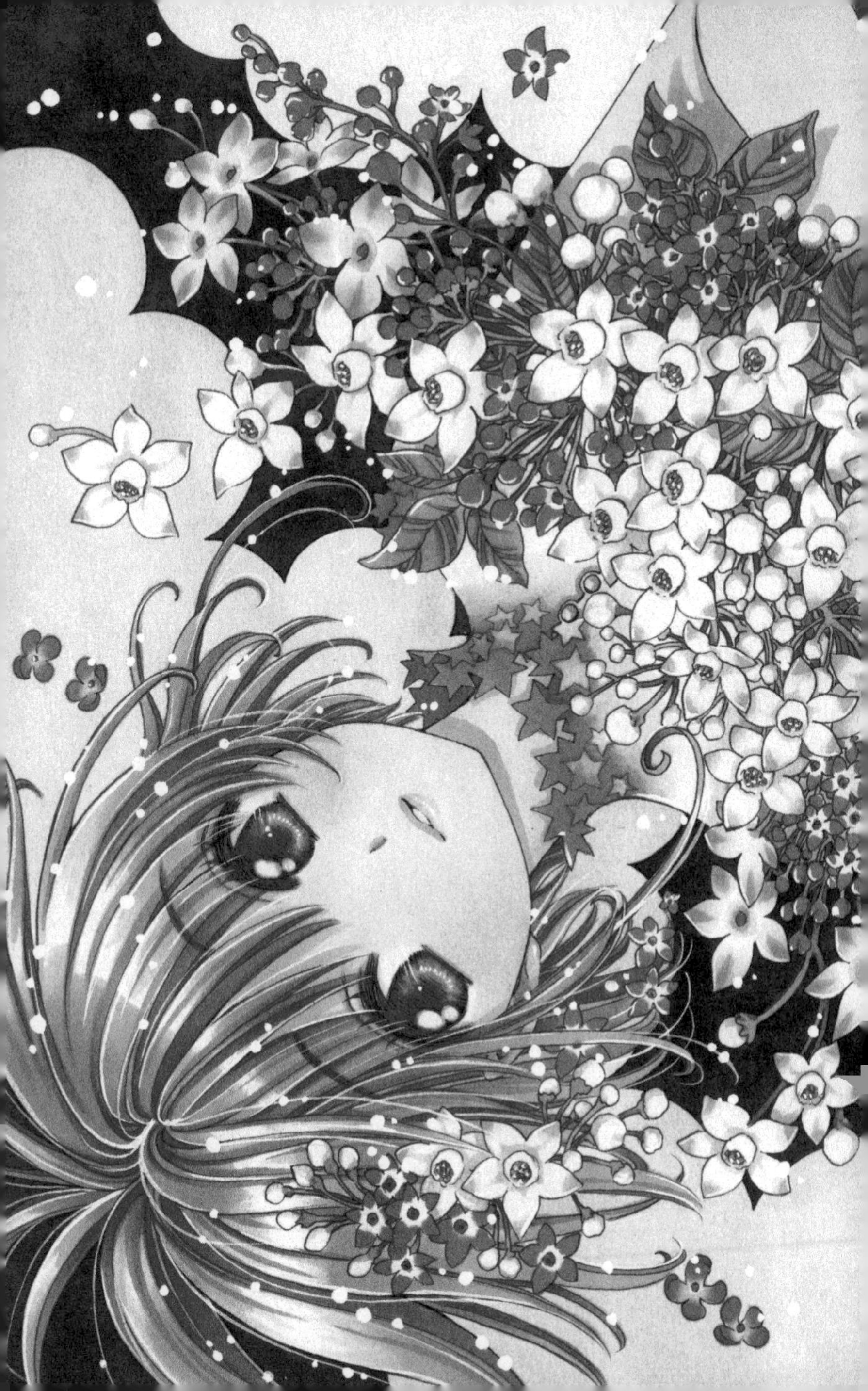

Cardcaptor Sakura

CLEAR CARD

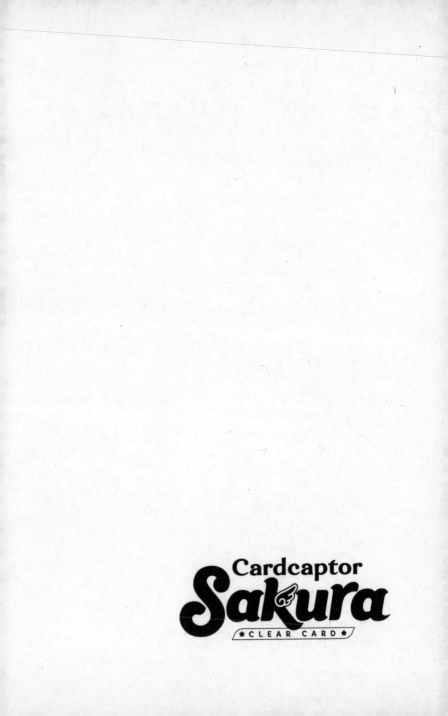

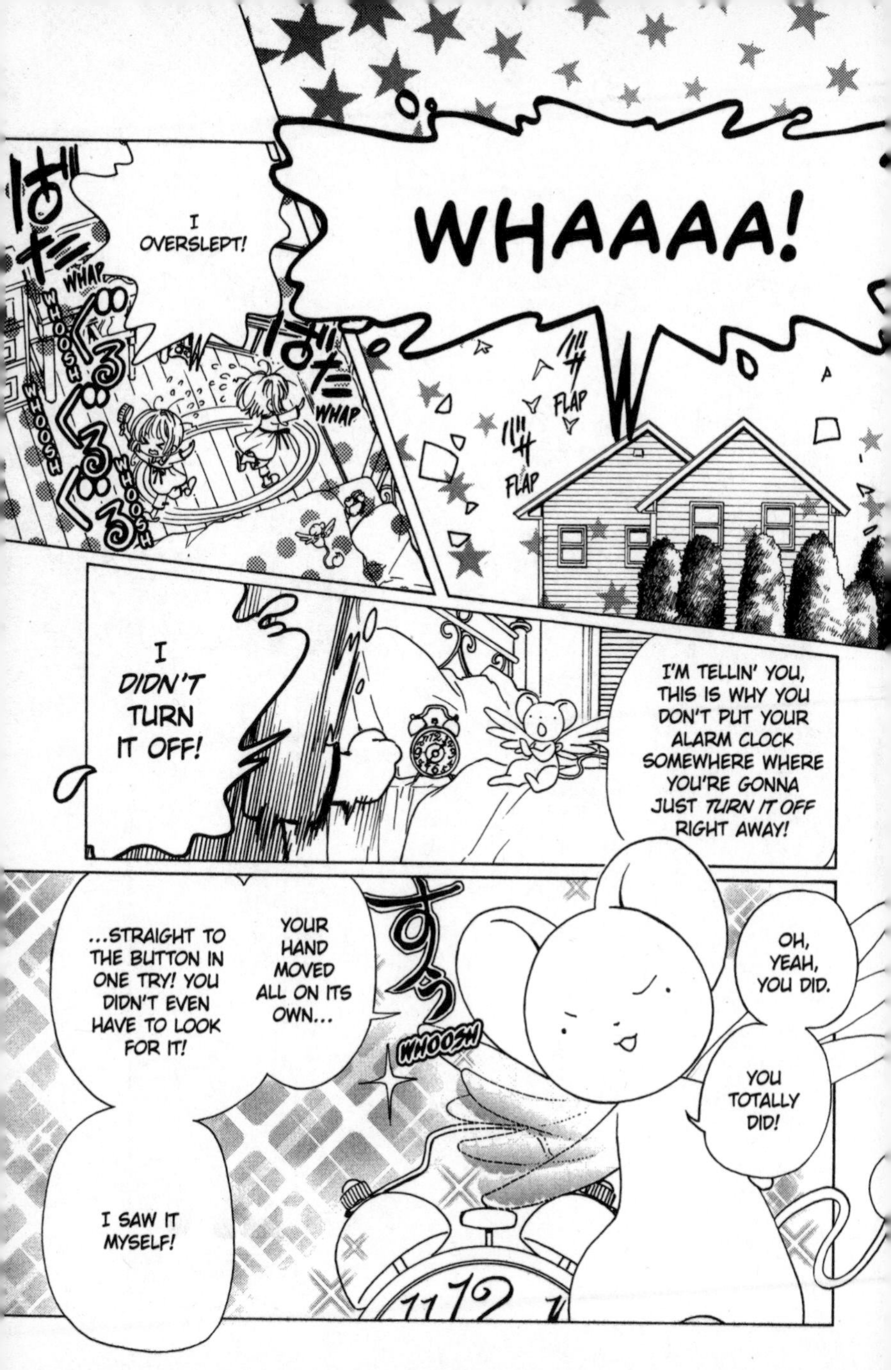
WHAAAA!
FLAP
FLAP
I OVERSLEPT!
WHAP
WHAP
WHOOSH
WHOOSH
WHOOSH
I'M TELLIN' YOU, THIS IS WHY YOU DON'T PUT YOUR ALARM CLOCK SOMEWHERE WHERE YOU'RE GONNA JUST *TURN IT OFF* RIGHT AWAY!
I *DIDN'T* TURN IT OFF!
OH, YEAH, YOU DID.
YOU TOTALLY DID!
WHOOSH
YOUR HAND MOVED ALL ON ITS OWN...
...STRAIGHT TO THE BUTTON IN ONE TRY! YOU DIDN'T EVEN HAVE TO LOOK FOR IT!
I SAW IT MYSELF!

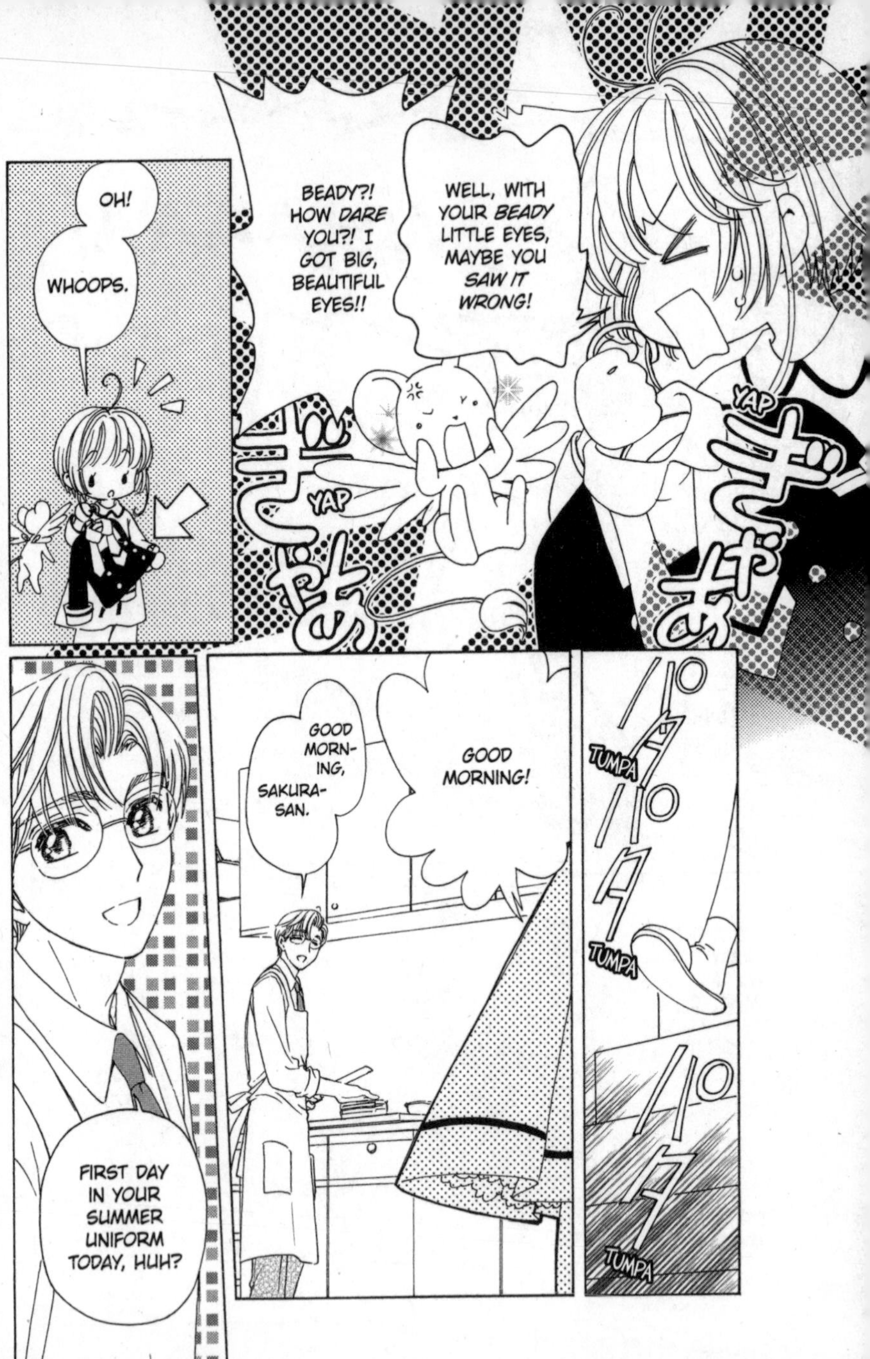
WELL, WITH YOUR *BEADY* LITTLE EYES, MAYBE YOU *SAW IT WRONG!*
BEADY?! HOW *DARE* YOU?! I GOT BIG, BEAUTIFUL EYES!!
YAP
ぎゃあ
YAP
ぎゃあ
OH!
WHOOPS.
TUMPA
パタパタ
TUMPA
パタ
TUMPA
GOOD MORNING!
GOOD MORN-ING, SAKURA-SAN.
FIRST DAY IN YOUR SUMMER UNIFORM TODAY, HUH?

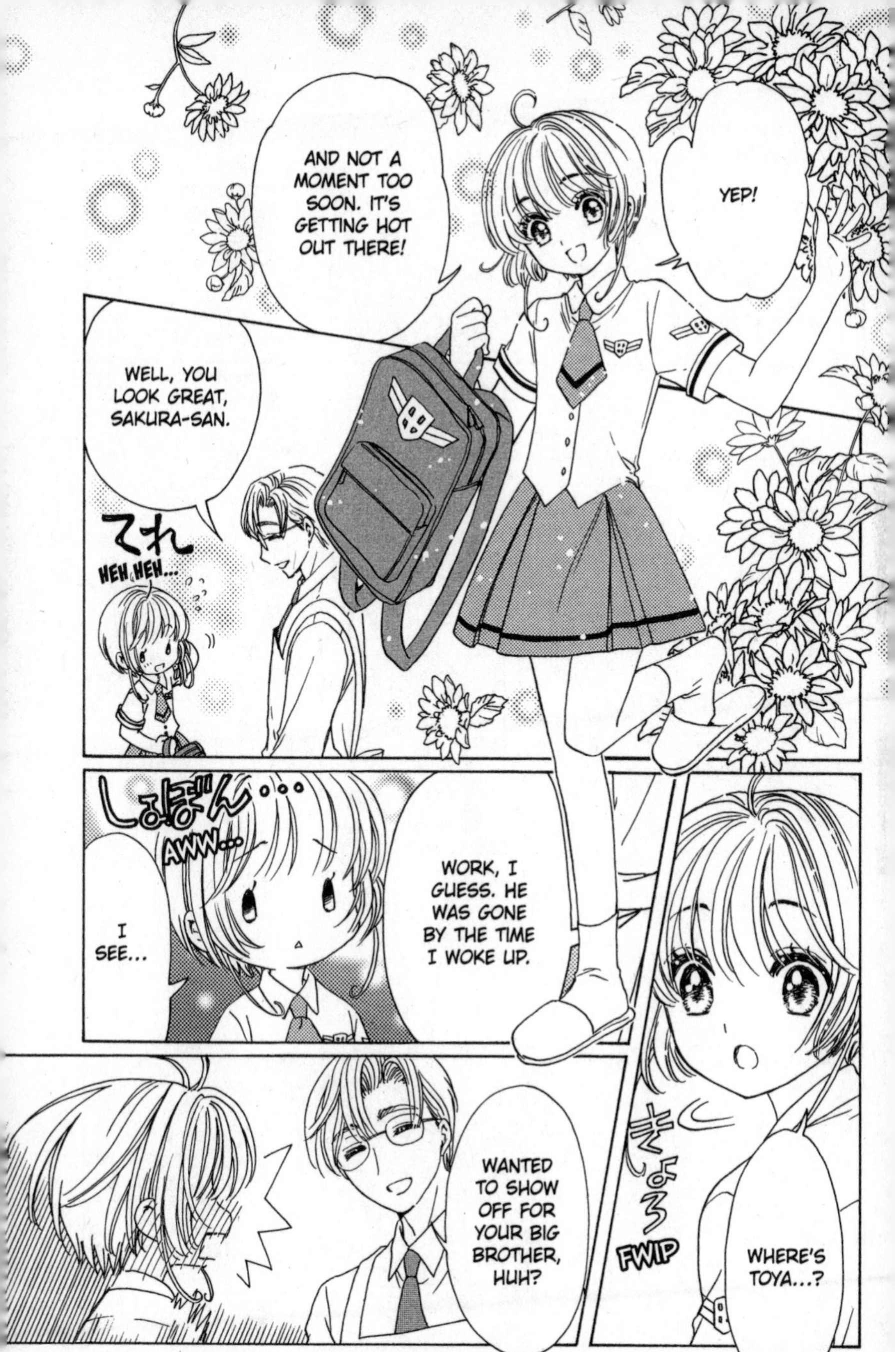
YEP!
AND NOT A MOMENT TOO SOON. IT'S GETTING HOT OUT THERE!
WELL, YOU LOOK GREAT, SAKURA-SAN.
てれ
HEH HEH...
WANTED TO SHOW OFF FOR YOUR BIG BROTHER, HUH?
きょろ
FWIP
WHERE'S TOYA...?
WORK, I GUESS. HE WAS GONE BY THE TIME I WOKE UP.
しょぼん…
AWW...
I SEE...

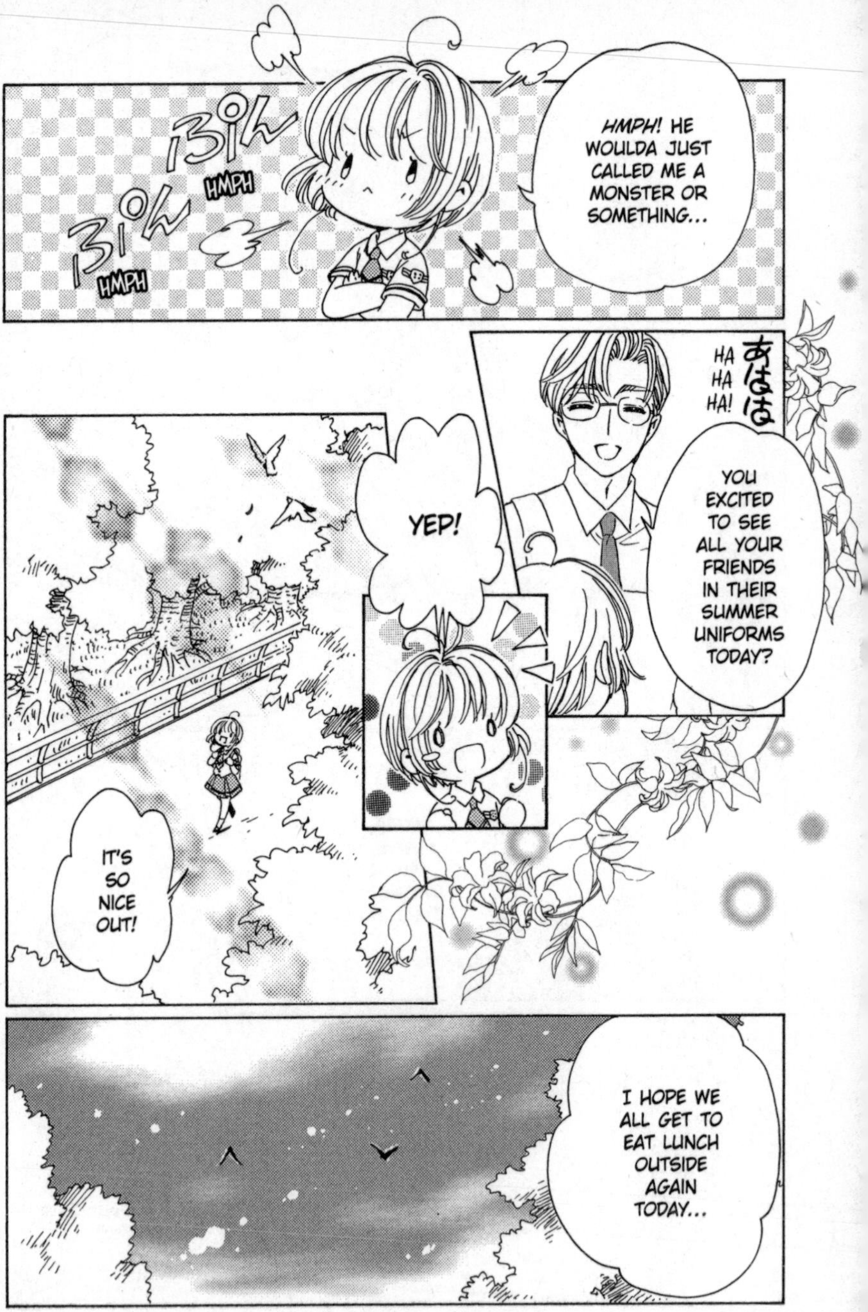
HMPH! HE WOULDA JUST CALLED ME A MONSTER OR SOMETHING...
ぷいん
HMPH
ぷいん
HMPH
あはは
HA HA HA!
YOU EXCITED TO SEE ALL YOUR FRIENDS IN THEIR SUMMER UNIFORMS TODAY?
YEP!
IT'S SO NICE OUT!
I HOPE WE ALL GET TO EAT LUNCH OUTSIDE AGAIN TODAY...

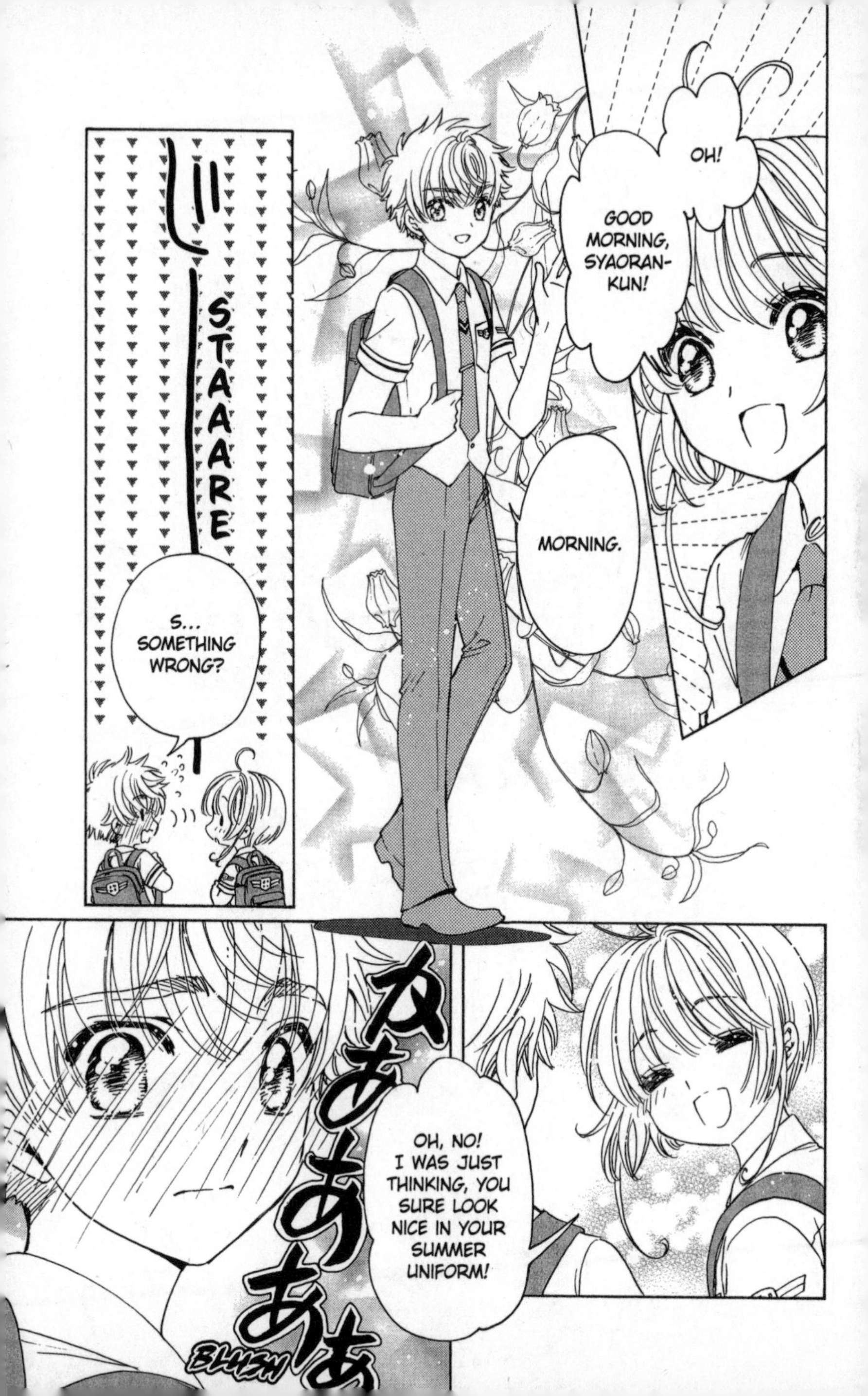
OH!
GOOD MORNING, SYAORAN-KUN!
MORNING.
じー
STAAARE
S... SOMETHING WRONG?
OH, NO! I WAS JUST THINKING, YOU SURE LOOK NICE IN YOUR SUMMER UNIFORM!
BLUSH

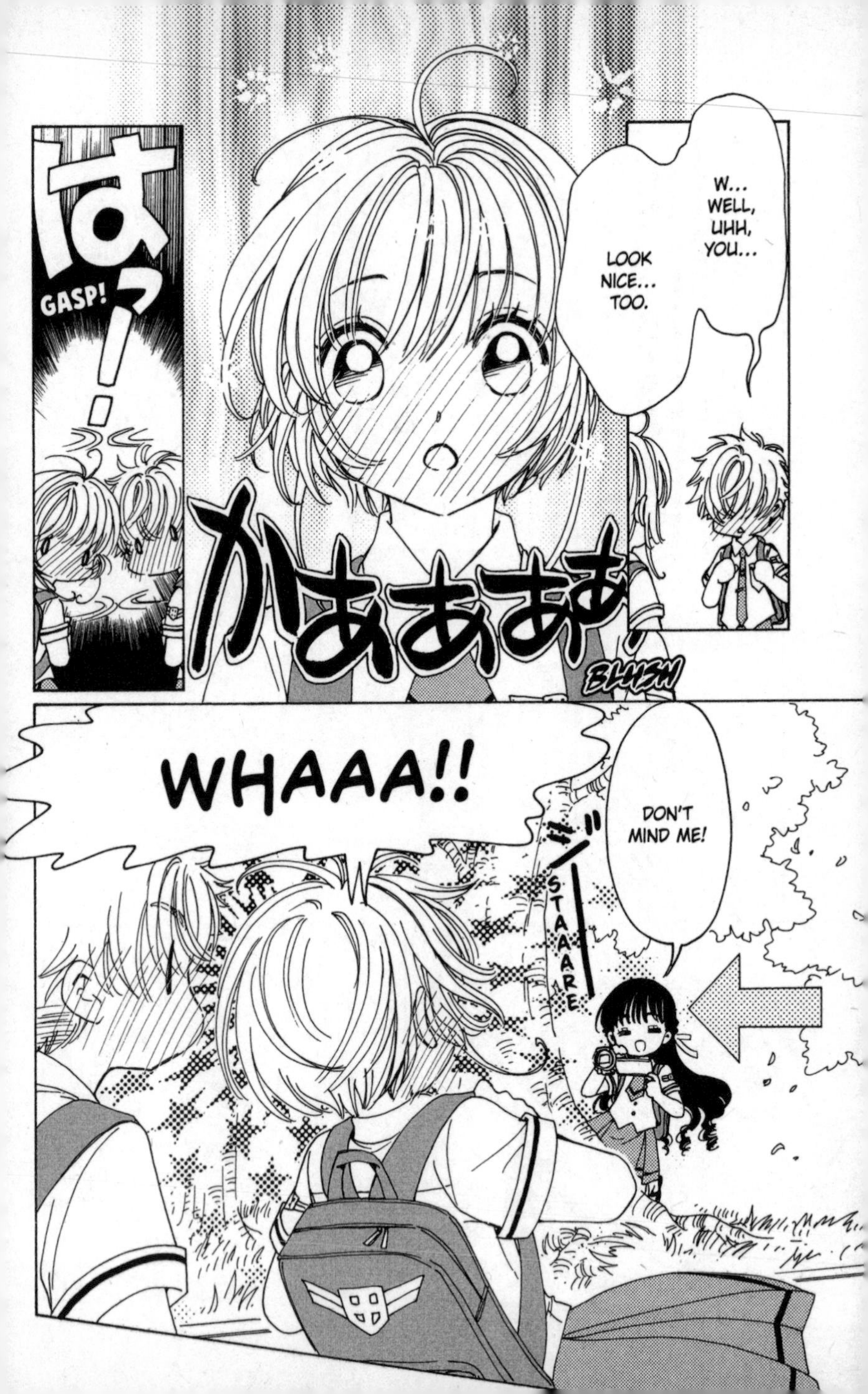
W... WELL, UHH, YOU...
LOOK NICE... TOO.
かあああああ
BLUSH
はっ!!
GASP!
DON'T MIND ME!
ジー
STAAARE
WHAAA!!

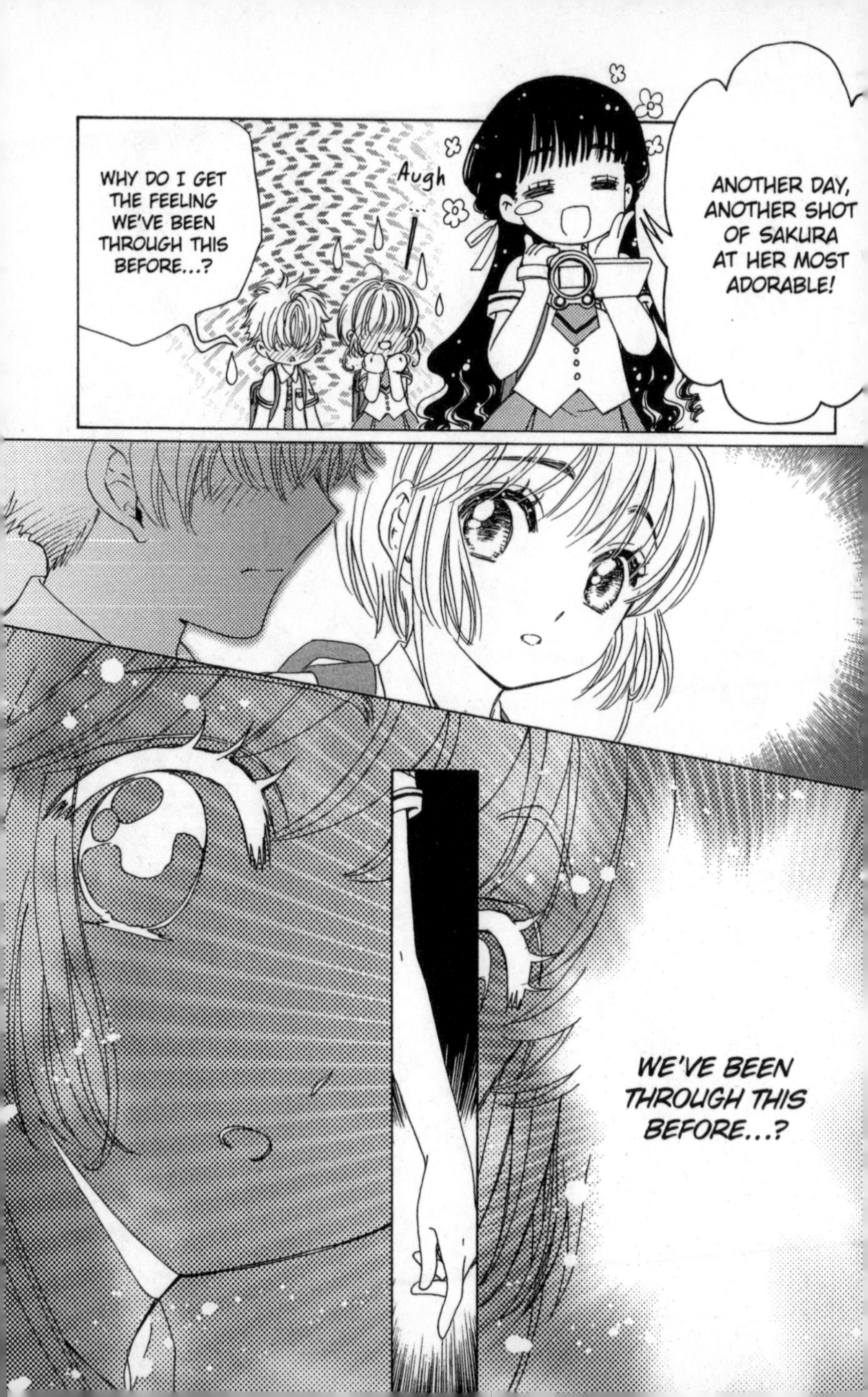
ANOTHER DAY, ANOTHER SHOT OF SAKURA AT HER MOST ADORABLE!
Augh...
WHY DO I GET THE FEELING WE'VE BEEN THROUGH THIS BEFORE...?
WE'VE BEEN THROUGH THIS BEFORE...?

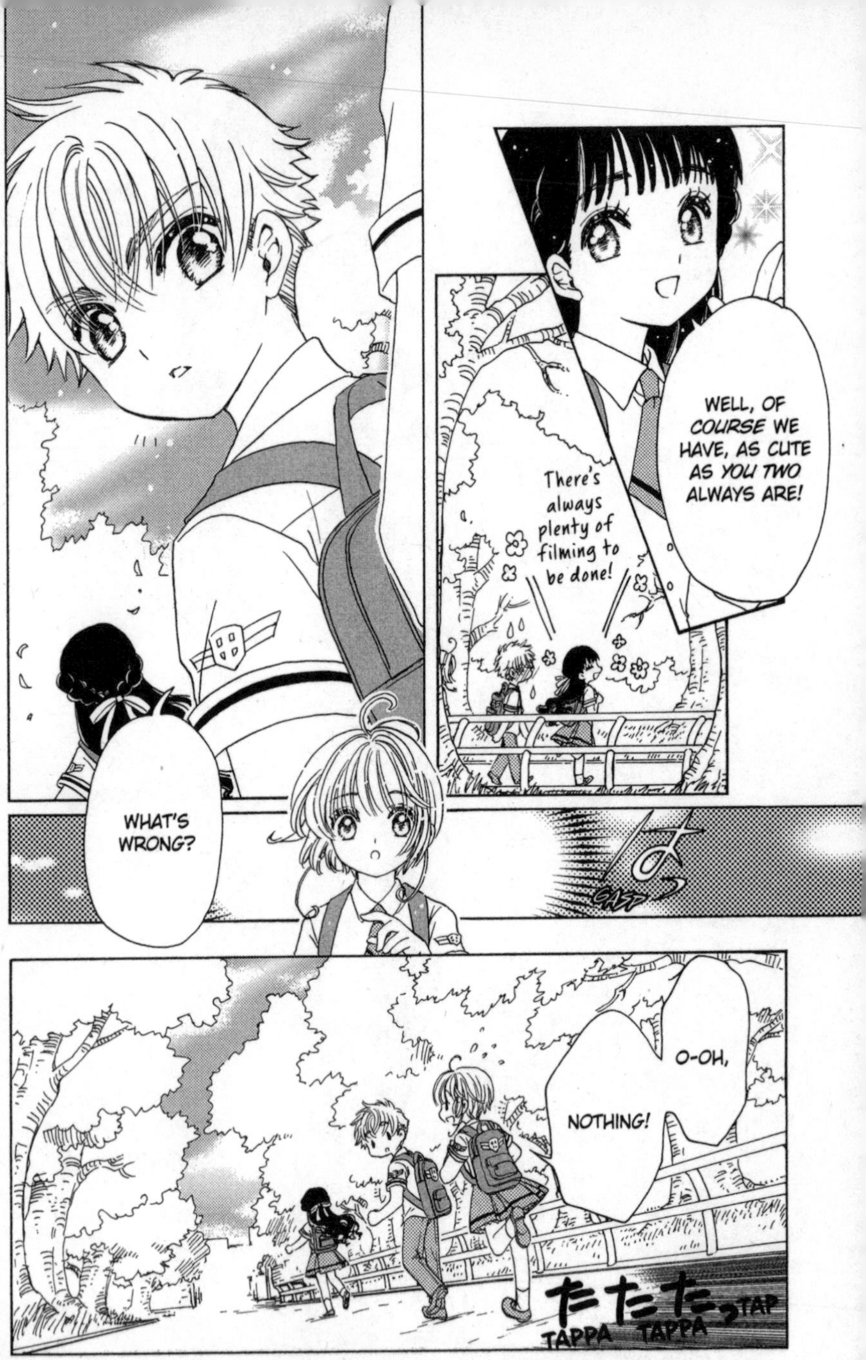
WELL, OF COURSE WE HAVE, AS CUTE AS YOU TWO ALWAYS ARE!
There's always plenty of filming to be done!
GASP
WHAT'S WRONG?
O-OH, NOTHING!
TAPPA TAPPA TAP

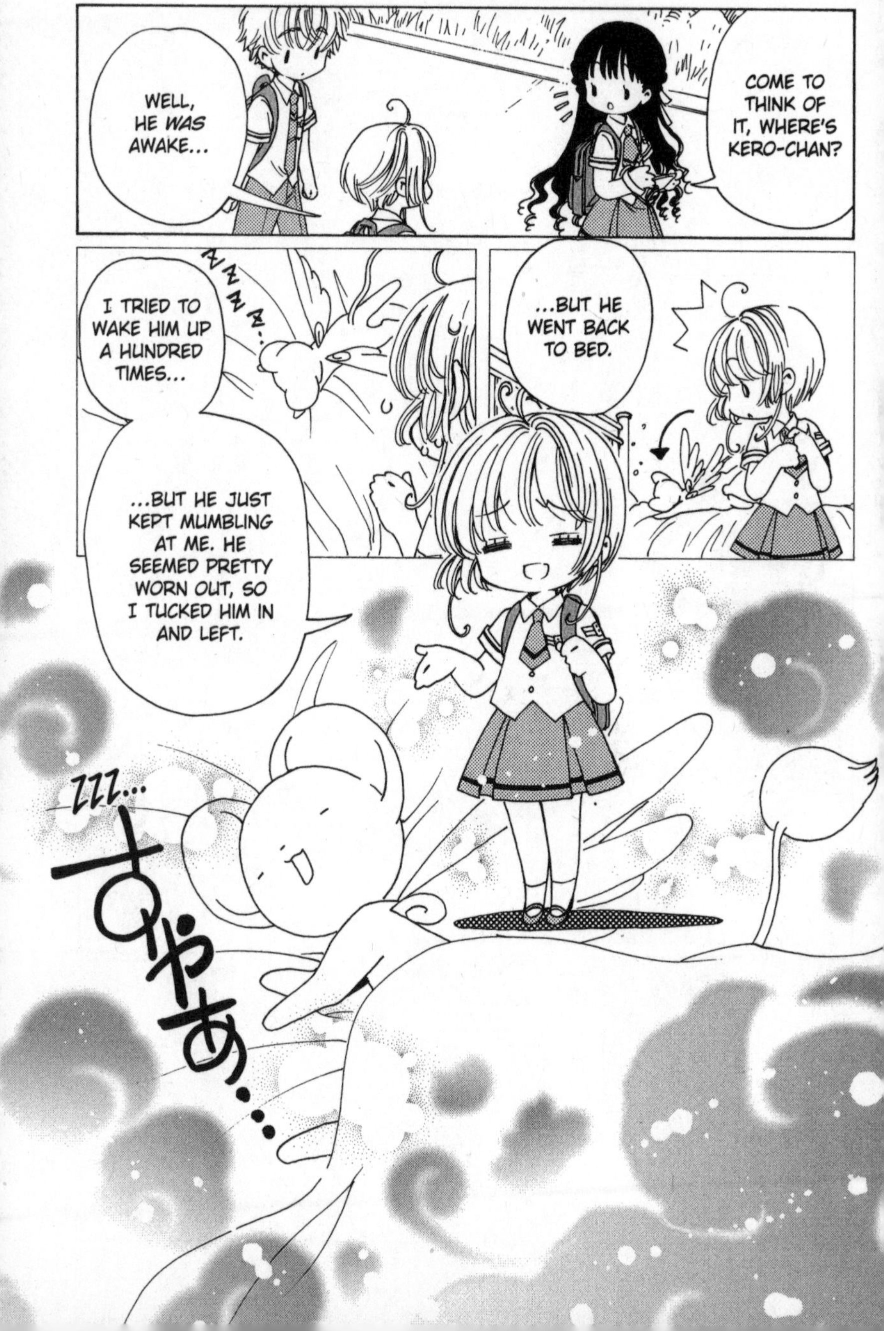
COME TO THINK OF IT, WHERE'S KERO-CHAN?
WELL, HE *WAS* AWAKE...
...BUT HE WENT BACK TO BED.
I TRIED TO WAKE HIM UP A HUNDRED TIMES...
ZZZZ...
...BUT HE JUST KEPT MUMBLING AT ME. HE SEEMED PRETTY WORN OUT, SO I TUCKED HIM IN AND LEFT.
ZZZ...
すやぁ...

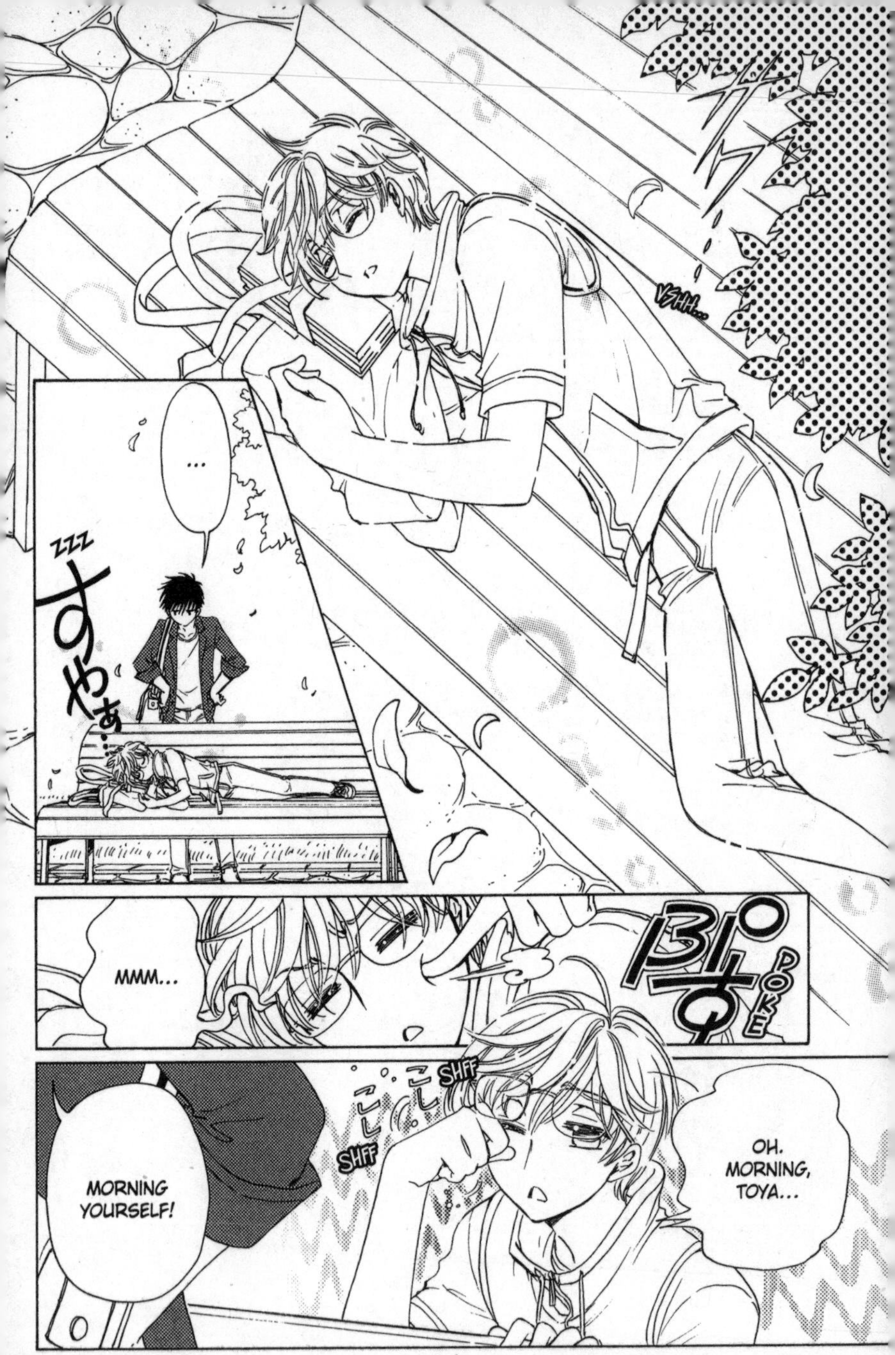
VSHH...
...
ZZZ
すやぁ…
POKE
MMM...
SHFF
SHFF
OH. MORNING, TOYA...
MORNING YOURSELF!

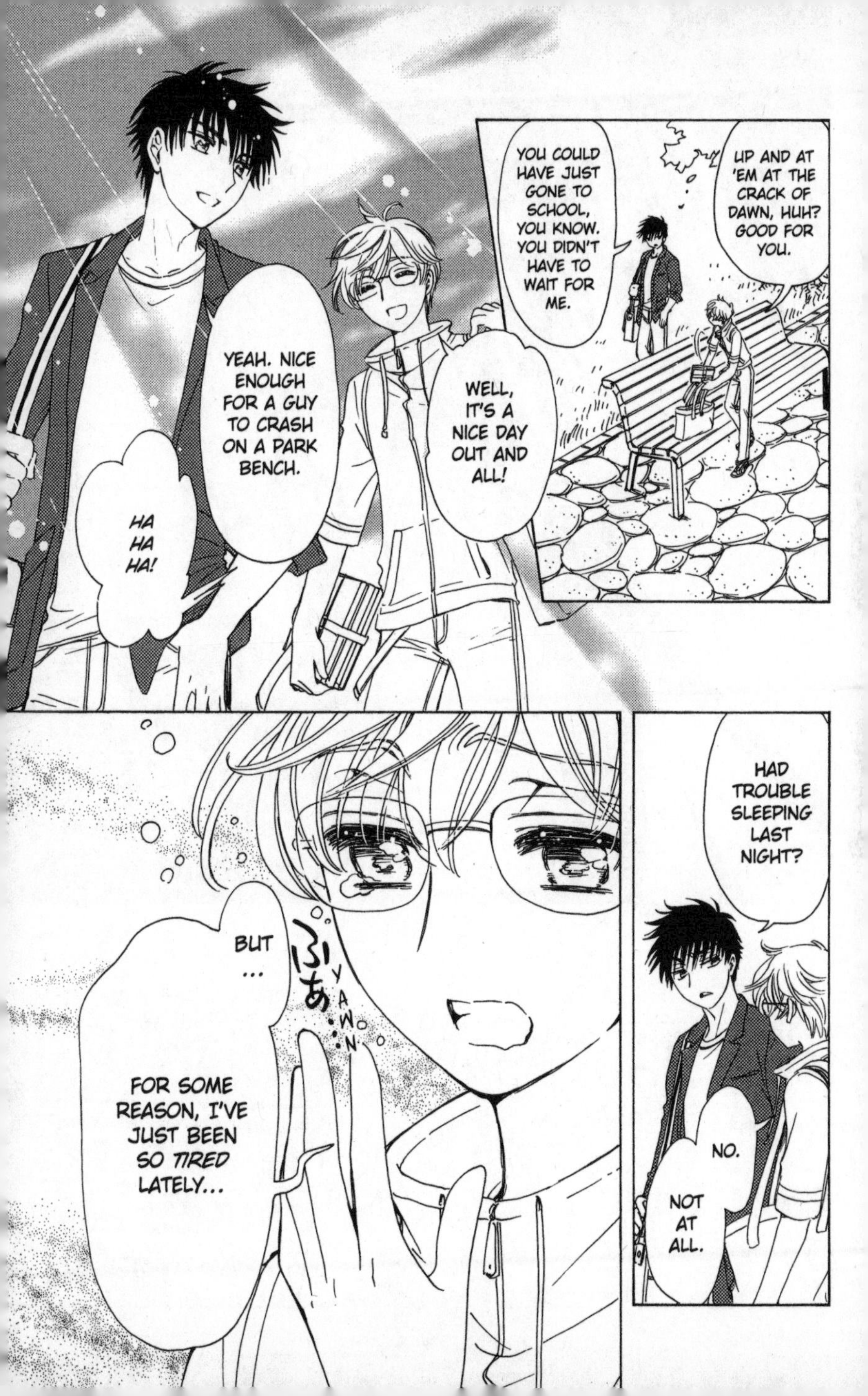
UP AND AT 'EM AT THE CRACK OF DAWN, HUH? GOOD FOR YOU.
YOU COULD HAVE JUST GONE TO SCHOOL, YOU KNOW. YOU DIDN'T HAVE TO WAIT FOR ME.
WELL, IT'S A NICE DAY OUT AND ALL!
YEAH. NICE ENOUGH FOR A GUY TO CRASH ON A PARK BENCH.
HA HA HA!
HAD TROUBLE SLEEPING LAST NIGHT?
NO.
NOT AT ALL.
BUT ...
ふあ
YAWN
FOR SOME REASON, I'VE JUST BEEN SO *TIRED* LATELY...

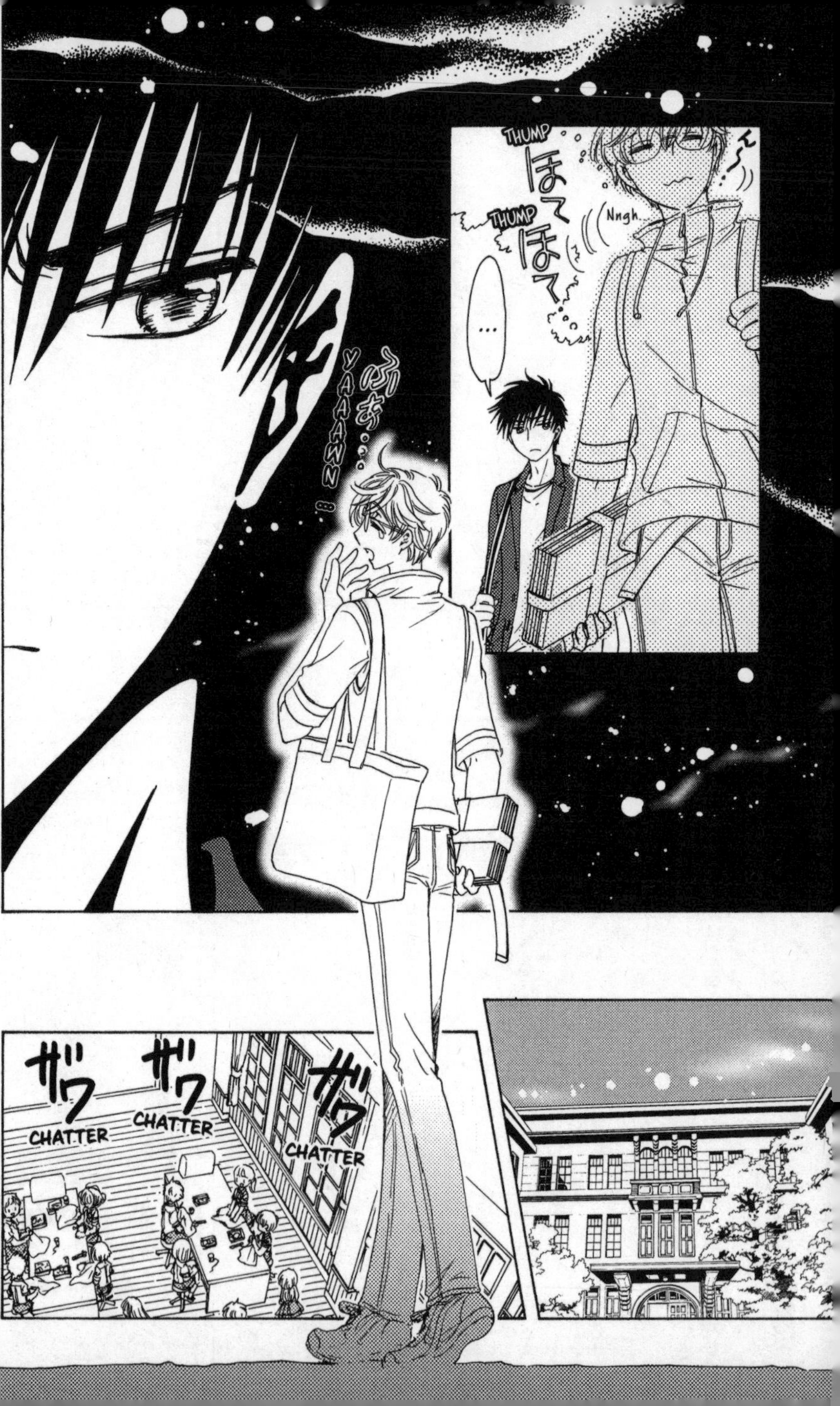
THUMP
ほて
THUMP
ほて
んー
Nngh
...
ふあ...
YAAAAWN...
ザワ
CHATTER
ザワ
CHATTER
ザワ
CHATTER

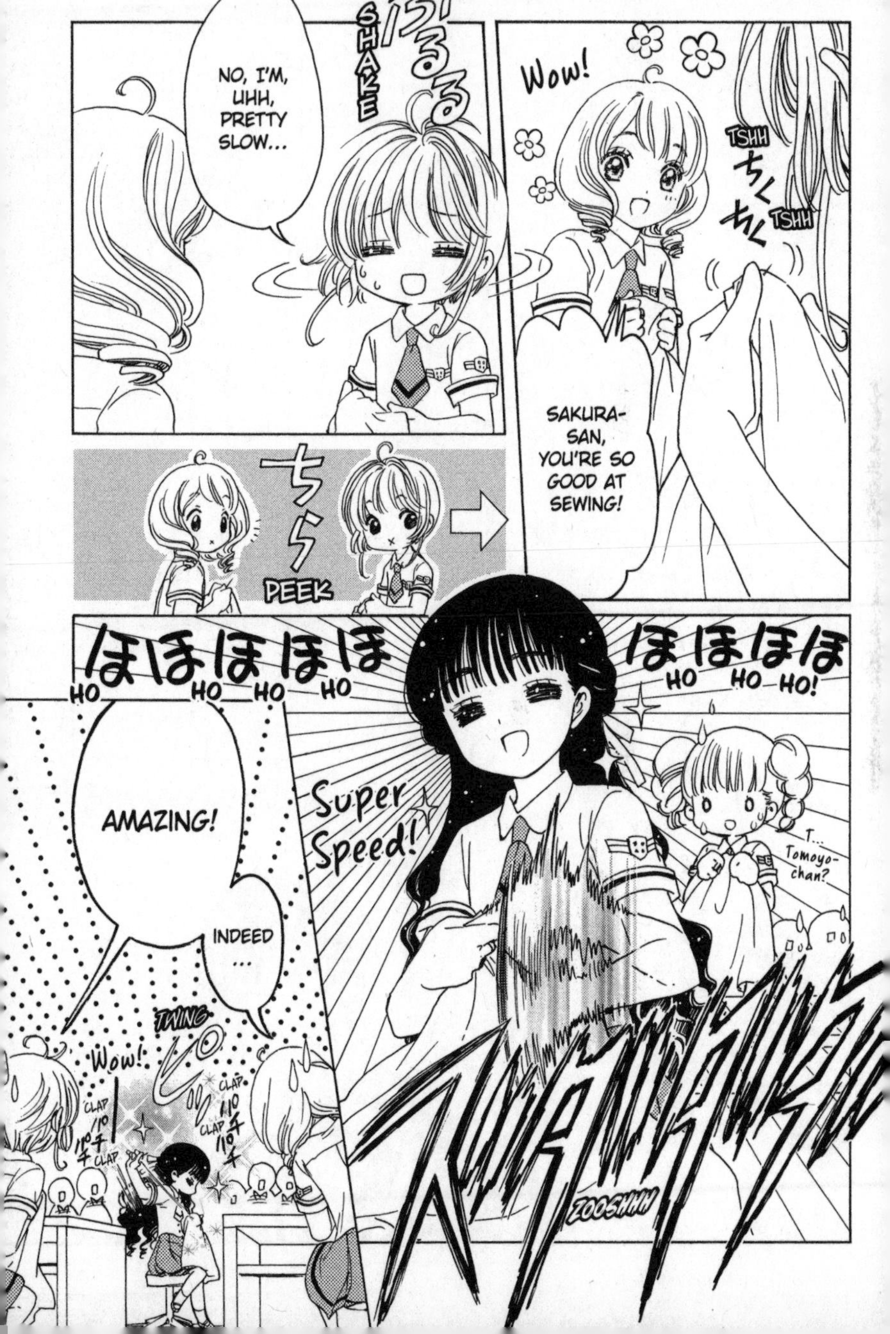
Wow!
SAKURA-SAN, YOU'RE SO GOOD AT SEWING!
ちくちく
TSHH
TSHH
ぷるる
SHAKE
NO, I'M, UHH, PRETTY SLOW...
ちら
PEEK
ほほほほ
HO HO HO!
ほほほほほ
HO HO HO HO
Super Speed!
T... Tomoyo-chan?
ZOOSHHH
AMAZING!
INDEED ...
TWING
Wow!
CLAP
CLAP
CLAP
CLAP

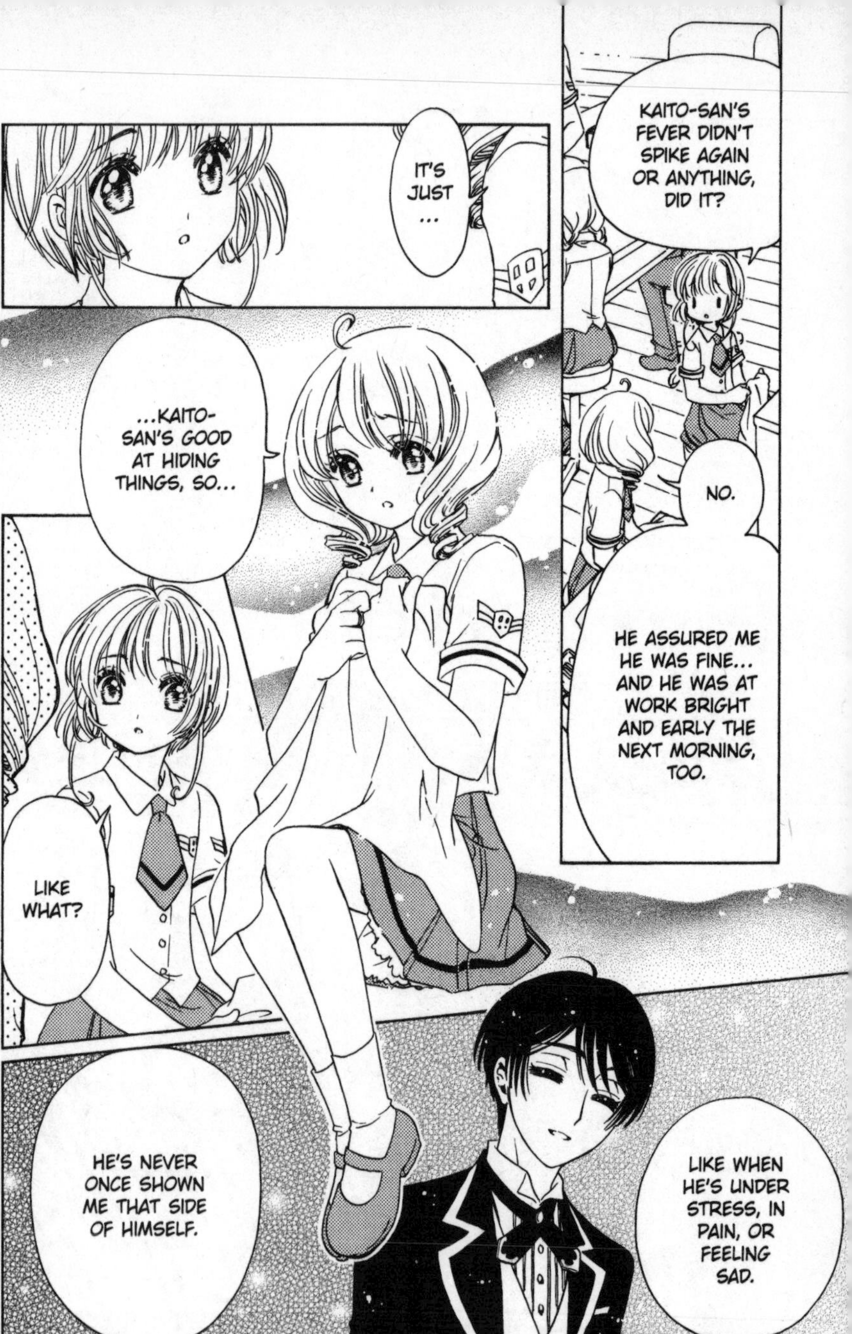
KAITO-SAN'S FEVER DIDN'T SPIKE AGAIN OR ANYTHING, DID IT?
NO.
HE ASSURED ME HE WAS FINE... AND HE WAS AT WORK BRIGHT AND EARLY THE NEXT MORNING, TOO.
IT'S JUST ...
...KAITO-SAN'S GOOD AT HIDING THINGS, SO...
LIKE WHAT?
LIKE WHEN HE'S UNDER STRESS, IN PAIN, OR FEELING SAD.
HE'S NEVER ONCE SHOWN ME THAT SIDE OF HIMSELF.

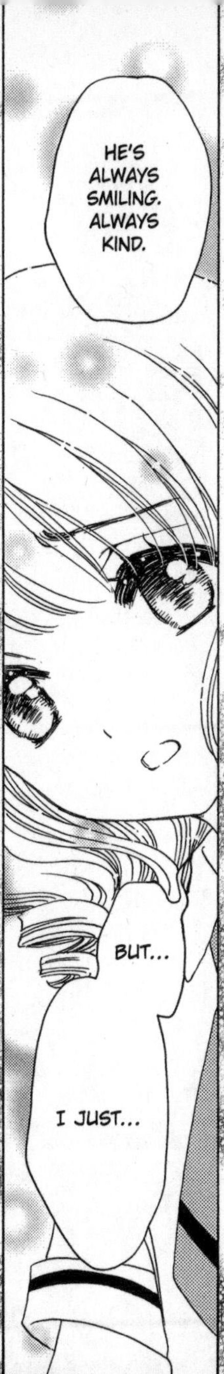
HE'S ALWAYS SMILING. ALWAYS KIND.
BUT...
I JUST...
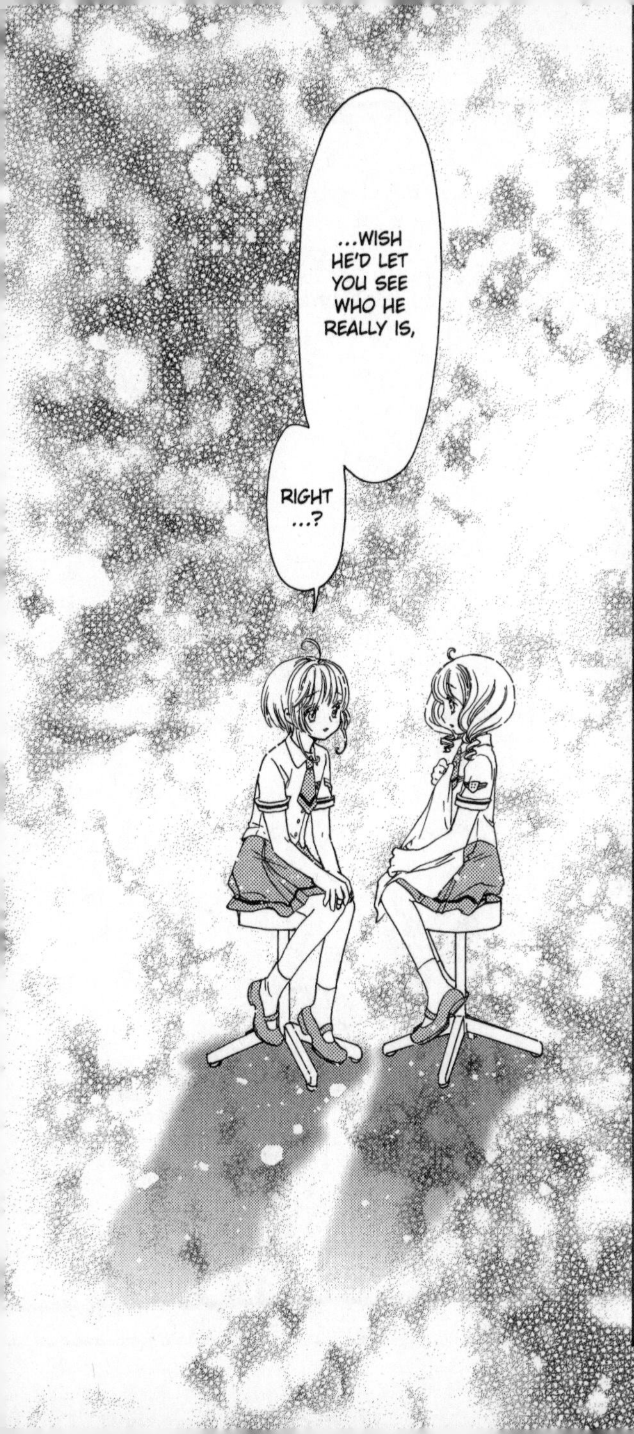
...WISH HE'D LET YOU SEE WHO HE REALLY IS,
RIGHT ...?

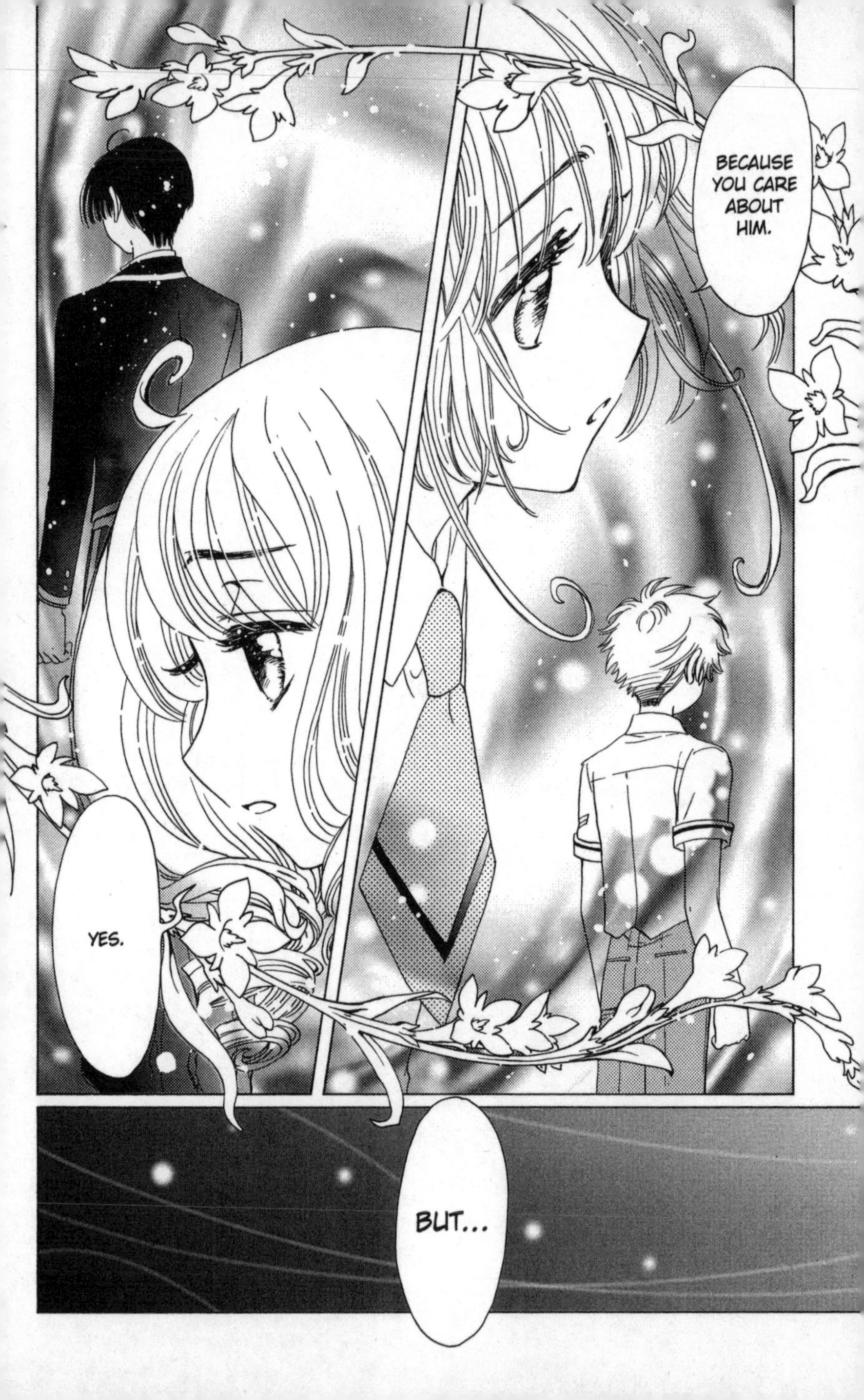
BECAUSE YOU CARE ABOUT HIM.
YES.
BUT...

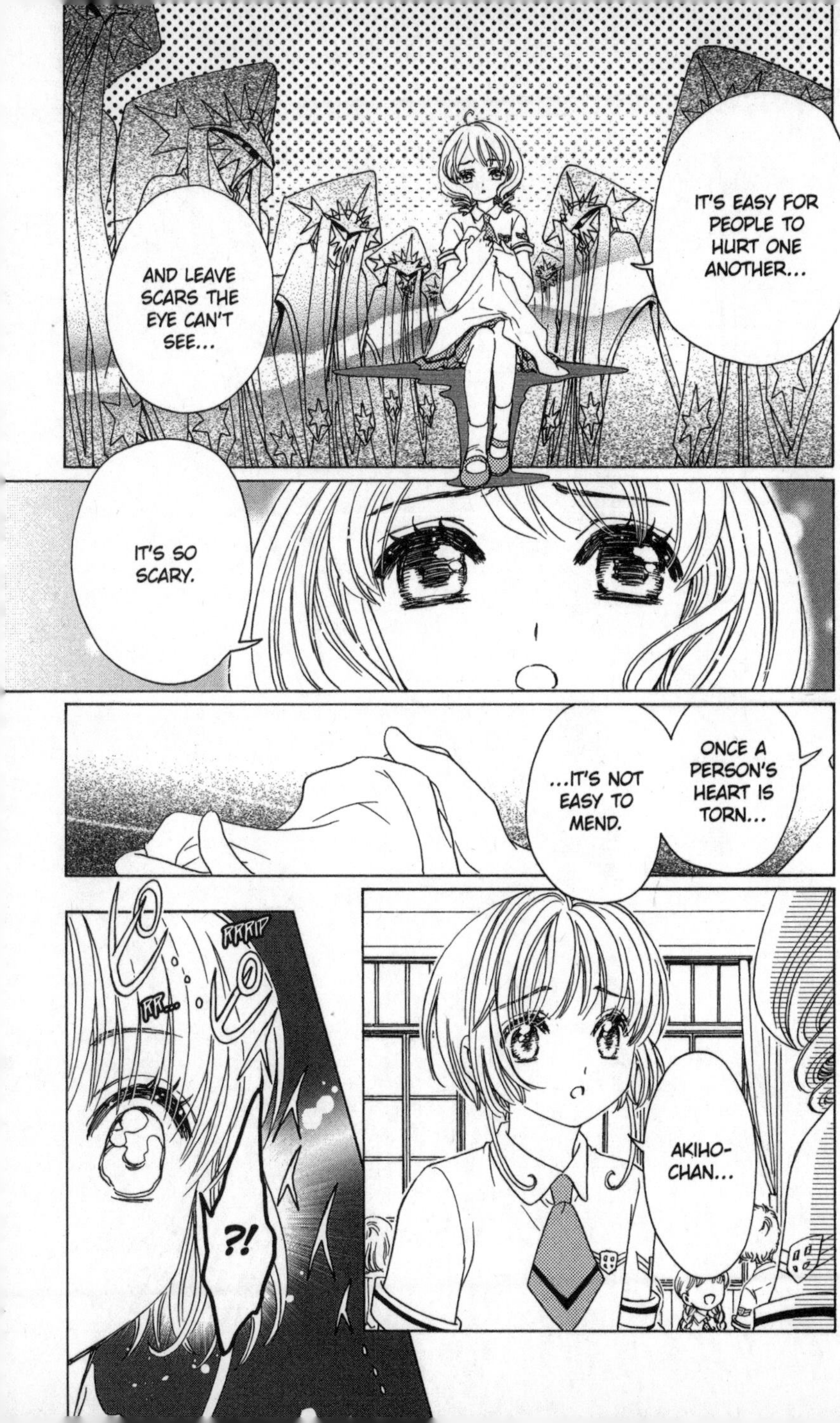
IT'S EASY FOR PEOPLE TO HURT ONE ANOTHER...
AND LEAVE SCARS THE EYE CAN'T SEE...
IT'S SO SCARY.
ONCE A PERSON'S HEART IS TORN...
...IT'S NOT EASY TO MEND.
AKIHO-CHAN...
RRRIP
RR...
?!

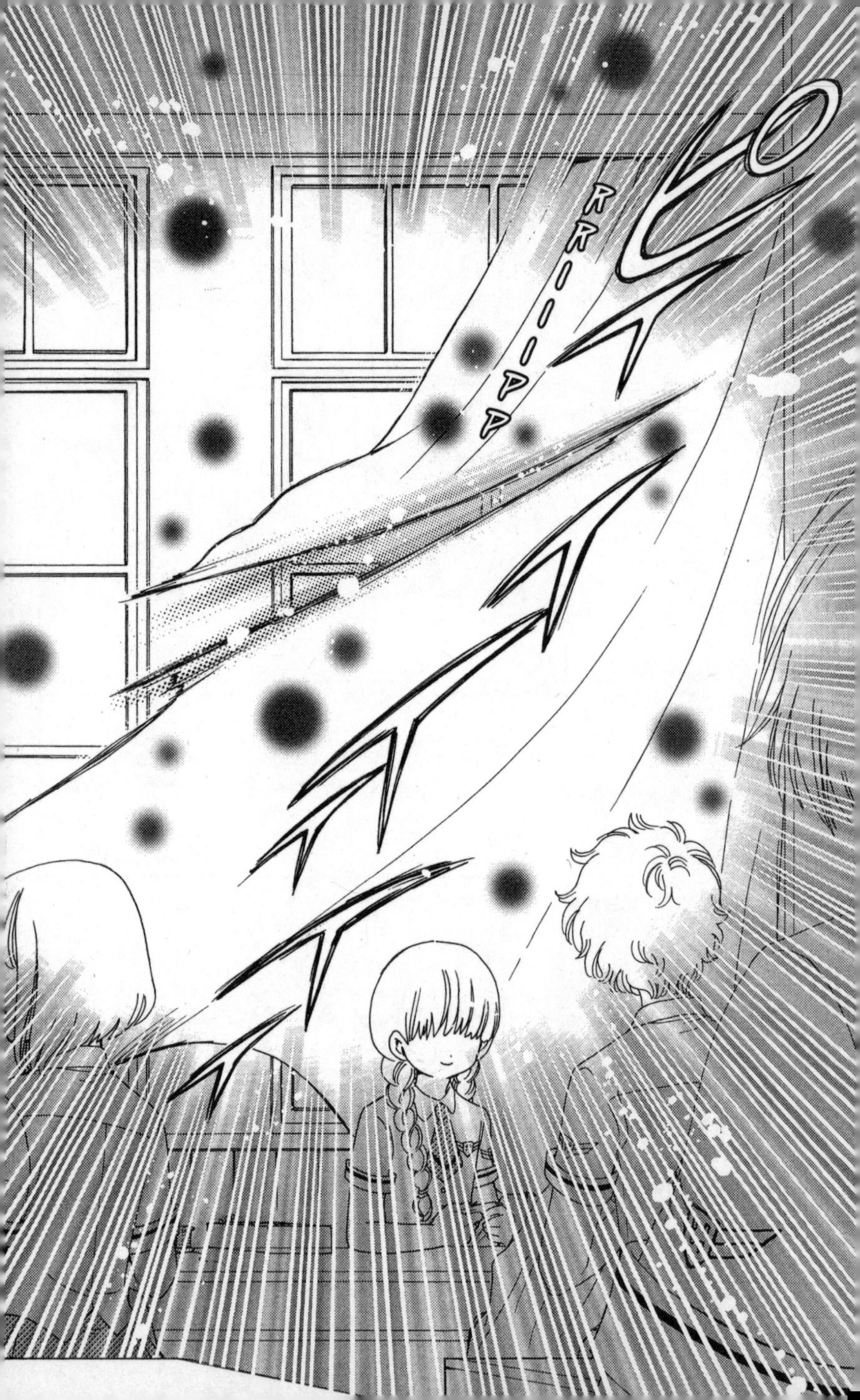
RRIIIIPP

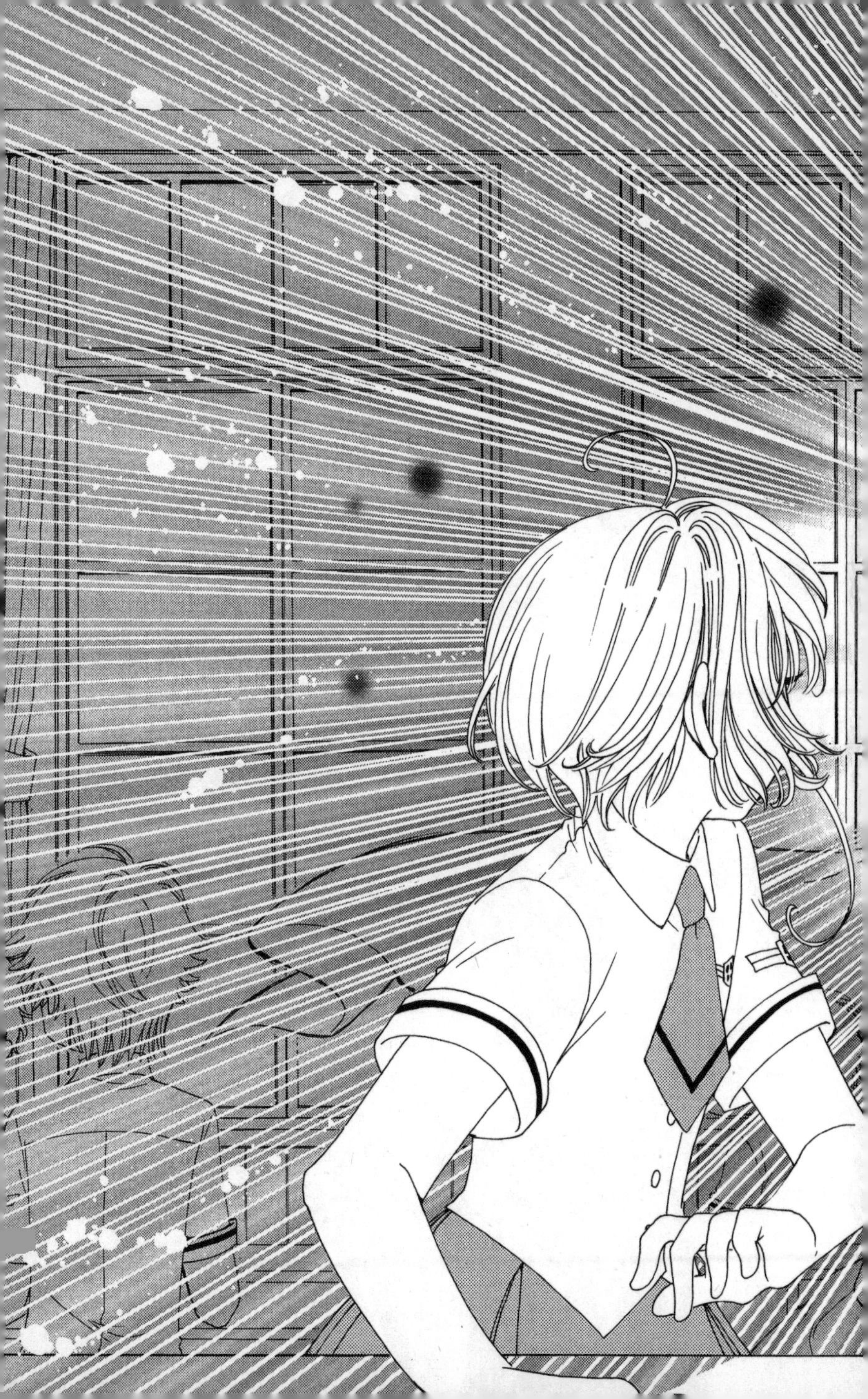

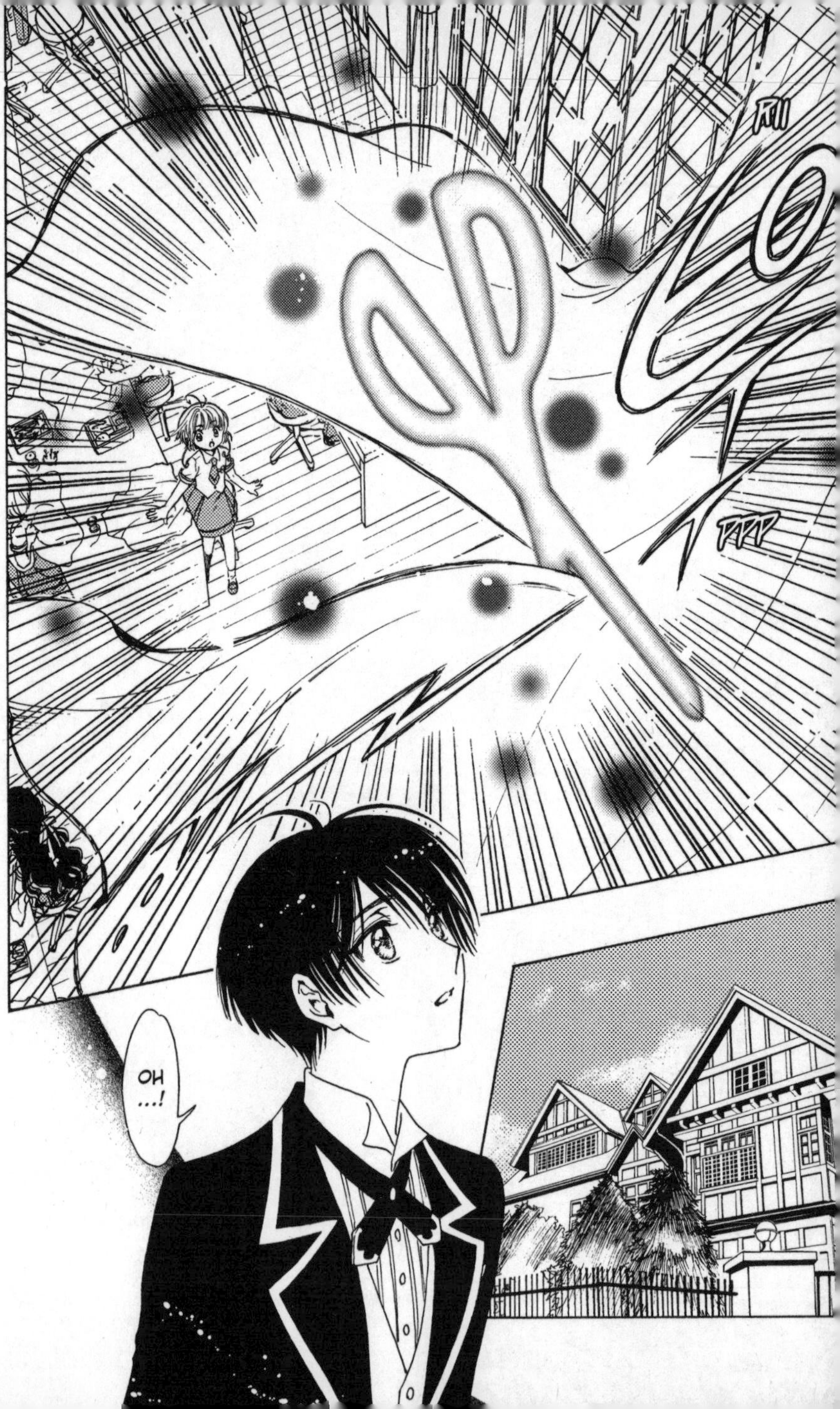
RII
OH ...!

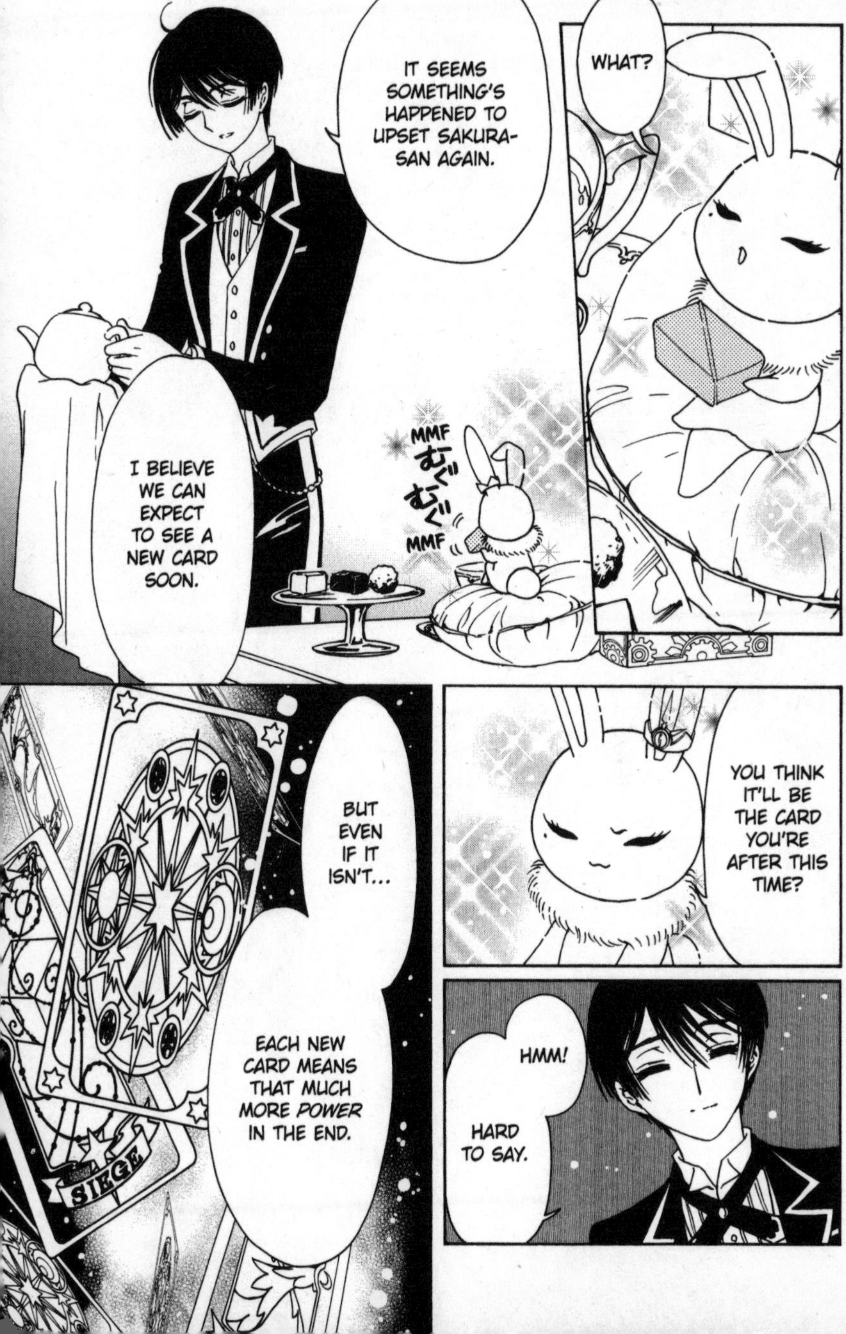
WHAT?
IT SEEMS SOMETHING'S HAPPENED TO UPSET SAKURA-SAN AGAIN.
MMF むぐむぐ MMF
I BELIEVE WE CAN EXPECT TO SEE A NEW CARD SOON.
YOU THINK IT'LL BE THE CARD YOU'RE AFTER THIS TIME?
HMM!
HARD TO SAY.
BUT EVEN IF IT ISN'T...
EACH NEW CARD MEANS THAT MUCH MORE *POWER* IN THE END.
SIEGE

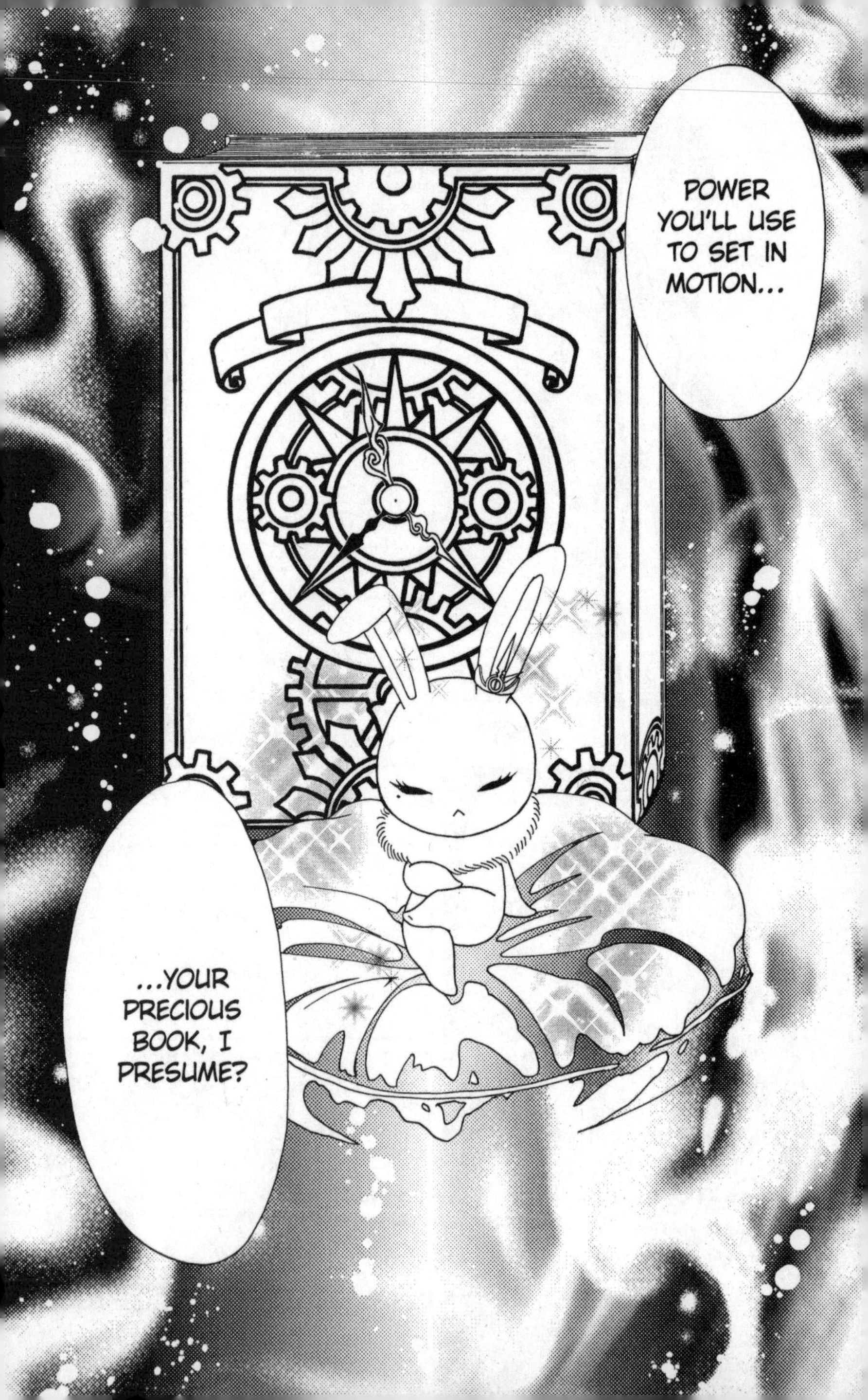
POWER YOU'LL USE TO SET IN MOTION...
...YOUR PRECIOUS BOOK, I PRESUME?

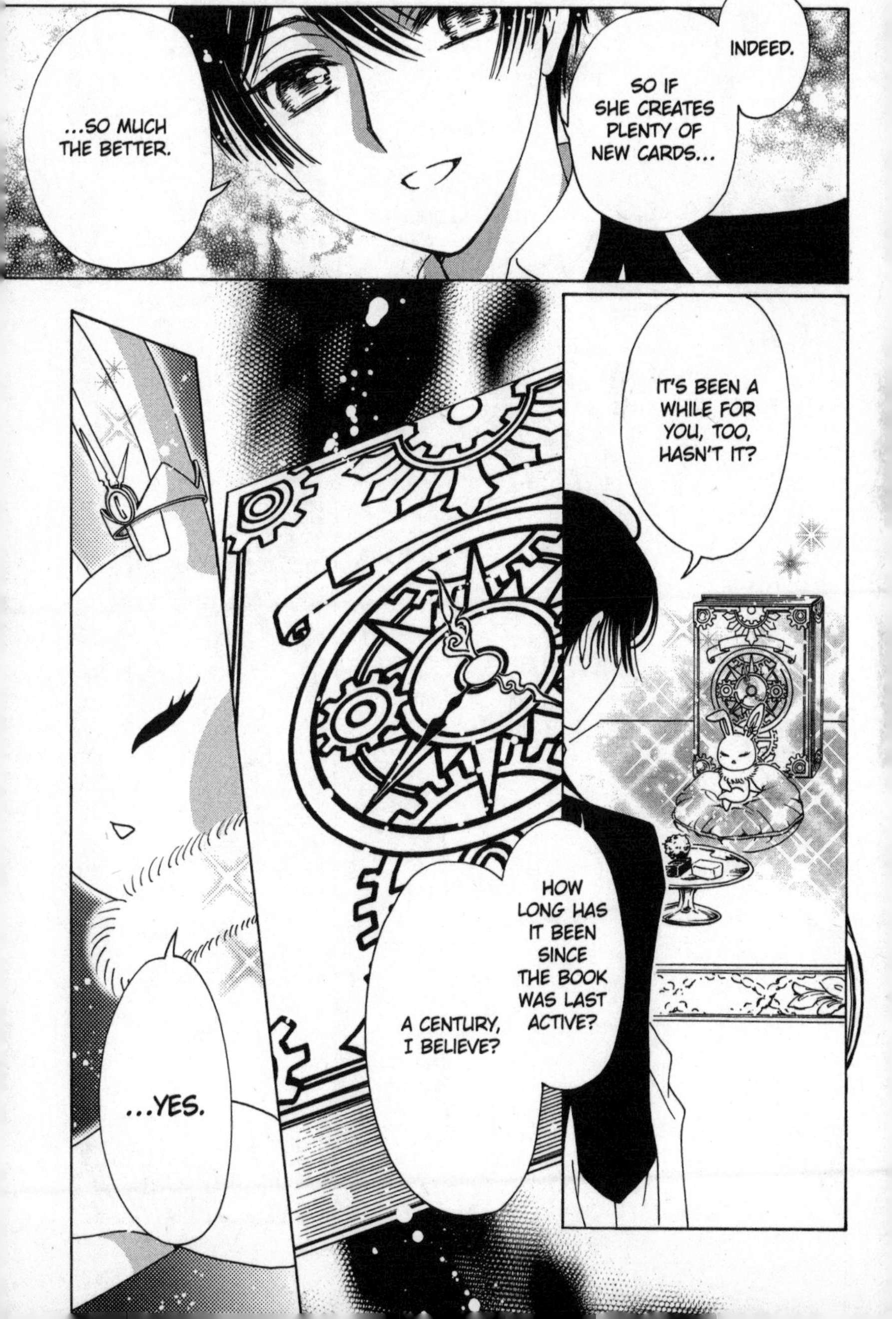
INDEED. SO IF SHE CREATES PLENTY OF NEW CARDS...
...SO MUCH THE BETTER.
IT'S BEEN A WHILE FOR YOU, TOO, HASN'T IT?
HOW LONG HAS IT BEEN SINCE THE BOOK WAS LAST ACTIVE?
A CENTURY, I BELIEVE?
...YES.

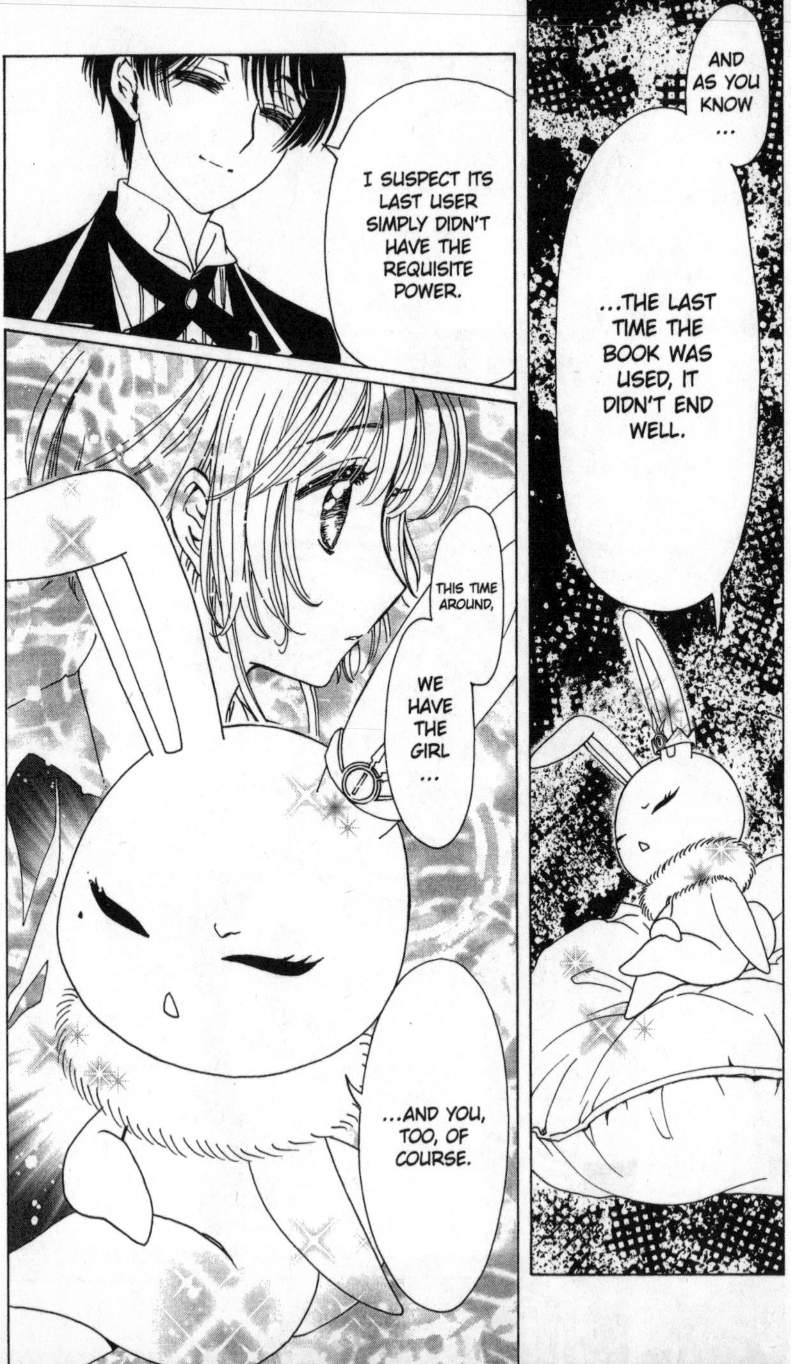
AND AS YOU KNOW ...
...THE LAST TIME THE BOOK WAS USED, IT DIDN'T END WELL.
I SUSPECT ITS LAST USER SIMPLY DIDN'T HAVE THE REQUISITE POWER.
THIS TIME AROUND,
WE HAVE THE GIRL ...
...AND YOU, TOO, OF COURSE.

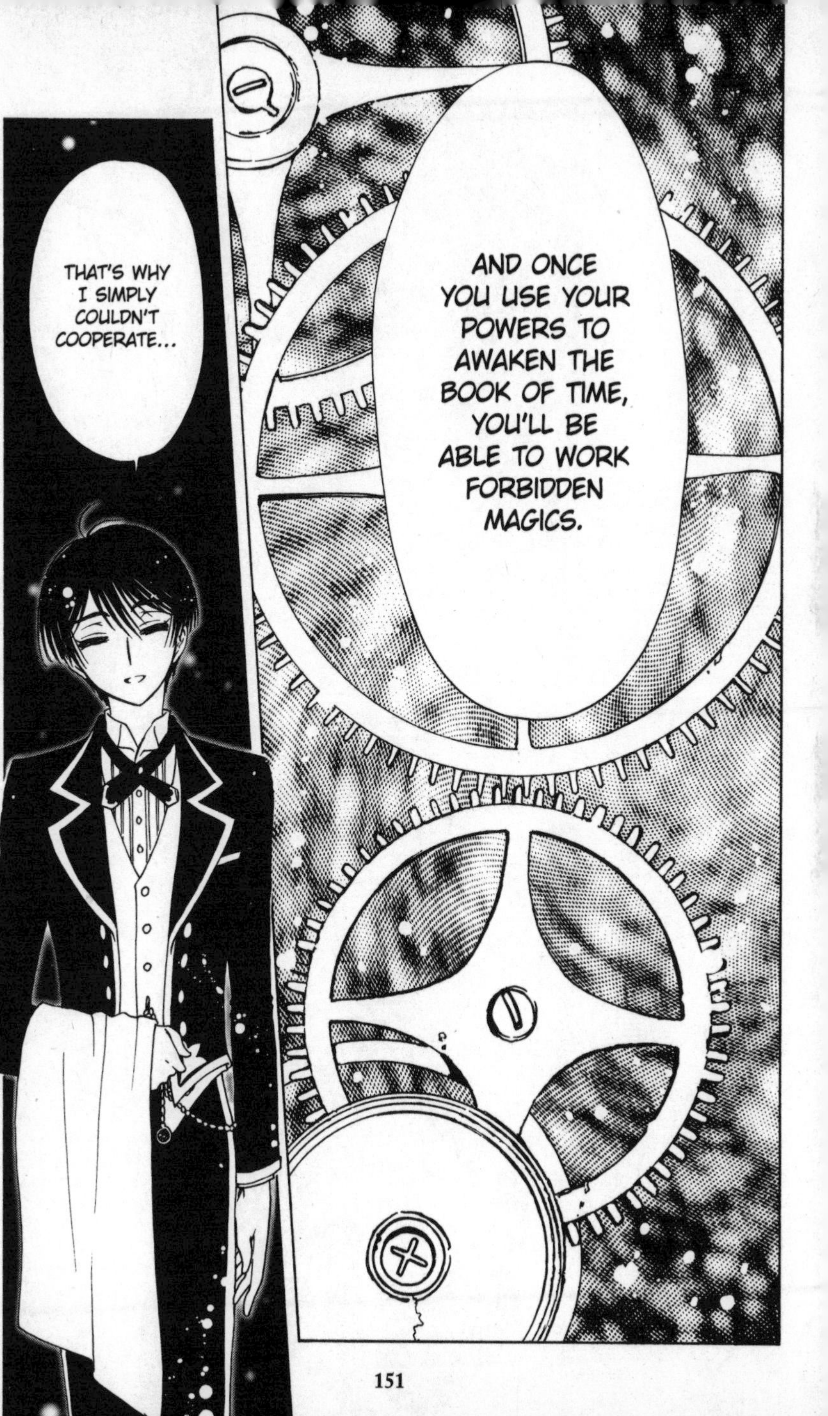
AND ONCE YOU USE YOUR POWERS TO AWAKEN THE BOOK OF TIME, YOU'LL BE ABLE TO WORK FORBIDDEN MAGICS.
THAT'S WHY I SIMPLY COULDN'T COOPERATE...

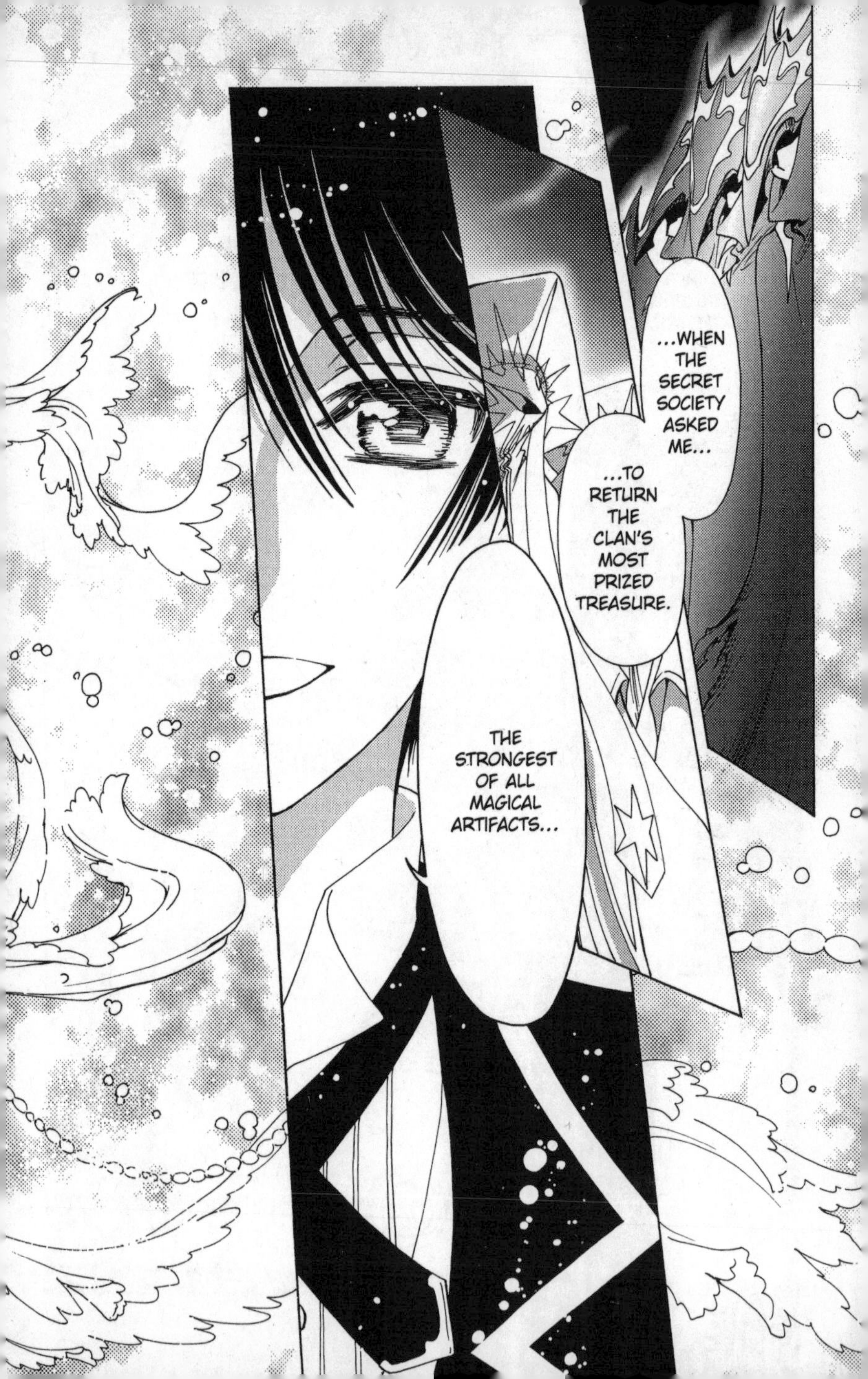
...WHEN THE SECRET SOCIETY ASKED ME...
...TO RETURN THE CLAN'S MOST PRIZED TREASURE.
THE STRONGEST OF ALL MAGICAL ARTIFACTS...

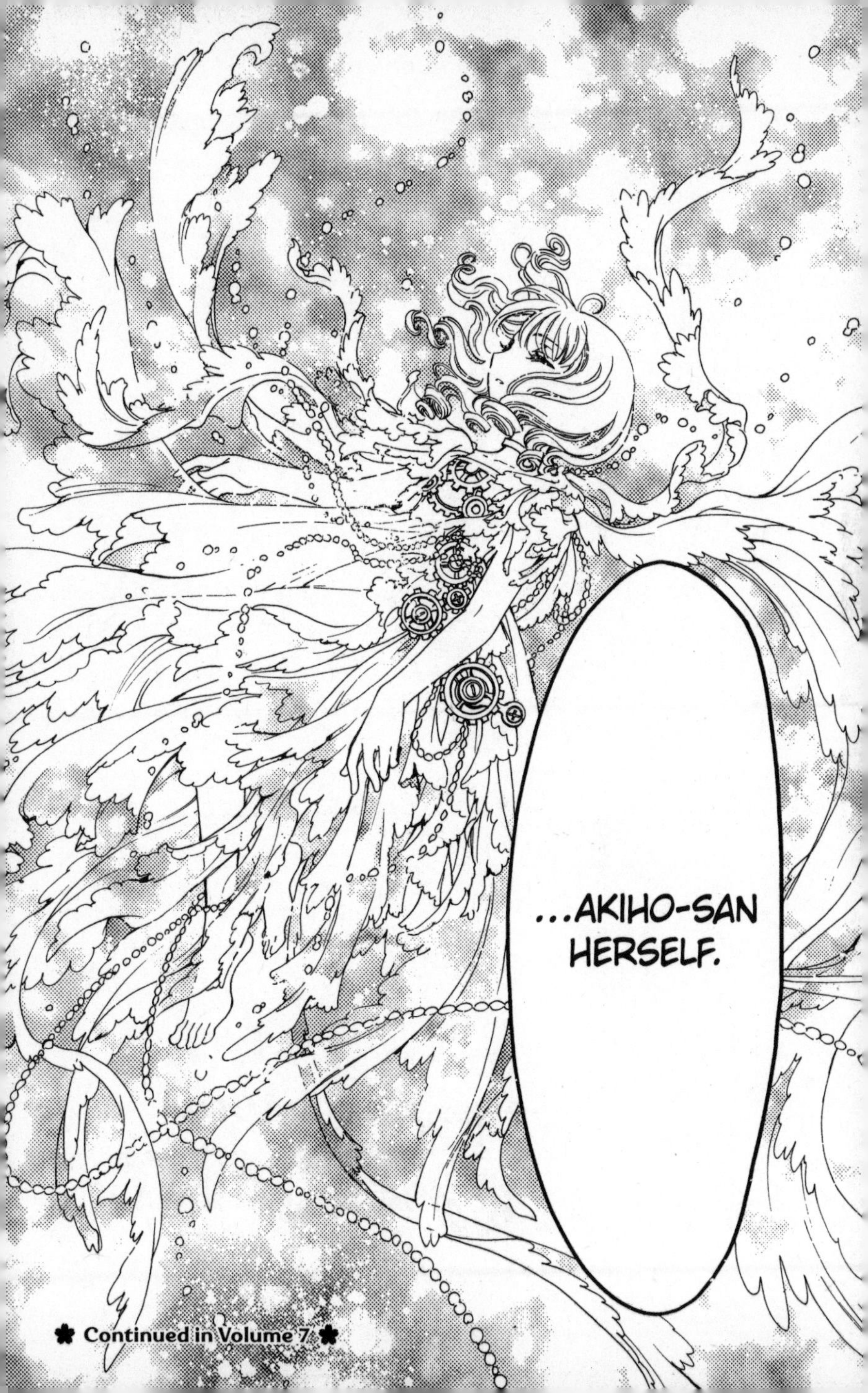
...AKIHO-SAN HERSELF.

✽ Continued in Volume 7 ✽

Cardcaptor Sakura

CLEAR CARD

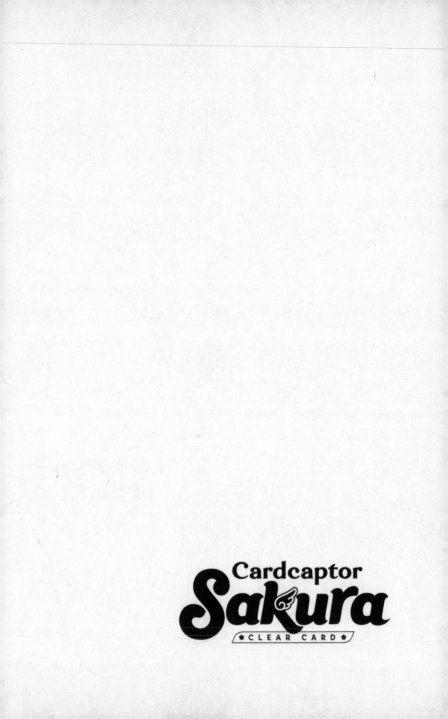

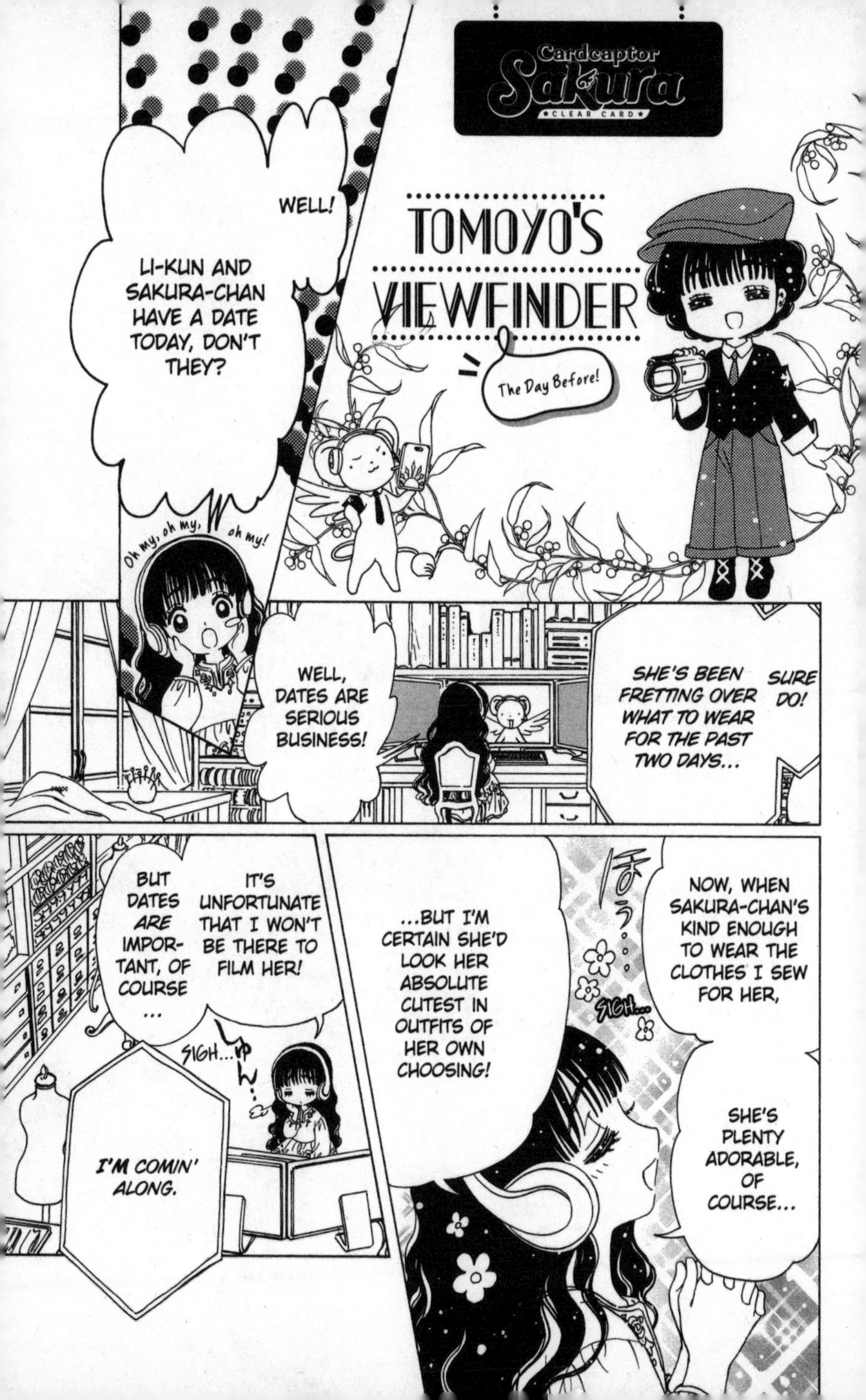
Cardcaptor Sakura
CLEAR CARD
TOMOYO'S VIEWFINDER
The Day Before!
WELL!
LI-KUN AND SAKURA-CHAN HAVE A DATE TODAY, DON'T THEY?
Oh my, oh my, oh my!
SURE DO!
SHE'S BEEN FRETTING OVER WHAT TO WEAR FOR THE PAST TWO DAYS...
WELL, DATES ARE SERIOUS BUSINESS!
NOW, WHEN SAKURA-CHAN'S KIND ENOUGH TO WEAR THE CLOTHES I SEW FOR HER,
SHE'S PLENTY ADORABLE, OF COURSE...
ほう…
SIGH...
...BUT I'M CERTAIN SHE'D LOOK HER ABSOLUTE CUTEST IN OUTFITS OF HER OWN CHOOSING!
IT'S UNFORTUNATE THAT I WON'T BE THERE TO FILM HER!
BUT DATES ARE IMPORTANT, OF COURSE...
SIGH...
しゅん…
I'M COMIN' ALONG.

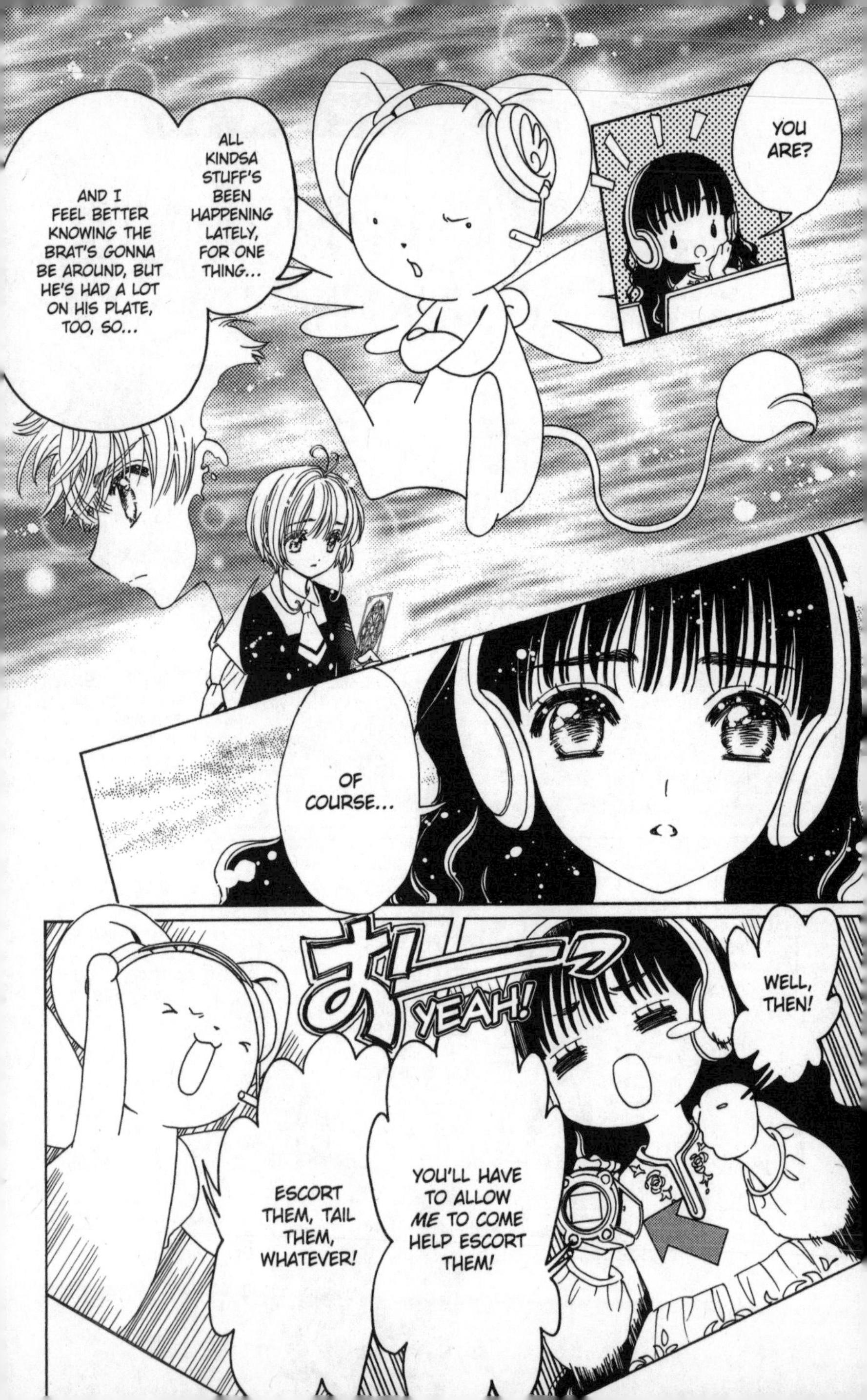
YOU ARE?
ALL KINDSA STUFF'S BEEN HAPPENING LATELY, FOR ONE THING...
AND I FEEL BETTER KNOWING THE BRAT'S GONNA BE AROUND, BUT HE'S HAD A LOT ON HIS PLATE, TOO, SO...
OF COURSE...
WELL, THEN!
YOU'LL HAVE TO ALLOW ME TO COME HELP ESCORT THEM!
お―っ
YEAH!
ESCORT THEM, TAIL THEM, WHATEVER!

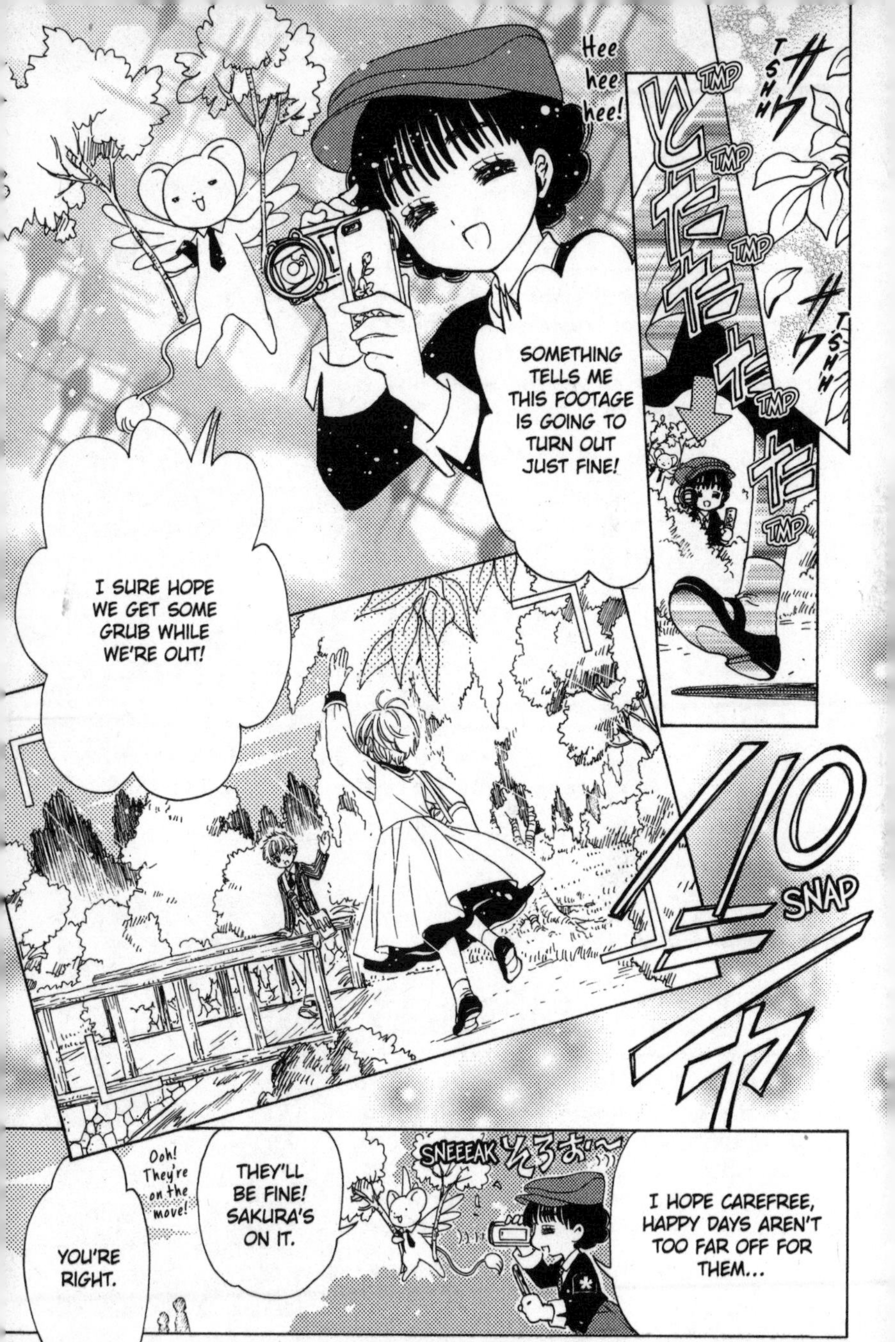
TSHH
TMP TMP TMP TMP TMP
TSHH
Hee hee hee!
SOMETHING TELLS ME THIS FOOTAGE IS GOING TO TURN OUT JUST FINE!
I SURE HOPE WE GET SOME GRUB WHILE WE'RE OUT!
SNAP
I HOPE CAREFREE, HAPPY DAYS AREN'T TOO FAR OFF FOR THEM...
SNEEEAK
THEY'LL BE FINE! SAKURA'S ON IT.
Ooh! They're on the move!
YOU'RE RIGHT.

✿ The End ✿

WAITING FOR SPRING

A sweet romantic story of a soft-spoken high school freshman and her quest to make friends. For fans of earnest, fun, and dramatic shojo like *Kimi ni Todoke* and *Say I Love You*.

KISS ME AT THE STROKE OF MIDNIGHT

An all-new Cinderella comedy perfect for fans of *My Little Monster* and *Say I Love You*!

LOVE AND LIES

Love is forbidden. When you turn 16, the government will assign you your marriage partner. This dystopian manga about teen love and defiance is a sexy, funny, and dramatic new hit! Anime now streaming on Anime Strike!

YOUR NEW FAVORITE ROMANCE MANGA IS WAITING FOR YOU!

THAT WOLF-BOY IS MINE!

A beast-boy comedy and drama perfect for fans of *Fruits Basket*!

"A tantalizing, understated slice-of-life romance with an interesting supernatural twist."
- Taykobon

WAKE UP, SLEEPING BEAUTY

This heartrending romantic manga is not the fairy tale you remember! This time, Prince Charming is a teenage housekeeper, and Sleeping Beauty's curse threatens to pull them both into deep trouble.

Cardcaptor Sakura: Clear Card volume 6 is a work of fiction. Names, characters, places, and incidents are the products of the author's imagination or are used fictitiously. Any resemblance to actual events, locales, or persons, living or dead, is entirely coincidental.

A Kodansha Comics Trade Paperback Original.

Cardcaptor Sakura: Clear Card volume 6 copyright © 2019
CLAMP · Shigatsu Tsuitachi Co., Ltd. / Kodansha Ltd.
English translation copyright © 2019
CLAMP · Shigatsu Tsuitachi Co., Ltd. / Kodansha Ltd.

All rights reserved.

Published in the United States by Kodansha Comics,
an imprint of Kodansha USA Publishing, LLC, New York.

Publication rights for this English edition arranged through Kodansha Ltd., Tokyo.

First published in Japan in 2019 by Kodansha Ltd., Tokyo, as
Kaadokyaputaa Sakura Kuriakaado Hen volume 6.

ISBN 978-1-63236-719-8

Printed in the United States of America.

www.kodanshacomics.com

9 8 7 6 5 4 3 2 1

Translation: Erin Procter
Lettering: Erika Terriquez
Editing: Alexandra Swanson and Tiff Ferentini
Kodansha Comics edition cover design: Phil Balsman